JEWISH EASTERN EUROPE
1830-1914

⊕ Provincial Capital ★ Major City • Settlement

⊕ Border ⋯⋯ Provincial Border ▨ Pale of Settlement

▨ Congress Poland

km

0   100   200

© **carta**, JERUSALEM

POLTAVE

Poltave

Pereyaslev

Dnieper

KIEV

Shpole

Rizhin

Talne

Barditshev

Uman

Zhitomir

Chichelnik

KHERSON

Nikolayev

Khmyelnik

Mezhbizh

Letitshev

Nemirov

Bratslav

PODOLIA

Bar

Tultshin

Kamenets-Podolsk

Ostre

Satanov

Dniester

Kremenets

Husiatin

Strusov

Chortkov

Tarnopol

Dubne

Brod

Horodenka

Lemberg

Kolomay

Sadeger

Chernovits

Sokal

Belz

Zholkve

Pshemishl

GALICIA

Lezhensk

Rimanov

Carpathian Mts

Nay Sandz

Kroke (Cracow)

HUNGARY

Munkatsh

Satmer

Sighet

BESSARABIA

Kishinev

Prut

Yas

ROMANIA

Danube

Odessa

Black Sea

C

D

E

THE SHTETL BOOK

THE SHTETL BOOK

An Introduction to East European Jewish Life and Lore

by

Diane K. Roskies and David G. Roskies

SECOND, REVISED EDITION

KTAV PUBLISHING HOUSE, INC.

Library of Congress Cataloging in Publication Data

Main entry under authors:

Roskies, Diane K. & David G.

Bibliography: p.
SUMMARY: Examines the history and way of life of
Jews in Eastern Europe.
1. Jews in Eastern Europe — Social life and customs.
2. Europe, Eastern — Social life and customs.
[1. Jews in Eastern Europe — Social life and customs.
2. Europe, Eastern — Social life and customs]
I. Roskies, Diane K. II. Roskies, David G., 1948-
DS112.S485   947'.004'924   75-11693
ISBN 0-87068-456-6

Design by EZEKIEL SCHLOSS

MANUFACTURED IN THE UNITED STATES OF AMERICA

TABLE OF CONTENTS

FOREWORD

This book was put together by two people who never saw a shtetl and never will. It is for this very reason that we were determined not to make do with generalizations and sentimentalism. Our book is about real places and events.

In choosing our material we hoped to provide two things: an in-depth study of one shtetl in Eastern Europe as it existed at a specific point in time plus an overview of the major patterns and events of East European Jewry. As a model shtetl we chose Tishevits in the Lublin province because there is more published material on this town than on any other, thanks in great measure to the exemplary efforts of Jacob Zipper and Yekhiel Shtern both of whom were kind enough to supplement their written works with verbal information. As for the general overview, our concern is not with the agricultural village nor the great urban centers of Jewish life, but with the market town. The time span is 1800-1914, but important developments leading up to this period are dealt with briefly, especially in unit three.

To maintain a consistent style throughout we shortened many of the texts and added explanations where necessary. For exact citation the reader should consult the sources directly. Except where otherwise noted, all translations are by David G. Roskies.

This is a book about Yiddish-speaking Jews. Since so much of the culture was verbal, or let's say because so much of what has survived of the culture is verbal, we included a basic Yiddish vocabulary of about one hundred words. We have spelled these words phonetically, the way they are spoken. Rather than devising a system of our own, we adopted the transcription of Uriel Weinreich's *Modern English-Yiddish, Yiddish-English Dictionary*. A glossary of these words appears at the end of the book. In addition, Yiddish songs, chants and proverbs are included throughout the text.

We would like to thank the staff at the YIVO Institute for Jewish Research for their help and encouragement in the final phase of our work, and for their permission to use many articles first published in the YIVO journals and photographs from their archive, most of which are now appearing in print for the first time.

Foreword to the Second Edition

Four years later, *The Shtetl Book* is still the only collection in English of primary and literary sources on East European Jewish social history. Our exclusive emphasis on the everyday life of ordinary Jews in the small town has provided a useful addition to the intellectual, economic and political histories, few though they be, of East European Jewry. The discussion of cultural geography and entertainment have been especially well received.

The Shtetl Book, it should be emphasized, was written with the classroom in mind. A detailed *Reader's Guide* accompanies *The Shtetl Book* and may be ordered directly from the publisher. The *Guide* gives background information on each and every selection and suggests ways of organizing the material for individual or classroom projects, in particular, how to use the data, maps and charts in the text to trace one's own East European roots.

Besides correcting errors of fact and usage, we have greatly improved the photographic material that supplements the text. This has happened thanks to the recent discovery of a fund-raising film made in 1929 of the shtetl

Kolbushov in central Galicia. We would like to express our deepest gratitude to David Salz of Brooklyn for providing us with still photographs made from the film footage. Finally, it is our pleasure to thank the following individuals for their helpful comments: Hillel Schwartz (Del Mar, California), Lucjan Dobroszycki and Dina Abramowicz (YIVO Institute for Jewish Research).

New York City, March 1979

PRONUNCIATION GUIDE

		As in	Example
Vowels			
	a	f*a*r	far
	e	b*e*d	shtetl
	i	*i*s	gvir
	o	*o*nly	dos
	u	f*u*ll	shul
Diphthongs			
	ay	wh*y*	dayen
	ey	th*ey*	dreydl
	oy	b*oy*	hoyf
Consonants			
	kh	Blo*ch*	bokher
	sh	fi*sh*	fish
	ts	le*ts*	tsitses
	y	*y*es	yid
	zh	mea*s*ure	Rizhin
	tsh	su*ch*	tsholnt

HOW JEWS FIRST CAME TO POLAND: THREE LEGENDS

A woodcut by S. Yudovin.

I. After the death of sinful King Popiel, the throne of Poland stood empty. The elders and leading citizens assembled in the town of Krushvits. The assembly sat for days but could not decide on a new ruler. Finally, they hit upon a plan. The first person to cross the bridge leading into town on the following morning would be crowned king. Three bridges led into the town of Krushvits. Guards were stationed at all three spots, and the members of the assembly waited breathlessly.

As chance would have it, a Jew named Abraham, who supplied the town with gunpowder, was the first person to enter Krushvits after sunrise. The guards seized him at once and brought him triumphantly to the impatient assembly. Abraham the gunpowder merchant was to become the new king of Poland.

"Wait a minute," he said to the members of the assembly. "I must have time to decide. Give me three days. Let no one disturb me. Then I will bring you my reply."

They gave Abraham a hut on the edge of town where he prayed to God for guidance. Three days and three nights passed and still Abraham did not appear. The assembly was growing impatient. What to do? Suddenly, a man named Piast, a respected citizen, jumped up from his seat.

"Citizens," he cried, "we cannot go on like this! A country without a ruler will perish. If Abraham won't come to us, we must go to him and demand an answer." And with that he grabbed an ax, rushed to Abraham's hut, and smashed down the door. Then Abraham appeared on the threshold and said:

"Poles, behold your citizen, Piast. He possesses a healthy spirit, for he dared to disturb me in my pious thoughts. Choose him as your ruler instead of me and you shall always be thankful to the Lord and to Abraham his servant."

And Piast was crowned prince over all of Poland.

II. During the Polish Piast dynasty, the Jews in Germany were being persecuted. When they realized that they had nothing more to lose they sent five leading rabbis to the Polish prince asking him for the right to settle there. The prince called his council together. At the end of three days the prince appeared before the rabbis and said:

"Our country is suffering from a great drought. If your prayers can bring rain, we shall grant you the right to stay here. If not, you must go elsewhere to live."

The rabbis returned to the inn where they were staying and prayed to God to grant the prince's request for rain. On the third day the skies clouded over and the first rain in months began to fall.

The prince kept his promise and, in the year 894, the first group of Jewish immigrants came from Germany. Later, the prince granted the Jews the privilege of free entry to Poland, protection, and the right to rule their own affairs.

III. It happened in 1492, when the Jews were expelled from Spain. Where could these Jews flee, if not toward the East? After wandering for months, they finally reached a land of many forests. Suddenly, a heavenly voice called out to them, in Hebrew: POH-LIN, here shall you rest. And from that day on the country was known as *Poyln* [Poland].

UNIT ONE
THE SHTETL TISHEVITS

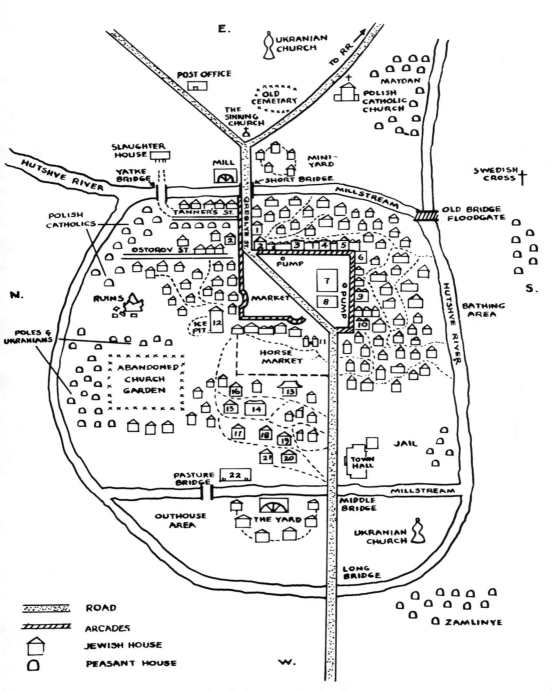

Map I: The shtetl Tishevits

KEY TO THE MAP OF TISHEVITS

1. Yitskhok-Khiel's station house
2. Tavern
3. Kerosene shop
4. Soda shop
5. Belzer shtibl
6. Government school
7. Stores
8. Iron goods store
9. Trisker shtibl
10. Radziner shtibl
11. Arn-Moyshe's station house
12. The brick building
13. Shul
14. Besmedresh
15. Rizhiner shtibl
16. Soup kitchen
17. Zhamele's house
18. Gershn melamed's beginner's kheyder
19. Yankev Yoshe's translation kheyder
20. Kalmen Dovid's beginner's kheyder
21. Peysekh melamed's translation kheyder
22. Bathhouse

1. A BIRD'S-EYE VIEW

The town of Tishevits is surrounded by water on all sides.
Which isn't to say that it's on an island, because islands are
usually formed by nature and Tishevits is more or less a
man-made affair. Originally the Hutshve River, which we
renamed Itshe Bombe's River in honor of Itshe Bombe,
flowed on three sides only.

Then, one day, it was decided that the city needed a water-
fall for which there were no suitable sites on the existing
river. That's when a millstream was dug on the eastern
side, which joined up again with the main river and completed the circle. Then a floodgate was built at the mouth of
the millstream where the Old Bridge now stands, and in
this way the water was diverted to run the mill.

Later on, another canal was dug by the peasants, and two
bridges were built to cross it: the Middle Bridge and the
Pasture Bridge. This made the town itself more compact
than before, because the *eyrev* now extended only as far as
the Middle Bridge and those who lived across the newly dug
river had to fend for themselves. This outside area is called
the *hoyf*, or Yard. And wouldn't you know it? No sooner had
the second stream been dug, then the Yard decided to build a
mill of their own! But more about that later.

2. THE LONG BRIDGE

The main bridge leading into the shtetl is the Long Bridge,
named "Long" not because the bridge itself is so long, but
because the road leading from it through meadows and fields
into town—is long. It leads from the gentile suburb of
Zamlinye into the Jewish town of Tishevits.

4

A unique view of shtetl architecture: Bath Street and Egypt Street in Vilkomir, Lite. Note the Greek Orthodox church in the background. Courtesy of S. Sarkin, Vancouver, Canada.

5

3. THE SHORT BRIDGE

The second busiest bridge is the Short Bridge on the other side of town. Though it stands right next to the large, noisy mill, with its huge wheel splashing night and day, the bridge itself is a modest, quiet affair. Except on market day, on Wednesday that is, when the peasants park their high wagons on the empty field opposite the mill and then make their way into town on foot.

Jews use the Short Bridge to reach the Old and New Cemeteries. Each funeral procession stops a few steps before the bridge. The coffin rests there for a few minutes, then the pallbearers hurry as if someone were chasing them over the bridge past the small church at the crossroad.

It's a little old church. The walls are covered over with moss. Once, though, it was taller than the old *shul* and its bells would peal as soon as a Jewish funeral passed by. Until, one day, a disguised *tsadek* cursed the church and caused it to sink deeper and deeper into the ground. However, the bell still rings. Hoarse and creaking though it sounds, it still manages to drown out the cries of the women mourners. That's why the coffin bearers always hurry by as if fleeing the plague.

Children who usually keep their distance from a funeral stay put at the bridge and watch the procession disappear from sight. On the way back from the cemetery, the mourners stop again before recrossing the bridge, this time to wash their hands. Someone pours river water over their hands with a large cup, as all Jews are required to do after having contact with a dead person. Then, shaking their wet hands in the air, they return to town.

4. WHEN THE MESSIAH COMES

Why do they stop at the bridge both going there and coming back? The only way to find out is to ask one of the old women when she's in a mood to talk. Then perhaps she'll explain that "when the Messiah comes, and may he come real soon, he'll ride into town on the Long Bridge. Then the entire community, young and old alike, will come running to greet him. Meanwhile, all our forefathers and mothers will rise from the dead and come to greet him—from across the Short Bridge. No one will be permitted to see them until they take the required bath in the river and hurry into *shul* to change into the specially prepared Messiah clothes. . . ."

5. THE OLD BRIDGE

The Old Bridge is a combination bridge and floodgate. Huge square logs protrude on both sides of the bridge. The water below roars and seethes as it passes through the grating. On the other side, barely a trickle of water makes it through the wooden structure, but the noise is a constant reminder that someday the river will overflow, wash away the floodgate and take half of the town with it. Then the peasants' fields and the orchard will become part of the river and the people of Greblye Street will have to take refuge on the roofs of their houses.

Jews don't use the bridge very often. It leads only to the village and who but a peddler has any reason to spend time with the peasants? Except when it's *shabes* [Sabbath] afternoon on a hot summer's day. Then the meadow is dry and in the orchards the apples and pears are begging to be picked. Mothers and fathers are fast asleep behind closed shutters and what better opportunity is there to make a dash for the village? Some of the peasants are friends from way back and let us climb the trees. They know that we'll pay them later on in the week. Others aren't quite as generous. They demand immediate payment for each pear and apple. Plums are more expensive. Even when we're afraid that our parents will find out—we still take a chance to grab a fast bite. By the time we're back at the Old Bridge on the way home, the growling in our stomachs is so loud it drowns out even the roar of the water and the barking of the dogs that some of the peasants have set on us: "The grubby *kapotes* who pollute Poland's farms with their dirt!"

Things aren't always so simple, though. Sometimes the peasant bullies show up from behind the orchard, armed with sticks. Usually, we head for home when this happens, except when there's no retreat. Then both groups attack each other. Part of our gang comes prepared for the showdown with small pieces of iron hidden in their sleeves, or better yet, a set of brass knuckles. The boys who own this type of hardware, mostly sons of horse-traders and butchers, stand off at the side. They're our reserves, so to speak. They wait for one of the attackers to approach. First, they bawl him out for picking on us. If that doesn't scare him, they beat him up good. Both sides fight, hats fly, clothes rip, until the first sight of blood. Then it stops.

From time to time, a bloodied lad comes running back to Greblye Street where the Jewish horse-traders and butchers are all out on their porches taking in the sun. Then all hell breaks loose: "The plague take them! They're not getting away with this!" Their broad shoulders straighten up. Despite the fact that its *shabes*, iron bars appear somehow in every fist, and for weeks afterwards the town will be alive with the news. The settlements in court will cost a fortune and the entire community will be forced to cover the fee. "They don't like it, those snobs, well they can lump it!" says Greblye Street with pride and pokes fun at the middle-class Jews who are embarrassed by the whole thing.

6. PASTURE BRIDGE

Not far from the Old Bridge is our bathing spot. In the summertime, all the shtetl kids go there for a swim. Middle-aged and older men generally swim next to the Pasture Bridge, while the women and girls, dressed in long night-shirts, bathe even further down.

The Pasture Bridge is constantly in need of repairs. It simply cannot manage to stand straight. A horse and wagon never crosses it, first, because it doesn't lead anywhere, except to the "pasture" and secondly because only an animal trained for obstacle courses could ever make it across. At that spot the water is not deep anyway. If you know how to swim, there's no danger. It only gets bad at the beginning of spring when the river unfreezes and heavy ice floes crash against the skinny beams that support the bridge. The whole structure starts shaking, and the March winds don't help any. Rotted pieces of wood fall off in every direction.

Everyone knew that someone was certainly responsible for the upkeep of the bridge. The town hall knew that too, and they would often block the road leading to the bridge in order to prevent an accident—"until such time as the party responsible repairs it." So who was "the party responsible"? The town hall explained that bridges were its responsibility when, and only when, the bridge in question *leads* somewhere. But this particular bridge leads nowhere, and only the shtetl Jews ever use it! Therefore, kahal is responsible. Kahal, on their part, quoted an ancient precedent that the bathhouse attendant was the man responsible; for, as long as people could remember, the bridge was called "The Bathhouse Bridge." The attendant, in turn, argued as follows:

"All right, if a plank falls off, I can hammer it back into place. After all, I'm a Jew, am I not? But as far as my official job goes, I'm responsible only for the bathhouse. And as proof, may I remind you that in Polish the *goyim* call the bridge 'Kahal's Bridge.'"

The fate of the bridge remains hanging in the balance. Even the *rov* cannot decide. "This does not call for a religious decision," he says, "but rather, for a compromise." Again, it's the same problem: number one, he himself is implicated in the case, because Synagogue Street where he lives is one of the streets that uses the "pasture" as its outhouse, and number two, the sides of the argument are not evenly matched.

Needless to say, a decision was never reached, and every time we crossed the bridge to "go to the bathroom" (Tishevits has no plumbing), we took our lives into our hands.

9

Scene at town bridge in Matshevis, Lublin Province. Instead of using the bridge, the horse and buggy are about to splash through the shallow stream where a woman is doing her laundry.

7. YATKE BRIDGE

Tucked away in a corner of town, resting on very high beams, is the Yatke [butcher shop] Bridge which leads to the slaughterhouse. Only the Oxen Path takes you there.

Hardly anyone uses the narrow Oxen Path. No one goes for a stroll there and regular wagons never drive through. Only the high peasant wagons with their thick wooden racks on two sides ever take this path. These wagons are full of bleating calves and sheep being led to the slaughter.

Sometimes, early in the morning, an animal is led on foot, with a peasant in front and a butcher in back. The peasant holds a rope tied around the animal's horns while the butcher tickles the beast with a twig. All of a sudden, the beast stops dead in its tracks. It turns its head back and utters such a frightening bellow that the path and neighboring stream seem to shudder. The peasant gets cold feet and lets the rope fall out of his hands. The butcher also gets nervous and starts tapping the animal from all sides with the twig as if trying to stop the bellowing from awakening the shtetl.

Another reason the path is so unpopular is that the bridge has a bad name. No one, absolutely no one, will go there alone at night since the incident with the *shoykhet* many years ago. What exactly happened is still uncertain. Something about a group of drunks who tried to get even with the *shoykhet* and the next morning he was found near the bridge almost dead. He left behind a widow and five little children. The skinners who work late hours at the slaughterhouse often report hearing strange voices on crossing the bridge at night. Some say, the drunks forced the poor *shoykhet to* sing *shabes* songs as they held him half dunked in the water. Others say they threw a sack over his head, and his stifled voice can still be heard.

11

8. THE REAL TRUTH BEHIND REB ARYE SHOYKHET'S DEATH

To understand what really happened that night on the Yatke Bridge, we have to go back many years to when Reb Peyshe was the chief supervisor of the slaughterhouse. Reb Peyshe was the kind of man who always got his way. All he had to do during a dispute was to grab his thick black beard in one hand and say:

"See this beard? Each and every hair in it is ready to fight to the finish for the sake of kosher meat."

After such a declaration no one, not the butcher, the *shoykhet*, nor even the *rov* would dare contradict him. They knew that Reb Peyshe was backed up by the most powerful khasidic *shtibl* in town and that the *rebe* himself had appointed him as supervisor.

Each khasidic *shtibl* had a *shoykhet* of its own. The supervisor was the one who kept watch over everything. His job was to examine the slaughter knives that all the *shokhtim* used and to make sure the butchers obeyed all the rules of Jewish law. Naturally, he got involved in any number of disputes, especially with the Rizhiner *shtibl* and its *shoykhet* Reb Arye. This should come as no suprise, because of all the khasidic groups who had "branches" in Tishevits, the Rizhiner *khasidim* were the most haughty.

"Who gives a hoot for a Polish *rebe?*" they would say sarcastically. "Why there's more happening by us on an ordinary Wednesday than by you on *yonkiper!*" [Yom Kippur].

"By us" meant in Galicia, in the town of Chortkov where their *rebe* could boast of more wealth than any Jew since the time of King Solomon.

The Polish *khasidim* from Belz, Trisk or Kotsk wouldn't take an insult like that lying down and sometimes faces got slapped in the heat of things. Then one day, news reached town that one of the Rizhiner heirs was planning to open a *yeshive* where secular studies like handwriting and arithmetic would be taught as well as Talmud. Soon enough letters of warning started arriving from the other khasidic

Main Street, Chekhenove, Warsaw province.

centers that the Rizhiner *shtibl* was declared "off limits."
Even ordinary Jews who never got involved in khasidic disputes and who trusted the word of the *rov* and the supervisor, even they stopped buying meat slaughtered by Reb
Ayre *shoykhet*.

The *rov* kept insisting that at no time did he ban Reb Arye
from slaughtering and that he had nothing but respect for
the *shoykhet's* learning and piety. It was no use. The boycott
was in full force.

Reb Arye himself, who was by nature a mild-mannered
person, was terribly upset by the whole thing. He finally convinced a group of Rizhiner *khasidim* to accompany him
to Reb Peyshe's house. If anyone could straighten things out,
it was Reb Peyshe the supervisor. But instead of helping
matters, Reb Peyshe added more coals to the fire. Straight-
ening up to his full height, he said:

"You yourself are to blame. Who asked you to worship
the golden calf?" (By this he meant the Rizhin brand of
Khasidism.)

This was the last straw. Leybush, one of the Rizhiner,
burst out at him:

"How dare you! Just you wait."

"You'll come crawling to us in your socks to beg forgiveness, you traitor, and see if it'll do you any good!"

The feud would probably have blown over just like all the
other feuds that Reb Peyshe got involved in. Except for a
new development. The Bere-Aba Clan, who were the main
butchers and the toughest guys around, were losing money
left and right on *treyf* meat. No matter how much livestock
was brought to the slaughter, at most one or two came out
kosher. Either the animals were diseased or the *shokhtim*
were messing things up, all except for one *shoykhet*—Reb
Arye. Neither Reb Ayre nor the butcher working under him
made a single lamb *treyf* through sloppy work. Now the
Bere-Aba Clan had a grudge against Reb Arye from years
back, because even before the feud he was never too friendly.

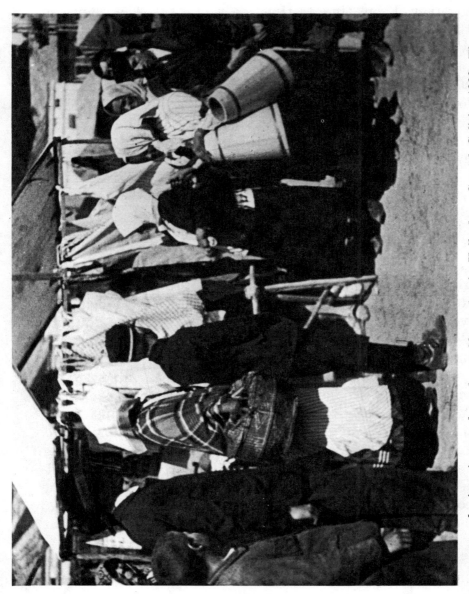

Peasant women buying piece goods at the weekly market in Kolbushov, Central Galicia, 1929. The woman carrying two milk cans had just sold their contents to a Jewish customer. Courtesy of David Salz, Brooklyn, New York.

He would refuse to perform the ritual slaughtering if any of the helpers showed signs of being drunk or acted up in any way. Now, during the boycott, he avoided the Clan altogether. From time to time, he would throw a glance in their direction, but that was all. Normally, his glances wouldn't have mattered, but because they were losing so much money every day, the Bere-Abas weren't thinking straight. They decided that Reb Arye was smiling at their losses. At the height of their anger, Reb Peyshe happened to walk into the slaughterhouse.

"What's the matter?" he asked. "Are you afraid of an evil eye? You can't stop a man from looking, you know."

"He'll make paupers out of us yet!" roared Leybe the Tall One. As he understood it, Reb Peyshe blamed their losses on Reb Arye's evil eye. "Listen to me, Reb Peyshe. We'll show him a thing or two." And with that he rushed outside.

Reb Peyshe lay low all week, even when he heard the butchers talking openly of an evil eye that someone had given them. He secretly rejoiced that the butchers blamed Reb Ayre. Now they wouldn't let him or the butcher who worked for him enter the slaughterhouse. That would teach Reb Arye a lesson as well as all the other Rizhiner troublemakers.

Even the *rov* couldn't change Reb Peyshe's mind. "What you're doing is forbidden," he warned the supervisor. "Firstly, because Reb Arye is a scholar and one must honor the Torah. Secondly, once you give the simple people an excuse, there's no knowing where they'll stop. And how long can you continue the feud? After all, their brand of Khasidism is also legitimate. Reb Peyshe, aren't you afraid of the consequences?"

"Afraid? Not me. They'll come in their socks to beg forgiveness!"

Sure enough, they did come in their socks, but not the ones he expected. It was the Bere-Aba Clan who appeared in this way at the Great *Shul*. The ark was opened and they swore on the Torah itself that they had nothing to do with the fact that early last Wednesday morning Reb Arye was found next to the Yatke Bridge half dead. What exactly happened to him and who exactly was responsible for doing it was never discovered. Reb Arye was found in a state of shock and died a few days later.

Only two people were missing at Reb Arye's funeral: Bere Good-for-Nothing and Reb Peyshe the Supervisor. Bere seemed to have vanished into thin air and rumors soon had it that the butchers weren't as innocent as they swore to be. As for Reb Peyshe, someone reported that the day after the funeral, he appeared at Reb Arye's grave begging the deceased for forgiveness. On his way out, he was met by Reb Elye, one of the leading Rizhiner *khasidim* who lashed out at him:

"Reb Peyshe, on account of a needless feud the Temple in Jerusalem was destroyed and we were exiled from our land. You think you can make up for the same sin with a few tears?"

"Then I too will go into exile!" cried the supervisor, breaking down completely.

"Don't be a cry-baby, Peyshe. We Rizhiner know for a fact, that whoever starts up with a *tsadek* will be cursed with a long life. And in this long life he himself will grovel in the mud while the *tsadek* he persecuted will rise to heights of greatness."

The next day Reb Peyshe disappeared and was soon followed by the rest of his family. He left behind an empty house which stood empty forever after. Soon it fell into ruin and only cats and dogs would be seen there. Another address was added to the shtetl list of places no one mentioned and no one ever approached.

9. THE MIDDLE BRIDGE

The Middle Bridge is lucky. Though it hovers over a deep part of the river and was the cause of many accidents, the bridge is kept in perfect shape.

The nearest major attraction is town hall, surrounded by a high fence. Crowds of petitioners can be seen there most of the day waiting for hours until Yarush the Town Clerk throws open the large glass door and announces with great pomp that Pan Biezhinski (the sour-faced major) is ready to receive complaints by the common folk. The bridge is always full of whispers. Nervous petitioners are consulting in hushed voices those who have an "in" with the Mayor. Market day is especially busy. That's when the entire peasantry from far and wide congregates in the nearby tavern and drinks whiskey out of large tea glasses. Their tongues loosen up and they give the local officials a piece of their minds.

It's a strong bridge all right, with double supports. On the side, protected by a railing, is the pedestrian lane. Wagons make a huge racket on the wooden planks, but the bridge itself doesn't budge. Though most of the town is visible from the bridge, it actually marks the outer boundary. The coachmen bringing their goods and passengers from the larger towns park their wagons near this bridge. Here the shtetl says goodbye to its inhabitants who set out for distant places. Here the shtetl welcomes a khasidic *rebe* or—not to mention them in the same breath—the governor, with symbolic offerings of bread and salt. In short, there's always something happening at the Middle Bridge.

The *eyrev* starts as soon as you cross the bridge, which means that as far as Jews are concerned, the town ends here. This, despite the complaints of the big shots from the Yard that they live just on the other side of the bridge and therefore the *eyrev* ought to include them too. No one listens, and this is why:

"Whoever heard of making an *eyrev* in the middle of nowhere?" Between us, though, it's only an excuse. It's the shtetl's way of getting even with the Yard for being standoffish and . . . different.

"What are they so arrogant about, anyway? They're not

Fancy stores in the Kolbushov marketplace, 1929. The tobacco store on the left, owned by a Jew before World War I, now belonged to a Gentile. In the center is an agency for Okocim Beer. Courtesy of David Salz.

khasidim that's for sure. If you ask me, they've gone off the deep end!" That is what some people say. Others have seen with their very own eyes that in Tall Khanina's library, the Vilne edition of the Talmud rubs shoulders with Moses Mendelssohn's Bible commentary!

But who needs to think up an excuse when the best proof is Khanina himself. He, the old owner of the mill, always makes his way into town dressed to the hilt. His beard well groomed, and on his head an indescribable hat which is neither Jewish nor *goyish*. Thus the town has quite a grudge against the population of the Yard. But the anger never comes out into the open. First, because a good many townspeople depend on the mill for their livelihood, and second of all, everyone knows that the Yard goes back to a long line of distinguished rabbis.

The Yard often entertains strange visitors from far-off places. They wear funny clothes and speak in a funny dialect. The women of the Yard are always dressed very well, with colored shawls and knitted suits that can stop traffic. They have a kind of royal grace of a Jewish nobility of bygone days. These women are very independent. They stroll about on the bridge with perfect freedom, talk to strange men without any bashfulness. Why even the clerks in the town hall stop and strike up a conversation with them. And that's nothing. Sometimes in the early morning or evening you can see them out in a rowboat singing loud and clear as if there weren't a man in sight and as if Jews weren't on their way to the *besmedresh* at that very moment.

Their husbands, tall and sturdy men, with well-trimmed beards, do make an appearance at the *besmedresh*, but keep their distance. They usually stand in a corner near the book shelves and leaf through the works by the Rambam and other philosophers. Seldom, if ever, do they sit down and study the way a Jew ought to—with body and soul.

10. THE MINI-YARD

The Yard-and-Mill is not the only area that the shtetl considers out-of-bounds. On the very opposite side of town, across the Short Bridge, past the sinking church, and facing the brown church with the golden dome is the area called the *heyfl* or mini-yard. The shtetl's argument against this neighborhood is this:

"Any Jews who choose to live within arm's reach of two churches and within ear's reach of their Sunday masses, do not belong within our borders . . ."

But the people of the mini-yard say:

"Both the Old and New Cemetery are far away from us. You can't disqualify us on that count. If not for the Short Bridge, the *eyrev* would certainly have included us because the path leading to the nearby suburb really begins past the Yard. The mini-yard isn't even built the way the suburb is. Our houses have a porch in front and a garden in back. Just like Tanner's Street across the bridge. Why couldn't we just be a continuation of that street, especially since some of us lived there for many years before we moved here?"

Go argue with a wall.

The mini-yard hasn't given up, though, and in the meantime, its members always go into town for services.

Actually, Tishevits is proud of the mini-yard and proud of its owner, Reb Mordkhe Broyer, the only man in town who is called by his last name. Reb Mordkhe settled in Tishevits as a young man. It was still a time when Jews could get rich in Poland by working for the *porets*, the Polish nobleman. The *porets* no longer owned serfs, but he still owned most of the land in Poland. Instead of taking care of his holdings by himself, the *porets* usually preferred leasing them to Jews. Thus, for instance, the *porets* would lease his forests for so many years to a Jewish lumber merchant. The Jews took charge of cutting down the trees and floating the logs down the Vistula River to the Prussian port of Danzig.

The local hotel and restaurant in Kolbushov, 1929. Courtesy of David Salz.

Reb Mordkhe was an agent for just such a lumber merchant. As soon as he settled in Tishevits, Reb Mordkhe made friends with the local *porets* and took charge of his lumber and grain. Soon enough, all the townspeople began using his safe as their bank. They deposited their down payments and dowries with him because Reb Mordkhe's word was as good as gold. And though everyone had perfect trust in him, he himself always insisted on giving receipts for every sum deposited in his safe, no matter how small. If someone asked him why he was so strict, he would explain:

"A man does not have full control over his life. One never knows what might happen."

His practice was proven right. One day the old *porets* dropped dead and his crazy son Yanush tore up all his papers. The *porets*' brother came running all the way from Paris—straight to Reb Mordkhe. Reb Mordkhe sat him down in a easy chair and rattled off an exact statement of who owed what to whom.

"How could you remember all that?" asked the young *porets* in amazement.

Reb Mordkhe promptly opened the safe and showed him copies of all the papers that had been destroyed.

"Every man has in him the desire to sin, especially when it comes to money," he said. "Memory alone is too weak to fight such a strong desire."

If not for his honesty, Reb Mordkhe could have made a fortune then and there. The old *porets* had lent him huge sums of money which he could have denied and no one would have been the wiser.

11. THE MARKET

Though we've covered a lot of ground until now, we still haven't reached the heart of Tishevits. We've looked at the six bridges leading into town, the two yards that were left out in the cold. We've mentioned some of the most important streets and memorable sites. But all this is nothing but a

Market day in Horkhov, Volin province. The shul is in the background with the peasant wagons parked all around.

shell without the yoke. What's missing is the very thing that makes a shtetl what it is—the marketplace. For without a market all the Jews would starve to death and all the peasants would be naked and barefoot. The market is the pulse, the meeting ground, the center of action.

Six days a week the market is nothing but an empty unpaved area surrounded on all sides by stores. Right in the middle is the grey, rusted water pump and next to it the firebell on top of a high pole with a long cord running down. The stores are run mostly by women. Stores of every conceivable kind: ironware and odds-and-ends; textiles and leather goods, flour and spices, shoes and hats, fruit and meat, furs and pelts; handmills that grind different grains and cereals all day long. And to top it all off, the pharmacy with its large black sign in *goyish* letters—the pharmacy with its hidden secrets and strong odors of medicine that make you cough.

The barber's pole with its peppermint-stick sign catches the eyes of all who pass by. We Jews hurry past the tall porch so as not to see Moyshe Barber standing there with a naked head and naked chin, as he shaves the faces of peasants and Jews who have left the path of righteousness.

Nearby is the local tavern with its glass door and constant noise. It too has a sign: a steaming hot samovar on top, a glass and plate below. On the plate, just begging to be swallowed, is a piece of red salami.

On Wednesday the market comes alive. The central area is filled with the high peasant wagons that arrive early in the morning. The wagons are packed with the produce and livestock of the entire area; horses, cows and chickens, grain and fruits, vegetables, milk products, eggs and flax. All this disappears into the Jewish storehouses, for a price, of course. The peasants crowd around the Jewish stalls and display tables piled high with fur and three-cornered hats with shiny beaks, short cotton jackets and broad velvet slacks, high boots and pieces of colored linen. The peasants haggle and barter until the deal is clinched with a clap of hands. For good measure they get an extra kerchief, ribbon, or a shiny white comb that reflects the rays of the sun. The faces of the peasant women glow with satisfaction while the Jewish merchants hustle and bustle around them so as not to pass up the sales they have been waiting for all week long.

One never knows when or where trouble might start. All of a sudden someone might feel that he's been cheated or someone else, after swallowing a herring too many, might throw it all up, swearing a blue streak against his own mother and all the Jews. One word leads to another and the whole fair might explode into violence, God forbid. When that happens, all it takes is for one of the Bere-Aba Clan to appear and things quiet down. If not, the peasant will soon find himself flat on his back in one of the alleys.

The job gets done so quickly and quietly that hardly anyone notices. The fair continues: horses neighing, pigs squeaking, ducks quacking, hens crowing and voices shouting from the tavern with the steaming samovar. Nothing to worry about—the guys from Greblye Street are keeping a watchful eye out for all possible trouble makers.

On market day, the children don't play outside. They don't even go swimming. The banks of the river are crowded with horses and young peasants. It looks as if the peasantry has taken over the whole town with all its six bridges. If it's very hot, the older boys can always cool off in the *mikve*.

12. THE HOUSE OF BRICK

It towers over the entire market. Three stories high at the very point where the market ends and Greblye Street begins. To be quite honest, there isn't a brick in it. All three stories are made of wood, but two sides of the building are protected by tin-plate, painted over to resemble a brick wall. Which is good enough for us.

Somehow, the Brick House belongs and yet doesn't belong to the rest of the shtetl—just like its owner, Berish the No-

Market with an alarm bell in the foreground, Lukov, Lublin province.

tary Public. He lives on the top floor with the huge airy rooms that are opened to the *khasidim* of our town only on *simkhes-toyre* [Simkhat Torah] or when Reb Dovidl Rizhiner comes for a visit. The very fact that Reb Dovidl, a direct heir of the Rizhiner dynasty, lodges in the Brick House once every few years, gives the building a very special status.

"The Rizhiner are royalty, you must understand. They hardly ever mix with the people. If one of them does decide to make a trip, you can be sure there is a good reason for it. And wherever he goes, his royalty goes with him. Just think how privileged we are that Reb Dovidl brings his royalty here as well."

This is what *khasidim* say as they look up at the Brick House with grateful smiles.

On the Friday of Reb Dovidl's visit, the market becomes quiet by midday. When Reb Dovidl begins reciting the Song of Songs, the entire market, all the side streets and all the bridges, is still.

Sure, in the Radziner *shtibl* people will make faces and poke fun: "A King in Slippers," referring to Reb Dovidl's soft shoes and quiet way of speaking. In the *shtiblekh* of Trisk and Belz, jealous voices will say: "What's the big deal? You never hear him teach anything new."

But the rest of the town knows that Reb Dovidl, in his own quiet way, inspires awe wherever he goes. Why even his arrival is something special. The upholstered carriage on rubber springs comes all the way from across the border. And the driver is a rich *khosed* from Galicia. Reb Dovidl himself is not particularly tall or impressive-looking, but he carries with him unmistakably the greatness of his royal family.

Berish the Notary, on the other hand, is the tallest man in town, just like the house he lives in. Even his wife is tall and always beautifully dressed. Berish writes petitions to the government and other documents for the courts. In the large, perfectly clean room where he receives his clients, you can see a piece of paper on the wall that states in black and white that "Citizen Berko Schwartz is authorized to give legal advice and to attend civil suits." This in itself is enough to separate Berish from the rest of us.

The front of his house looks out over the market, but the windows on the side face the Horse Market with its hog stalls and its red rooster on top of the pole. Those unlucky Jews who live near the Horse Market and see the red rooster everyday of the year are especially careful on Christmas Eve. On that night they keep their curtains tightly closed and don't let the children even take a peek outside. From all the surrounding suburbs the church bells ring loud and clear and when that happens the rooster comes alive. First a whirlwind spreads the rooster's wings and sets it spinning on its wire feet. Then the rooster stretches its bright red throat and gives out a bloodcurdling COCK-A-DOODLE-DO! If we Jews didn't know from experience to keep our ears plugged at that very moment, who knows what price we'd pay?

Jewish children always cross the Horse Market on the run. Who can stand the sight of white sides of lard hung on huge hooks? And who can stand the smell when the hogs are being skinned and boiled? There's only one place to go to escape the stench and the noise, and that's the Brick House.

No matter what's happening all around, the house itself maintains a calm, quiet dignity. One look at the fancy stores on the first floor is enough to make you forget there ever was a market. The small display windows wink at you with their white shoe boxes, long bales of textiles, and all kinds of leather goods. The doors of the stores are always kept closed. You can't just run in whenever you please. It takes a while till you shake off the noise of the market and you open a door with a polished knob that sets off a bell inside the shop. As soon as you walk in, the door snaps shut behind you as if to say: The market noise mustn't enter, even for a split second.

There's no rushing and no bargaining in these stores. Here you go by the rules of the big city where the boxes with red and blue tags all come from. The stores are owned by Yankl Merchant, a lively character with a blond beard and silver pince-nez.

"It's the latest style," he says as he sits comfortably in the store watching the saleslady serving you. Sometimes he gets up from his chair, removes his pince-nez and says: "We don't bargain here," if he hears a customer complain about the price.

He seldom serves the customer himself unless it's a *porets* or one of the women from the Yard. Then he greets the customer with a big smile as if he were waiting for him all day. In perfect Polish he sings the praises of his international merchandise.

It's even rare for him to show his face outside except when he's expecting a new shipment. This is the day the shtetl tailors and shoemakers fear the most. Who knows what new style he's imported that will rob them of their last meagre earnings?

But if you're really in a hurry or if the smell of lard has gotten into your system, then avoid Yankl Merchant and his stores altogether. Pass them by. Only a few feet more and you'll be among Jews of your own kind: Khone the iron-goods dealer, Khayim of the soda shop, and Khaytshe the *gabe's* wife who owns the kerosene store. Her store never closes.

Abridged and adapted from Jacob Zipper.

UNIT TWO
THE GEOGRAPHY OF YIDDISH

The Spinker rebe and his followers. Sapunta, Romania.

It was a kingdom. It stretched from Amsterdam to Shklov and from Strasbourg to Odessa. It was the largest empire in the history of Europe and lasted for almost a thousand years. And all without a king or parliament, an army or civil service. In fact, it only existed in the minds and mouths of its speakers, and they kept it a secret from everyone else. It was a language kingdom made up only of words.

1. THE FOUR GROUPS

The earliest records indicate that Yiddish evolved in the Rhine Valley among Jewish settlers from Italy and France. This later became known as Old Western Yiddish and was made up of three groups. The oldest and most respected of the three were the Hebrew-Aramaic words from the Jewish religious heritage. You may recognize a good many Hebrew-Aramaic loanwords that are used in Yiddish in their Ashkenazic pronunciation: sholem (peace), *khazn* (cantor), *ganef* (thief), *yontef* (holiday). Not all Hebrew-Aramaic words in Yiddish are outright loanwords. Some have actually been created by Yiddish-speaking Jews: *metsiye* (bargain), *klezmer* (musician), *khevre-man* (fellow or brat), and *porets* (nobleman). Now they have been "borrowed back" into modern Hebrew with their Yiddish meanings.

The second group of words were those brought by the Jewish settlers from Western France and Northern Italy—from their own Jewish versions of Old French and Old Italian. This influence remains today particularly in Jewish family names. The French name Bonhomme became Bunem in Yiddish. The Italian names Senior and Angelo became Shneyer and Anshl. Even the Yiddish name Yente, which seems to be 100% Yiddish, can actually be traced back to the name Gentille.

The third group was perhaps the most powerful because it was the language of the area those Jews had immigrated to. There were several distinct dialects of German in the Middle Ages, and no one is quite sure which one or ones were most important in the growth of Yiddish. At any rate, there was ample room for a new language to develop alongside the native tongue, and Yiddish thus became a Germanic language in much the same way that English is related to German. Compare these two sentences and you will notice a great similarity:

English: My brother says: open the door and thank him for the fish.

Yiddish: Mayn bruder zogt: efn di tir un badank im farn fish.

Why did Jews in the Rhine Valley, in the medieval cities of Worms, Mayence, Cologne, and Speyer, need a language of their own? The late Max Weinreich, the foremost historian of Yiddish, explained that the Jews of these cities chose to live apart from the *goyim.* They had to be close to a *shul,* they needed their own courts of law, their own slaughterhouse, a ritual bath, and, when the time came, a Jewish cemetery. Settling in groups was the natural thing to do in the Middle Ages. What Jews wanted in particular was, not isolation from the Christians, but insulation from Christianity.

These Jews developed a built-in system to express the distance between Jewishness and goyishness. They summed it up in one word—*lehavdl,* to differentiate. When a Jew mentioned something sacred and profane in the same breath, he divided them by plunking *lehavdl* in the middle. "The rabbi and *lehavdl* the governor took part in the ceremony."

That's not all. Ashkenazic Jews (Jews who originally came from Germany) developed a double vocabulary for their world and that of the *goyim.* Their world was called *di yidishe gas,* the Jewish Street, as opposed to *dos mokem,* the non-Jewish town. Jews celebrate a *yontef*, a holiday, while the word for a non-Jewish holiday is *khoge* (an Aramaic loanword). When a Jew dies, his body is placed in an *orn* which is then buried in a *besoylem* or *beysakvores* (cemetery). A non-Jew is placed in a *trune* and is buried in a *tsvinter*.

As long as most Yiddish-speaking Jews lived among German speakers, Yiddish was considered just another variety of German. Ashkenazic writers in Hebrew referred to Yiddish as *loshn ashkenaz*, "the language of Germany." In Yiddish itself, *taytsh* was the current name; it still lives in expressions like *taytsh-khumesh*, the Yiddish version of the Pentateuch; *fartaytshn*, to translate into Yiddish, to explain; and *staytsh*, how is that?

If we had a time machine to whisk us back to Mayence in the year 1025, we could tape the following interview with a *bokher* in Rabeynu Gershom's *yeshive*:

Interviewer: What language do you speak?

Yeshive-bokher: Why the same language as the gentiles, of course!

Interviewer: Exactly the same? Don't you have specific words that are unknown to the *goyim*?

Yeshive-bokher: Well, I must admit there are a few such words, such as *toyre*, Torah; *mitsve*, commandment, good deed; *tfile*, prayer. But all these words come from Hebrew.

Interviewer: Really? How do you say "to bless"?

Yeshive-bokher: Bentshn.

Interviewer: Is *bentshn* Hebrew or German?

Yeshive-bokher: I guess neither. Then where does it come from?

Interviewer: From the Jewish language your grandparents brought along from France and Italy.

Yeshive-bokher: Come to think of it, here are some other examples I just thought of. We say *yidishn*, to circumcise; *reynikayt*, the scroll of the Torah; *opgisn negl-vaser*, to wash one's hands in the morning.

Interviewer: Very good! These expressions, though based on Germanic words, could hardly be considered German, because they have been coined by Jews for specifically Jewish needs.

Yeshive-bokher: So we don't speak German after all?

Eastern Yiddish was established four hundred years later by the Ashkenazic Jews who began to settle in Poland and the Grand Duchy of Lithuania. The Slavic languages Polish, Ukrainian and Belorussian thus became the youngest group to influence the makeup of Yiddish. You may know some of the Slavic loanwords: *nu,* well; *tshaynik,* teapot; *zeyde,* grandfather; *bobe,* grandmother; and *yarmlke,* skull cap. Thanks to the Slavic influence, Yiddish developed several diminutive forms. Almost any noun or name can be made smaller by adding a suffix. *Yung* means youth; *yingl* means a youth or boy and *yingele* means a little boy. *Beygl* becomes *beygele,* a little bagel. Avrom (Abraham) becomes Avreml, Avremele or the more chummy—Avremtshik. Similarly, *mame* (mother) can become *mamele, mamenyu* or even *mameshi.* The -nik ending from Slavic has found its way via Yiddish into other languages: kibbutznik, alrightnik, no-goodnik.

Based on Max Weinreich
(1953, 1967).

2. THE GEFILTE FISH LINE

No kingdom, even one made up entirely of words, can exist without showing signs of strife. The transition from Western to Eastern Yiddish happened smoothly enough. But something occurred in the eastward migration that was to create two rival camps of Yiddish speakers, and the *gefilte fish* line was to mark the boundary between them.

On the face of it, what could be less controversial than the preparation of fish for *shabes,* which goes back at least to Talmudic times? But for some reason that has yet to be discovered, Jews west of the border indicated in Figure 1 made a sweet type of fish with sugar. The easterners wouldn't go near the stuff since they seasoned their *gefilte fish* with pepper.

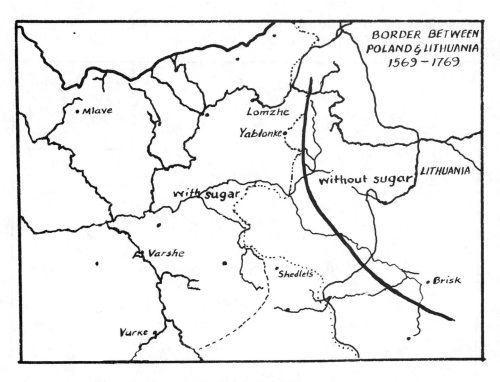

Figure 1. Seasoning of Sabbath Fish. Marvin Herzog, p. 19.

Another food found in all East European homes was *farfl*. These are pellets or flakes of dough, usually cooked in broth. *Farfl* was prepared in different ways from place to place. In the central, Polish-Ukrainian-Romanian area, the squares are cut from flat sheets of dough. In an area north of the center, where Poland passes into Lithuania, the pellets were made by chopping the dough. In the extreme northeast and southwest, an extremely old method dating back to medieval Germany was used: a hardened ball of dough is grated down to size. [The Israeli and American noodle industries, by the way, have adopted the cut-square pattern.]

Why would one group of Jews adopt the peasant's way of making *farfl* while another group would keep their *farfl* recipe from Germany? Was there some type of communication barrier dividing the groups, say a river or a mountain range? Or perhaps the clue to the differences lies in

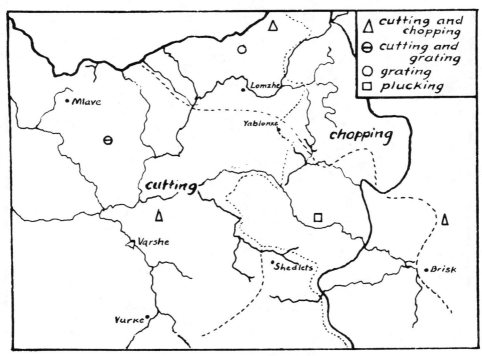

Figure 2. Preparation of farfl. Marvin Herzog, p. 19.

history rather than topography (the layout of the land). These questions become all the more perplexing when we realize that the Jews who prepared a spicy fish and chopped their *farfl* spoke a different dialect of Yiddish from those who ate sweet fish and cut their *farfl.*

For a further clue to explain these differences we must go back 200 years to the little town of Mezhbizh in the Ukraine. This is where the religious movement Khasidism began, a movement that affected all East European Jewry.

This map shows the spread of Khasidism from Mezhbizh where the Bal Shem Tov lived, westward into Poland, and then towards the northeast. Khasidism was a mystical movement that spread by means of wandering preachers—*magidim*—and of the disciples of the Bal Shem Tov. The

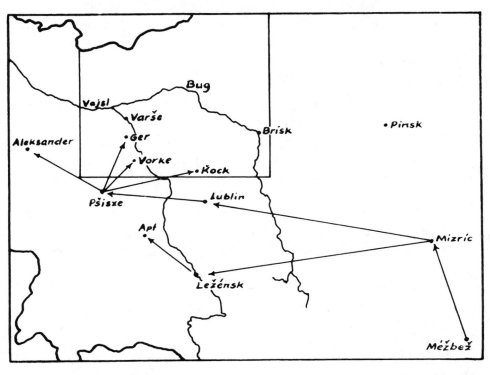

Figure 3. The spread of Khasidism into northern Poland. Marvin Herzog, p. 22.

major followers became khasidic *rebeim*, settled in other towns, and they in turn encouraged other students to spread the teaching. The following chart shows the teacher-student relationship between the early khasidic masters. The *rebe* was known for the town where he settled down and began attracting his followers. Thus, Dov Ber, the "Magid of Mezritsh" had two main pupils, one who settled in Lezhensk, the other in Lublin. Each, in turn had one main pupil who established their own centers in Apt and Pshiskhe, and so on.

You should keep in mind that not all Polish Jews became *khasidim*. Those who didn't, the so-called *misnagdim*, were every bit as "religious" as the Jews who followed the teachings of a khasidic *rebe*. Even so, there are reports of entire communities being converted to Khasidism after a single visit by a *rebe*. As different brands of Khasidism developed, one town might have followers of several different *rebeim*, as was the case in Tishevits. The spread of one particular school, that of Ger, is illustrated in figure 5.

Now what does all this have to do with the *gefilte fish* line? We have already seen that it marks the boundary between Polish Jews and those who settled in Lithuania as well as between their respective Yiddish dialects. Now if we compare Figures 1 and 2 with Figure 3 we will see that the line dividing Jews on fish, *farfl* and dialect is not far from the northeastern limit of the spread of Khasidism. Except for a few early converts, Lithuanian Jews never did take to what a khasidic *rebe* had to offer. Lite became a stronghold of *misnagdim*. Does this mean that *khasidim* "brought" sweet *gefilte fish* to northern Poland or that the movement stopped at the border of Lite because the Polish *khasidim* couldn't understand Litvish Yiddish? We know that Litvish Yiddish (the Lithuanian dialect) is much older than Khasidism, but when exactly did the *gefilte fish* line come into the picture—before or after the rise of Khasidism? There is as yet no way to know.

Many other differences could be illustrated between Polish and Lithuanian Jewry, and certainly between them and all of the other Jewish groups of Eastern Europe. It's not always clear how customs and speech patterns were related. The important thing is to realize that basic differences did exist between the various Jewish communities of Eastern Europe.

Abridged from
Marvin I. Herzog

GENEALOGY OF KHASIDIC MASTERS

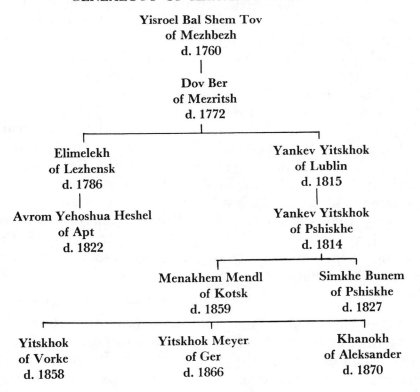

The teacher-student relationship between khasidic masters. The lines do not indicate family relations. Marvin Herzog, p. 23.

3. YIDDISH DIALECTS

Do you know where we are? We've reached Brod! We must be near America. A fine city, this Brod. The city, the streets, the people are nothing like those back home. Even the Jews aren't like those back home. Actually, they're the same Jews. In fact, you can even say they're more Jewish than our own Jews. Their *peyes* are much longer than ours. Their *kapotes* nearly reach the ground. They wear strange hats, belts and shoes and socks instead of boots. The women all wear wigs. But their language! You should hear their language. They call it "German." It's nothing like what we speak. Actually the words are the same as ours but with "ahs." For instance, *vos* is *vas*, *dos* is *das*, *shlofn* is *shlafn*, *broyt* is *brayt*, *fleysh* is *flaysh*, *Meyer* is *Mayer*, a *beheyme* is a *behayme*, a *sheygetz*—a *shaygets*, *milkhk* is *melkh*, *likht* is *lekht*, a *yid* is a *yeed*, a *yidene*—a *yeedene*, *kind* is *kund*, *tinterl* is *tunterl*, a *tsibele* is a *tsaybele*, a *sirnikl*—a *shvibele*. You should only hear them speak! When they talk, they sing. It sounds as if they're always chanting the Torah.

We caught on soon enough. First came our friend Pinye. He started speaking "German" almost the first day we arrived. It was easier for him, because he had studied some "German" at home. My brother Elye says, that even though he never studied "German" he can understand just as much as Pinye. I listen to others speaking "German" and I'm picking it up. In a foreign country, says Pinye, you've got to learn the language.

Sholom Aleichem (1920).

What happened to Motl and his family is that for the first time in their lives they came face to face with *galitsyaner* Yiddish, the Yiddish spoken by Jews in Galicia. The "German" they heard on the streets of Brod was mostly Yiddish, except for the first three words on the list. A real *galitsyaner* would say: *vus*, *dus*, and *shlufn*. The dialects of Yiddish differ from each other mainly in their pronun-

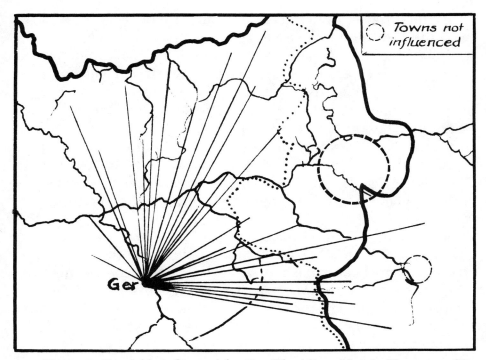

Figure 5. Shtetlekh influenced by Ger Khasidism. Marvin Herzog, p. 25.

ciation of vowels. The 'ey' sound Motl was familiar with from his Ukrainian dialect became 'ay' (as in 'sigh') in *galitsyaner* Yiddish. Hence the words for meat, *fleysh*; animal, *beheyme*; and gentile boy or smart-alec, *sheygets*, as well as the name for Meir—all sounded somewhat different. *Galitsyaner* Yiddish also has a long and short *i* while Motl's Yiddish has only the short variety. (*yid*, Jew, becomes *yeed*). Apparently, Motl got so carried away with the vowel changes, that he made up some of his own. If *ey* was pronounced *ay* in *galitsyaner* Yiddish, why not make all *i*-sounds into *u* or *ay?* He therefore changed *kind* (child) into *kund*, *tinterl* (inkwell) into *tunterl* and *tsibele* (onion) into *tsaybele*. Finally, the dialect spoken in Brod had different names for certain objects like a match, which Motl was used to calling a *sirnikl* and Brod Jews called *shvibele*.

Besides dialect differences, Motl might have encountered a totally different vocabulary among the *khasidim* of Galicia (the long *kapotes*, strange hats and belts and the shoes and socks are signs of khasidic dress). For *khasidim* did have Yiddish expressions all their own. Here are some examples: *rebe*, a khasidic rabbi; *gabe*, the *rebe's* secretary; *hoyf*, the *rebe's* residence; *shiraim*, whatever food the *rebe* leaves over on his plate; *kvitl*, a written request given to the *rebe*; *pidyen*, money given to the *rebe* for his advice or blessing. For *misnagdim*, except when talking about Khasidism, the words meant different things or weren't used at all.

Many Jews followed the example of Motl and his family. They traveled to other countries. In this way the dialects became somewhat mixed. In America, many "mixed marriages" took place between Jewish immigrants from different regions. Though there aren't too many cases on record of a *litvak* (a Jew who speaks the Litvish dialect), marrying a *galitsyaner!*

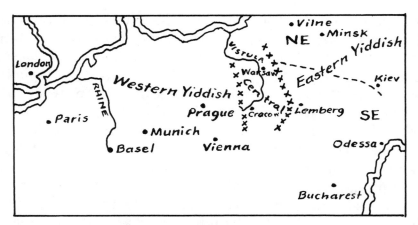

Figure 6. The major dialects of Yiddish. Uriel Weinreich, (1971) p. 43.

4. JEWISH GEOGRAPHY

Ask the average Pole where Khelm is and he may or may not know. But any Jew can tell you, whether he's ever been to Poland or not, that Khelm is the most famous foolstown in the world. It might seem strange that two nations living on the same soil would have an entirely different relation to the same place, but that's the way it happened. Jewish geography is simply not the same as *goyish* geography. For one thing, Jewish memory defies geographical change. The historical boundaries of the Grand Duchy of Lithuania (1569-1772) are preserved in Jewish geography as Lite— even two hundred years later! Secondly, other towns and cities besides Khelm that were unimportant to the *goyim* were actually towering cultural landmarks for the Jews. What Jew hadn't heard of such khasidic centers as Rizhin, Lyadi, Korets, Lezhensk and Ger? What Jew could hear the names Mir, Valozhin and Ponevizh, centers of Talmudic scholarship, and not respond with a sigh of pleasure?

5. SHTETL NICKNAMES IN LITE

How are nicknames created?

A. An actual event. Some nicknames are connected with a happening or true story that made an impact on the surrounding *shtetlekh*. It's obvious that such names as "Treyper *shames*" (the *shames* from Treype), "Musnik oath-breakers, Simne corpses, Sereye arsonists (people who purposely set fire to buildings) and Rakishek cymbalists" originate in some event. Unfortunately, I have no idea what these events were. But here's one I do know:

The town of Kelem (not to be confused with Khelm) is nicknamed "Kelmer sleepers." Tsar Alexander I was expected to pass through the town and the townspeople prepared themselves several days in advance. Finally the Tsar did come, but he arrived in the middle of the night and the people of Kelem slept through the whole thing!

B. First impression. Sometimes a nickname is coined by someone who passes through the shtetl for the first time and notices something peculiar about the place. Being a stranger to town, he notices things that a native never thinks about twice. For instance, the visitor sees what seems to him to be a fantastic number of goats. When he returns home, he can't stop talking about the "Ramigole goats" or the "Vidokle goats" or the goats of Tsaykishek or Zosle. Perhaps the visitor is insulted by something the townsfolk said to him or better yet, he gets sick from a dish they offered him. You can be sure this man will spread the news about "Vabolnik broth, Subotsh *kugl*, Masyad crackers and Shkud *farfl-tsimes.*"

Say the stranger was robbed. Don't you think he'll paint the whole town as a den of thieves? Sure enough we have: "Vidz thieves, Zelve thieves, Yaneve thieves, Posval thieves," and "Plungian thieves."

A group of beggars shows up in town and does not get the reception it expected or the community leaders won't even let the group go about its business. The beggars move on and spread the word far and wide: "Maliat pigs, Maliat charity," or "Krok pigs". (I can vouch for the fact that the tiny shtetl of Krok was swarming with pigs, at least when I visited there.)

C. Stereotype. Sometimes a nickname isn't far off the mark: it really does sum up the type of people who live there. Jews of the neighboring towns decide that the shtetl in question is full of boors who know nothing of the Torah. The result: "Utyan bear-trainers, Yaneve boors, Vizhun drivers, Vilkiye clod-hoppers."

Or else the townspeople are considered to be snobs and braggarts—"Aniksht show-offs, Bolnik or Vilkovishk roosters" or an even better one: "Salok moon" because the people of Salok are convinced that their moon is different from everyone else's!

The old community of Keydan, which once played such an

important role in the history of Lithuanian Jewry, is most certainly a town of braggarts. They always say with great pride: "We Keydaner..." while they poke their thumb at their chest. Well, from poking so long they develop a hole— "Keydan holes"—while on the other side they form a hump— "Keydan hunchbacks"!

Those places that became modern before the others, where the *haskole* [Haskalah] movement spread to first, were nicknamed: "Raseyn aristocrats, Raseyn sinners, Kalvarye Germans, Shavl *treyf*-eaters."

D. Profession. Other nicknames reflect the economic state of the shtetl, how rich or poor it is, or they reflect the main work of its inhabitants. "Pumpian sacks" and "Vilkomir bums" mean that in both places most people live off charity. "Latskeve rich men" means the same thing because the name is ironic. "Troke cucumbers" tells us that many Troke Jews were in the cucumber business. Similarly, "Aniksht woolens." Then there are the nicknames about smuggling. "Yurbarik smugglers" is indeed an accurate nickname, as are "Shaki and Gorzd horse thieves." In the last two places, many Jews sold horses and brought them over the border to Germany. As we know, selling and stealing are almost one and the same in the horse trade.

Some of the larger towns had a higher standard of living. The neighboring *shtetlekh* were the first to notice this and complain: "Ponevezh turkey-gobblers, Raseyn gluttons, Shaki honeylickers."

E. Substitutes. How many towns can you call by the name "pigs"? Eventually you start thinking up substitutes. Besides "Tsaykishek goats," as mentioned before, there are also "Tsaykishek he-goats." When a shtetl has the bad luck of being known as a foolstown, it's also called a town of wise men. If Ragole is known for its bad lunches, why not: "Ragole dinner"?

F. Associations. Finally, there can be all kinds of associations people have with one town or another. In Yaneve, for

47

instance, there was a large family of Bene-Zuske's children. Hence the whole town was called "Bene-Zuske's." There's a shtetl called Layzeve which sounds very close to a popular creature that makes you scratch, i.e. *layz* (lice). The nickname: "Layzeve scratchers." We mentioned *"Shkud farfl-tsimes"* earlier. Now *farfl* is a type of round noodle and the marketplace in Shkud was paved with round cobblestones. That's easy enough to figure out. And since Shkudvil sounds almost the same as Shkud, you have by association: "Shkudvil *farfl-tsimes*"!

Leyb Zamet.

6. LUBLIN PROVINCE

Lublin is a province full of famous places, including the most famous shtetl of all—Khelm. Other towns, such as Goray and Tomashov, not to mention the provincial capital, Lublin, are known to the readers of Isaac Bashevis Singer (*Satan in Goray, The Magician of Lublin*). The famous Yiddish writer I. L. Perets was born in the city of Zamoshtsh. But the Jews of Lublin province had altogether different associations with the cities and towns of their region. Each town had its usually nasty nickname and it's reason for being called that—by the people of the *other* towns.

Thus Zamoshtsh, for instance, was hated and feared by tradition-minded Jews for being the center of *haskole*, enlightenment. Why the very name of the city gave it away as a hotbed of sin and corruption! Take the letters as they appear in Hebrew: *zayin, mem, vov, shin, tsadek*, add up their numerical value and you get 443, the same as *apikoyres* (heretic)! Hence the flattering nickname: *zamoshtsher freser* (gluttons).

Even towns with an excellent record managed somehow to get caught with a bad name. Kuzmir was built in the fourteenth century by King Kazimir the Great. Jews and non-Jews alike knew of its glorious past. For many, many years, beautiful silver candlesticks and a gold curtain over the ark were kept in the old synagogue. Despite all these points in its favor, the inhabitants were called *"kuzmirer apostates"* and all because of one man named Khatskele, who converted to Christianity and left a black mark on the town forever afterwards.

Of all the towns I can remember, only one had a good name and that was Reyvits, a small and quiet shtetl. The local rulers did not kill the Jews during the terrible Khmelnitski massacres and for this reason the town was immortalized in the expression: "As quiet as Reyvits."

Abridged from Sh. Khalamish (1951).

7. SOURCES OF THE YIDDISH PROVERB

Just as Yiddish as a whole is made up of four main groups, the Yiddish proverb also originates from four sources. The first is the Hebrew-Aramaic religious tradition. The Mishna and Talmud, especially *Ethics of the Fathers*, are full of sayings that were "Yiddishized" by Ashkenazic Jews. Second, are medieval German proverbs that were adopted in the Middle Ages and remain part of the Yiddish proverb collection to this day.

Slavic proverbs, the third source, may even appear in their natural form, without being translated. A Yiddish speaker will often cite a saying in Ukrainian, Polish, or Belorussian and introduce it with the phrase: *a goy zogt a vertl*, "As the peasant says...." Some Yiddish speakers know ten Ukrainian or Belorussian proverbs to every Yiddish one. In fact there is reason to believe that some of these Slavic proverbs were actually made up by Jews!

The *khasidim* had a special attitude to the gentile peasant. According to khasidic teaching, not only a scholar but even the uneducated Jew—why even the illiterate gentile peasant—could worship God in his own way. Which means

49

that the songs and sayings of the peasant must contain many hidden religious secrets. A khasidic proverb says just that: *a goyish vertl iz lehavdl a toyre:* a peasant proverb is like a quote from the Torah.

As long as the *goyish vertl* is cited in its original tongue, identifying it as Slavic is pretty easy. But as soon as gentile proverbs appear in their Yiddish form, it's anybody's guess whether the source is German, Polish, or Ukrainian. Therefore, the second and third sources of the Yiddish proverb can be considered as one–any gentile proverb that Jews picked up and translated either in Western or Eastern Europe.

The fourth source is probably the most interesting because it is based not on literature or borrowing, but rather on the lives of Jews themselves. Here are some examples.

Hobn tsu zingen un tsu zogn.   האָבן צו זינגען און צו זאָגן.

Literally: To have to sing and to say.
Meaning: To have no end of trouble.

This proverb dates back to the Middle Ages when wandering troubadours "sang and said" their heroic epic poems. The more dramatic an event was, the more it suited his story. If someone would be "singing and talking" about an event it must really be exciting.

Men zol im afile brenen un brotn.

מען זאָל אים אַפֿילו ברענען און בראָטן.

Literally: Even if he should be burned and roasted.
Meaning: Nothing can change his mind.

This refers to the tortures Jews suffered during the Spanish Inquisition in the Middle Ages.

Meylekh sobietskis yorn.   מלך סאָביעצקיס יאָרן.

Literally: in the years of King Sobieski.
Meaning: "in olden days."–"As old as Grandma Moses."

Jan Sobieski was a Polish king in the seventeenth century. At least a dozen other kings could have been chosen

50

as a symbol of the past, but Sobieski was particularly good to the Jews, so the honor went to him.

Opton emetsn af terkish.   אָפּטאָן עמעצן אויף טערקיש.

Literally: To treat someone in the Turkish manner.
Meaning: To play someone a dirty trick or to double-cross.

A reference to the sad experience of the Jews with the Tatars, a Turkish tribe that lived in the Crimea, and over-ran Eastern Europe in the seventeenth century.

Firn shtroy keyn mitsrayim.   פירן שטרוי קיין מצרים.

Literally: To carry straw to Egypt.
Meaning: (an English equivalent) To carry coals to New-castle.

The reference is biblical. What could be more useless than carrying straw to Egypt, where it was used by the Jews when they had to make bricks for Pharoah.

Raykh vi Koyrekh.   רייך ווי קורח.

Literally: As rich as Korah.
Meaning: As rich as a king.

Korah was a Levite who organized a revolt against Moses in the desert and suffered a miserable death (Numbers XVI). Why does he deserve a proverb in his name? Not for this, but because the Talmud tells legends about his fabulous wealth.

Az men fregt a shayle, iz treyf.

אַז מען פֿרעגט אַ שאלה איז טרייף.

Literally: If you ask permission, the answer will be "forbidden."
Meaning: If you ask permission the answer will be "no"—so better just act on your own.

This proverb refers to the custom of consulting a rabbi on the "kosher" state of a chicken, a pot, a dispute, a wedding, etc. The answer was, more often than not, *"treyf"* —forbidden. This saying is used today even by Jews who no longer practice any religious rituals.

Az men klingt iz khoge.　　　　.אַז מען קלינגט איז חגא

Literally: When the church bells are ringing, the *goyim* are celebrating a holiday.
Meaning: Where there is smoke there is fire.

Uriel Weinreich (1971)
pp. 34-35.

8. A PROVERB AND WHERE IT COMES FROM

Where I come from in the Ukraine, in the province of Kiev, we had a popular saying: *A tap in vogn shat nit,* "A tap in the wagon does no harm." Well, this proverb was apparently created in our village of Marozevke with a total Jewish population of fifteen families. I heard the story from my mother of blessed memory, when I was still a child.

Once a Jew from Rizhin passed through our village and stopped over at the mill. The mill was a popular stopover for many Jewish travelers who could expect a glass of tea since the miller was a hospitable Jew.

On this particular night there was a full moon. One of our Marozevke Jews decided to take a walk. He was a boor and a miser whom everyone hated. He was so stingy that even on *yonkiper* [Yom Kippur] he refused to contribute for the *khazn's* salary! So this fellow goes up to the wagon that was parked in front of the mill, he feels inside and takes out a *tales* [tallith]. The stranger didn't notice this and went on his way. It wasn't until the next morning when he was about to say the morning prayers that he realized a Jew from Marozevke had stolen his *tales.* That very same morning, our local miser appeared in *shul* with a new *tales* which he never would have paid for himself.

Ever since then we would say: "A tap in the wagon does no harm." You never know what you can find in a parked wagon. While buying something, whether the merchandise looked good or not, the saying would often pop up: *A tap in vogn shat nit.* There's no harm in examining the stuff before buying or at least testing the merchant to see if you can bargain down the price.

The proverb spread to other towns and eventually reached the big cities of our region, Kiev, Barditshev, Uman, and others. And from there to all the other places where Jews lived. No one but we knew where it came from.

L. Beylis.

A tap in vogn shat nit

In olden days, each city and town had an entrance gate through which all travelers had to pass. The guards would search each incoming wagon to see if it was carrying any whiskey. A guard who was too lazy to make a thorough search would simply take his spear and poke around in the wagon. This type of light "tap"—says the proverb—can do no harm.

Ignaz Bernstein, p. 115.

9. THE ANATOMY OF A YIDDISH PROVERB

When are proverbs used? When you want to show how a specific situation illustrates a general rule which the listener already knows. Say you were late for classes and in the rush you brought the wrong books. The teacher would look at you and say: "Haste makes waste." You made a specific mistake which illustrates the general rule of haste making waste, a rule you've heard many times before. If you and the teacher knew Yiddish, the proper response would be *fun aylenish kumt keyn guts nit aroys*, "no good results from hurrying."

There are any number of forms that a proverb can take. It can be an "If" proverb and concern situations from everyday life:

Az men hot gute skhoyre, hot men nit keyn moyre.

If you have good wares, no need to be scared. (An honest man has no need to worry.)

A proverb can be a comparison between two things:
Beser mit a klugn tsu farlirn eyder mit a nar tsu gevinen.
Better to lose against someone smart than to win against a fool.

Or it can be an imperative sentence, telling you what to do:
Freg nit dem royfe, nor dem khoyle.
Don't ask the doctor, ask the patient.
Gefin dem din, der heter kumt shpeter.
First find the rule, the exception comes later.

A proverb can also be in the form of a rhetorical question (when you don't expect an answer):
Az men iz in kas afn khazn, tor men keyn omeyn nit zogn?
If you're angry at the *khazn*, is that a reason not to say "amen"? (Compare with: Don't bite your nose to spite your face.)

Another form of proverb is the "A is not B" type:
An oylem iz nit keyn goylem.
The people is not a robot. (Meaning: the people has a mind of its own.)
A nemer iz nit keyn geber.
A taker is not a giver.

Based on Beatrice Silverman
Weinreich (1964).

10. POOR IN ONE RESPECT, RICH IN ANOTHER

My mother came from poverty which was not only total but also (as far as the tsarist authorities were concerned) God-given and, therefore, not to be changed. Her mother knew Yiddish, Ukrainian, and a very bare smattering of prayer-book Hebrew. She mastered not only modern Yiddish **(the stories of Sholem Aleichem being read and reread** with particular relish), but also the very old Yiddish of the *Tsene-rene,* a Yiddish version of the Bible for women.

My mother's father knew even more languages. First of

all, his prayer-book Hebrew was extremely good. In addition he also had a somewhat shaky control of Talmudic Hebrew-Aramaic (he never could devote to the Talmud the years of study that it requires) and of Polish and German as well (picked up during annual trips to his khasidic *rebe* whose court was in faraway Congress Poland). Finally, for the purposes of negotiations with the local nobleman, police officer, and other petty tsarist bureaucrats, he had acquired (entirely on his own and as a matter of pure survival) a knowledge of Russian, both spoken and printed. His Yiddish, of course, was as good as his wife's although he did not use the Yiddish of scholarly Talmudic discussions.

My mother's brothers, she had four, learned Yiddish (spoken and printed) at home, Hebrew-Aramaic (printed only) in the *kheyder* supported by the Jewish community, spoken Ukrainian from the non-Jews (particularly on market days) and Russian (spoken, written, and printed) from a university student who came daily to give them lessons in exchange for a hot kosher meal.

My mother, being a girl, did not get lessons in Hebrew-Aramaic. She was permitted to listen to the Russian lessons (but not to participate in them officially.) On the other hand, she alone was taught to write Yiddish so that letters could be sent to far-flung family members in America and in other parts of the Ukraine. Her Yiddish teacher was a pious woman at whose house several girls met every weekday afternoon in order to learn basic prayers (Hebrew), *Tsene-rene* (Old Yiddish), and letter writing (also a rather old and formal Yiddish).

My mother's childhood was scarred by poverty (two sisters and one brother died of hunger in infancy), war and revolution (five different armed bands controlled and terrorized her village during the period 1917–1919), disease (typhus, cholera, tuberculosis, malnutrition, etc.) and utter powerlessness and subjugation by the gentile world. Her health has always suffered as a result of her childhood experiences. Nevertheless, her knowledge of languages grew to include English (spoken, written and printed), Latin (printed) and, most recently, Modern Hebrew (spoken and printed). Of all the languages which she ever learned she has only forgotten Latin—studied during four years in an American high school.

Joshua Fishman.

UNIT THREE
JEWS AND GENTILES

A Jewish shoemaker serving his non-Jewish customer in the village of
Falenits, near Warsaw.

1. KNOW THY PORETS

In the centuries-old drama of Polish Jewry, one figure occupied center-stage for well over two hundred years. This was the Polish nobleman, or as the Jews called him, the *porets*. The first Jews who settled in Poland came either on the invitation or under the protection of the king himself. They settled in the royal cities of the kingdom such as Cracow, Poznan, and Lemberg. Even with the king's protection, though, these Jews had a hard time with the church and with local Christians. This is where the Polish noblemen entered the scene.

On their huge estates the nobles began to establish and encourage the development of new townships. A network of "private towns" was created. But who would settle these new towns? Not the peasants, because the nobles wished to keep them right where they were—enslaved to the land. The only alternative was to attract settlers from afar, and Jews fitted the bill perfectly.

The Jews, for their part, jumped at the chance to escape the outbreaks of fighting and hatred they faced in the old royal cities. Now they could move to places where they sometimes became the majority, or even the whole of the population. New charters were granted by the kings and nobles to communities and settlers in these new towns so that by 1650–1700, everywhere in Poland Jews had the same legal rights as the Christian middle class.

The Jews of Tishevits were granted a charter long before the "private town boom" came into full swing. King Zigmund August issued the following decree on their behalf in the year 1565:

WHEREBY WE, the King are most anxious to further the well-being of the municipality by encouraging a larger population, be it therefore decreed that we hereby permit the Jews

—to live both inside the city and out,
—to own houses, gardens and land,
—to buy and sell various goods by measure and weight,
—to distill and sell beer, mead, and whiskey,
—to engage in animal slaughter and sell the meat and
—to benefit equally with the town burghers from their privileges as well as to share their burden.

HOWEVER, the Jews are strictly forbidden to run for or accept public office.

FURTHERMORE, in order that the Jews not suffer any hindrance in their business, be it therefore decreed that fairs shall be held, according to custom, every Tuesday. If, for some reason, the day is to be altered, it shall never be changed to a Sabbath.

Up until this time, Jews were an urban people: they all lived in the royal or private cities. But now that the nobles took them under their wing, a new frontier also opened up outside of the protected towns. The vast lands of the Ukraine stood open which the nobles were very anxious to exploit. Even their vast estates closer to home could yield a fantastic income if there were only someone to take charge. The nobles themselves weren't interested, and besides, they didn't know how.

And so the *rendar* came into being. The nobles leased their estates or special branches of their estates to Jewish lessees called *rendares*. Western Europe was anxious to import agricultural products, lumber and especially alcoholic beverages from Poland. The *rendar* took over. This *rendar* often became not just an employee of the *porets*, but his business adviser as well. Of course not every Jew rented an entire estate or forest belonging to the *porets*. You could earn a good living simply by leasing a tavern and having the exclusive right to brew and sell whiskey. These taverns were spread out all over the countryside, and in this way Jews entered directly into the lives of the peasants. In 1764, in the Lublin district where Tishevits is located, 89 percent of all village *rendares* were inn or tavern keepers. The rest, about 11 percent, leased mills and dairy processing from the nobles.

In the stories that follow, you will meet good noblemen and bad. Generally speaking, the *porets* became worse as time went on. For as long as power and money were his alone, the Jew was both a helpful agent and a helpless victim. But once the *porets* lost his power to the Russian tsar and his money to gambling, there was no more reason to spare the Jew than to paint the manor house or to feed the horses.

2. THE RENDAR OPENS THE GATES OF HEAVEN

The *porets* had an only daughter, and one day she fell seriously ill. The finest doctors were called in, but they could find no way of saving her. Then the *porets* called for the priest so that he should pray to God for his daughter. Even this didn't help.

Once the *porets* realized that all his efforts had failed, he went to see his *rendar* and said to him: "Yankl, here's a hundred rubles. Ride straight into town, call together ten Jews, divide the money among them and ask them to pray for my daughter."

Yankl took the money, harnessed his horse and buggy and set out for town. By the time he reached the town, it was already late at night and there was no one to be seen in the marketplace.

As Yankl was searching high and low, he noticed Yosl the Horse Thief standing in a corner. Yankl called him over and said that he had a legitimate offer to make him.

Yankl told him the whole story and asked him to assemble a *minyen* to pray for the daughter's health.

Yosl liked the idea. He got together nine of his gang, went off to *shul* with them and they began reciting Psalms.

The next morning, the *porets'* daughter began to recover. As soon as he noticed that she was out of danger, her father, the *porets*, rushed off to his *rendar* and said to him with great joy:

"Yankl, let's go into town. I want personally to reward each of the ten Jews who prayed for my daughter."

Yankl turned pale when he heard this. But he got his wits about him and admitted the whole story about the horse-thief and his buddies.

The *porets* burst out at him: "Are you mad? Couldn't you find any better Jews?"

The *rendar* replied: "Dear *porets*, listen to me. I'll show you that I did the right thing. When I got into town, I noticed that the gates of heaven were locked with double and triple locks so as not to admit the prayers for your daughter. What to do? Then it hit me—who could possibly do a better job at lock-breaking than Yosl the Horse Thief and his gang? So I found Yosl and he and his buddies did a pretty decent job of it. They broke open the locks of the heavenly gates and brought the real cure for your daughter."

Naftoli Gross, pp. 343–344.

3. THE EVIL RENDAR

In one of the villages there lived a wealthy Jewish *rendar* whose lease included a large estate and many villages. The peasants worked his fields, took care of his yard and stables, and served him in his home. The owner of the estate, a *porets*, lived out of the country, and the Jew would send him the money once a year. But the peasants related to the *rendar* just as they did to the *porets*: they shook in their boots for fear of him.

As his wealth increased so too did his wickedness and his miserliness. He wouldn't even hear of giving charity. Two black dogs who always barked at the entrance to his yard were the terror of all passers-by. The *rendar's* cruelty became known far and wide.

As his wickedness grew so too did his pride. He would often have a carriage harnessed with six horses to take him for an excursion. The jingle of the bells could be heard all around and they gave word to the peasants that the *rendar*, the agent of the *porets*, had set out on the road. Their fear reached such a pitch that they would cross themselves. And the *rendar*? He scorned both Christians and Jews. As he stroked his chin he would think to himself: Who can do me harm? My wealth is great and it will protect me from everything. Why, even if the *porets* were to remove the estate from my hands, I would still have enough money in the banks.

The *rendar's* wife was by nature a good soul and would have lent a helping hand if it weren't for the fear of her husband that prevented her from doing good.

One day a fire broke out in one of the neighboring *shtetlekh*. The Jews of the town were reduced to ruin; they emerged naked and barefoot. People from far and wide, as soon as they heard of the fire, rushed in to offer assistance to the unfortunate victims.

The leaders of the community decided: Let's pay a visit to the *rendar*. Perhaps his heart will be moved by the size of our calamity. But no sooner did the messengers reach his gate than the two black dogs pounced on them, ripped their *kapotes* and set their fangs into them. And the *rendar*? He stood at the window and enjoyed the sight. He turned to his distraught servant who could barely keep the dogs in check and said: What did they want, those city beggars? What

The Satmer rebe, dressed in a fur coat, greets His Majesty, the King of Romania. The local priest stands on the extreme left and the funny Austrian helmet can be seen in back of the rebe's head.

did they think, that I'd hand out alms? They'll never come here again.

And the messengers? They cursed the *rendar* with a bitter curse: May God's vengeance be upon him.

As the years passed his wickedness increased and his heart became ever more hardened, until it turned into a heart of stone.

One day, one of the cows in the *rendar's* stable died and a stable hand came running to tell the *rendar* the news. The *rendar* laughed and said: "Go into town and tell the news to father." What he meant was the boy's father, by way of a joke. For the rich *rendar* wanted to show that one cow more or less made no difference to him at all.

The boy misunderstood and thought the *rendar* had meant the parish priest, whom the common folk call "father." What did he do? He hurried into town, went straight to church and announced: "There is a corpse in the *rendar's* yard."

The priest thought: There are many workers in the village. One of them must have died. This is why I am being summoned. What did he do? He put on his black cloak, took the icon in his hand and set out to perform the ceremony. He was accompanied by his page boys and choir as is customary in delivering the last rites.

The procession set out for the *rendar's* home with measured steps, chanting hymns and laments along the way.

Imagine how surprised they were when they reached the spot and discovered that the corpse in question was nothing but a carcass. This was a clear sign that the *rendar* not only ridiculed the gentiles but also had nothing but disdain for their religion. They began at once to ring their bells and the courtyard soon filled up with peasants. There was no stopping them now. They stripped the *rendar* and his family of their clothes and banished them from the estate. But not before giving the *rendar* a taste of his own medicine.

They locked him and his family up in the hen-house and kept them there all day. The peasants threw them food as one would feed a dog. The *rendar* was quick to realize that this was no mere mortal punishment, but that a power greater than man was settling the account with him. He realized too late that one must always give a helping hand to a person in need.

After all his property including his money in the banks was confiscated by the church, the *rendar* had no choice but to go begging. He, his sons, and his family set our collecting alms. And the black dogs? Well, seeing as how no one took care of them, they dropped dead from starvation.

As he wandered through the countryside he had time enough to recall the curse of the messengers who had come asking for help. Now the town that had burned down was rebuilt while he remained in this sorry strait for the rest of his life.

From the shtetl Lebedeve (near Vilne). Devora Fus.

4. THE PORETS PUTS HIS RENDAR TO A TEST

Three noblemen were once seated over a glass of wine and began to discuss their "little Jews." They entertained each other for a long time with jokes and stories about the Jews they employed.

"Wait a minute!" exclaimed one of the three, "I'll show you how I treat my *rendar*. This will really give you something to laugh about!" He called in one of his serfs and gave him a message to deliver to Yankl the *rendar*.

"Tell him that on Friday I'll be paying him a visit with my friends. Have him prepare enough food to fill us up till here" and drew his hand to the top of his throat to show exactly how full he meant.

The serf ran off to tell Yankl the news. When the *rendar* heard what important guests he'd be entertaining, he instructed his wife to prepare the best they had: *gefilte* fish, meat, wine and whiskey. Let them stuff themselves until they burst.

Friday the *porets* arrived on schedule with his two companions. The table was already set with every conceivable type of food. The noblemen sat themselves down and began stuffing it all in.

Once they had eaten and drunk their fill, the nobleman called Yankl over: "Serve the *mamelige* pudding!" he cried.

Yankl stepped back in fright. "Dear *porets*, I've prepared such expensive fish and meat. Why do you ask for *mamelige* too?"

"You so-and-so!" the *porets* screamed. "I said *mamelige*. I'll give you a whipping, that's what I'll give you!"

Yankl and his wife pleaded and cried, but to no avail. The *rendar* was tied down to a bench and given twenty-five lashes. The noblemen laughed their heads off.

A few days later the *porets* informed his second *rendar*, Srolke, that on Friday he would expect to have a feast prepared for himself and his friends. Srolke had already heard what happened, so along with all the delicacies he prepared *mamelige* too.

Came Friday, the noblemen showed up, sat down to the feast and began stuffing it all in. After they had finished, the *porets* called to Srolke: "Now bring in the cabbage!"

Srolke nearly fainted dead away. He caught on to what the game was, but it was too late. He pleaded with the *porets* that after such a sumptuous meal there was no need for cabbage but the *porets* cut him off and yelled: "You so-and-so, I'll beat the life out of you!"

And the *rendar* was given twenty-five lashes. On the third week, the *porets* wanted a repeat performance with his *rendar*, Mordkhe. But Mordkhe didn't prepare a thing. Hearing what had happened to the others he realized that the *porets* was living it up at the expense of his Jews. So what's the point of preparing for him?

Friday, when the *porets* and his friends arrived, they found an empty table. The guests asked with astonishment: "Where's all the food?"

The *porets* was especially angry and said: "Hey Mordkhe, what have you prepared?" The *rendar* replied very quietly: "Dear *porets*, I've prepared my backside for you. You didn't come here to eat but to beat. So beat away!"

Naftoli Gross, pp. 367–368.

5. THE KHMELNITSKI MASSACRE

When Poland annexed the Ukraine in 1569 the Golden Age of Polish Jewry went into full swing. A new frontier had opened up: the vast Ukrainian countryside. Jews played a very important role in colonizing these lands through their position as *rendares*. Under the protection of the Polish *porets*, the Jews could even control the lives of the Ukrainian peasants. Naturally, this type of power could easily be misused.

About seventy years after the colonization began, that is, in the 1640s, the Ukrainians began organizing the overthrow of the foreign rule. The Ukrainians were Greek Orthodox. They hated the Polish nobles, who were Roman Catholics, and hated their agents, who were Polish Jews. In May 1648 the peasant revolt erupted under the leadership of Bogdan Khmelnitski.

Khmelnitski, at the head of a Cossack army and strengthened by an alliance with the Tatars, scored tremendous victories against the Polish army. The revolt spread over the entire Ukraine. It swept over three hundred Jewish towns and took 100,000 Jewish lives. Hundreds of thousands were crippled, forced to convert to Christianity or sold as slaves to the Tatars. The story of Nemirov became the symbol for all that happened.

Nemirov was a walled city, a fortress. Six thousand Jews took refuge there as the Cossacks ravaged the unprotected towns and villages. Khmelnitski sent a crack unit of 300 Cossacks to take the city. Since storming the fortress was impossible, the Cossacks entered by means of a trick. They marched bearing the Polish flag. The walls of the city were manned by Poles and Jews. But the Ukrainian, Greek Orthodox population of the city who knew of the deception, advised the defenders to open the gates for their "allies." On June 10, 1648, the Cossacks entered the city and, with the active help of the local Ukrainians, they murdered most of the 6,000 Jews in a matter of hours. Some Jews escaped death by converting and others by fleeing to Tultshin. But the vast majority were butchered with knives or drowned in the river. The Torah scrolls were trampled and the parchment taken to be made into sandals.

The slaughter did not go unavenged. The Polish general Wisniowiecki, a friend of the Jews, received word of the terrible events. He marched on Nemirov with 3,000 soldiers and executed the Cossacks and their collaborators. Two years later, in 1650, the Council of the Four Lands and the Council of Lithuania declared the 20th of Sivan, the date of the Nemirov massacre, as a day of mourning and fasting for all Jews. In addition, the two councils declared a three-year period of mourning, during which time Jews were not to wear fancy clothes, to hold feasts, or even to play music at a wedding.

The scars of the Khmelnitski massacres were very deep. The local and national Jewish governing bodies—kahal and the councils—were faced with thousands of refugees, deserted women, babies born as the result of rape, captured Jews who had to be ransomed, and converted Jews who wished to return to Judaism.

With Poland weakened by the wave of Cossack attacks which were renewed four times, the Muscovite (Russian) army got hungry for a share of the spoils. They attacked in 1654 and were followed a year later by a Swedish invasion. The Muscovite forces massacred Jews, expelled them, and banished them to the Russian interior where they were forcibly converted or sold into slavery.

The Golden Age of Polish Jewry came to a sudden end. Many facets of Jewish life, such as education and economics, never fully recovered from the blows. Eventually the survivors did return to the plagued areas and grew to a population of millions in the eighteenth, nineteenth, and twentieth centuries. But the story of Khmelnitski was never forgotten.

6. THE GRAVE IN NEMIROV

In many towns in Podolia and Volin we found, near the *shul*, a mound of earth surrounded by a fence. These are known as *khosn-kale* graves and the same story is told everywhere:

During the massacres of 1648–1649, Khmelnitski and his hordes overran Podolia and Volin and wiped out entire Jewish communities. In one of these raids a bride and groom who were standing under the *khupe* in the *shul* courtyard, were murdered together with the entire wedding procession. Later the bride and groom were buried on the very same spot—right next to the *shul*. Soon it became customary for every bride and groom, before being led under the canopy with their parents, to circle the anonymous grave seven times. Following the ceremony, the musicians strike up a lively tune and the newlyweds dance around the grave to the delight of the bride and groom who are buried there.

We found just such a grave near the *shul* in Nemirov. The townspeople told us the whole story.

In the year 1648 one of the most prominent Jews in the city prepared a meal for the poor in honor of his daughter's wedding the following day. While all the poor people were celebrating, the Cossacks burst into Nemirov and took the city by storm. The groom rushed to his bride and together

70

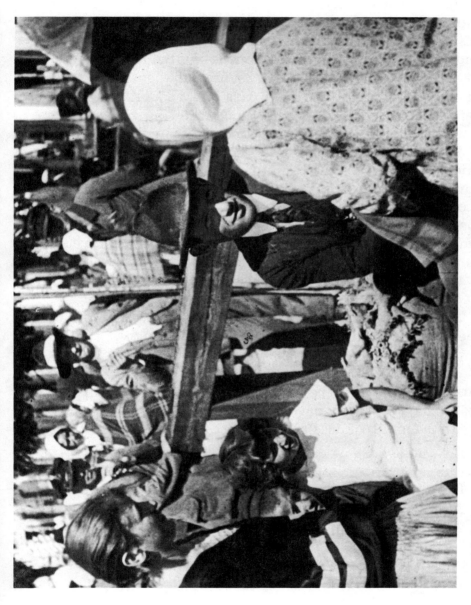

A young Jew buying vegetables from a peasant woman at the Kolbushov market, 1929. Two Polish policemen watch in the background. Courtesy of David Salz.

71

they were able to flee to the large *shul*. Many Jews had arrived before them, for the *shul* was built like a fortress to protect the Jews in just such times of distress. Even this walled fortress, however, could not withstand the enemy onslaught and the Cossacks managed to break in. The bride and groom were again able to escape—to the nearby river. They found a fisherman's boat on the bank, got in, and let the river take them—without oars or a rudder. The murderers caught sight of them, began throwing rocks and a few men jumped into the river to catch their victims alive.

At this point the bride realized they were doomed and said to her groom: "Any minute now we will fall into their hands. If I were certain that they would spare you on my account, I would choose to stay alive. But I have no doubt that you will be killed at once and I will be tortured and molested as they always do to women of our people. I would rather die with you than live in shame without you. If you really love me, do not refuse me and let us both sanctify God's name."

The groom embraced his bride and they both jumped into the surging river.

On the third day, after the Cossacks had left, the few remaining survivors found their bodies washed up on the river bank. They were buried near the *shul* and a mound was made over their grave. On the first anniversary of their death a tombstone was erected there with this inscription:

Beloved children, dearest bride and groom
Pure souls—
In their lives they lacked nothing.
They were about to be led to a bedecked canopy.
After their death, the very depths of the river could not
    contain them.
Not slain but drowned victims were they.
Only their bodies are separate; their souls are united
    forever.

19th of Sivan; Year: 5408

Abraham Rechtman, pp. 169–171.

7. COUNT POTOTSKI AND THE NEMIROV SHUL

Nemirov, a famous town in Podolia, belonged to Count Pototski. As often happens, a fire broke out in the town and the church burned down. The Christian population appeared before the count and asked him to rebuild their church. The good count agreed and a new site was chosen on a mound in the center of town.

All winter long the building materials were made ready —mortar was made into bricks and lumber was sawed into planks. After *peysekh*, once the snow had melted, the ground was soft enough to dig the foundation. The count sent workers to start digging.

But as soon as a shovel hit the ground, the workers began to sink. They were barely dragged out alive. The next day they tried it from another side and the same thing happened. After the third try failed they reported the events to Pototski and the count ordered the work to be stopped.

Count Pototski was no fool. He knew there had to be a reason for all this. First he questioned the oldest citizens in Nemirov, Jews and non-Jews. Then he consulted the old chronicles. Finally he checked the old town maps until he discovered that on the very hill he had ordered to be the site for the new church, there once stood a *shul* that Khmelnitski's Cossacks destroyed in 1648.

The good count was taken aback. What had he done? Surely the God of the Jews would wreak vengeance upon him for trying to build a church on such holy ground. Pototski was at his wit's end.

The next day happened to be the second day of *shvues*. All the Jews of Nemirov had assembled in the large *besmedresh* and were in the middle of reading the Book of Ruth as Count Pototski suddenly appeared. He walked up to the rabbi and with a quivering voice told all the congregants what had happened. He begged forgiveness for his wrongdoing and swore that he would never have ordered the

73

Shul **in Yoneve, Lite.**

church to be built there if he had known what he now knew. As proof of his sincerity, he offered to help the Jews build a new synagogue on the same mound and to donate all the building materials.

The rabbi assured him that according to Jewish law he had committed no sin and accepted his offer.

And so it was. Right after *shvues* the entire congregation assembled at the mound. The old rabbi performed the ground-breaking ceremony and pretty soon the foundations of the ruined *shul* were uncovered. A beautiful new *shul* was then constructed on the old foundations. At the dedication, the count and his court were honored and joyous guests.

Abraham Rechtman, pp. 76–78.

8. THE TREASURE

The fact that there was a treasure right here in our little village was indisputable. How did we come by a treasure? Khmelnitski brought it, that Ukrainian who rebelled against Polish rule. Khmelnitski buried it here a long time ago. For thousands of years, people had been collecting treasure after treasure, and then Khmelnitski came and took them away and buried them.

"Who was Khmelnitski?"

"You don't know about Khmelnitski? Why he was a monster, the Haman of his time . . . Any baby knows that. . . . Well, this monster, this Khmelnitski robbed the nobles and wealthy Jews. He stole millions, and he brought it here, to Voronki, and buried it one dark night in the ground under the light of the moon, on the other side of the *shul*. The spot is now overgrown with grass, and a spell has been cast upon it so that no one can find it."

"So, then it's lost for good?"

"Who says for good? Why do you think God created the *kabole?* The mystics know a trick or two for this sort of thing."

"What kind of trick?"

"You can be sure it's the right kind. They have a magic spell where a certain verse from the Psalms must be repeated forty times forty..."

"Which verse?"

"If I only knew! But even if I knew, it wouldn't help much. The way it goes, you have to fast for forty days, and you have to recite forty chapters from the Psalms on each of these days, and on the forty-first day, right after the sun has set, you've got to sneak out so that no one sees you...."

Sholom Aleichem (1955), pp. 16–17.

9. MUTUAL CULTURAL INFLUENCES

In folksongs, people often use or adapt foreign languages that they hear. A good number of khasidic songs are simply taken over lock, stock, and barrel from Ukrainian or Belorussian. A famous example is a song about Mark. The original lyrics are:

> Oh you stupid Mark
> Why travel to the fair?
> You don't buy, you don't sell,
> You only cause trouble.

For the *khasidim* this seemingly simpleminded stanza had deep religious meaning, for who was stupid Mark if not the personification of evil? The only way to overcome his influence was by turning to the Lord. And so the song continued with a passage from Psalms:

> My heart longs for You.
> My soul thirsts for You.

The *khasidim*, and particularly the more mystical ones,

often interpreted the simplest sayings of a peasant as a profound religious truth.

Once, Reb Zushe Anipoler was out taking a walk. He met a peasant whose wagonful of hay had turned over. The peasant asked Reb Zushe's help in turning the wagon over on its wheels.

"Hey Jew, lend a hand!"

"I can't," replied Reb Zushe.

The peasant threw him an angry look and said:

"You can all right, but you don't want to!"

Reb Zushe grabbed his head in his hands and began moaning bitterly:

"Oh Zushe, Zushe! You can all right, but you don't want to! You can serve the Lord if you only wanted to!"

What's true of folksongs is all the more true of folk melodies. Again the *khasidim* took the lead in borrowing and adapting peasant tunes for their own needs. From the tales of the Bal Shem Tov we can see how he and his followers showed great interest in peasant tunes. In one tale the Besht is out walking and he overhears a drunken peasant humming a tune. The Besht stopped and listened carefully to the entire melody. When the disciples asked him what it was that he had heard in the melody, the Besht replied:

"In a melody a man pours out his soul and confesses his wrongdoing. When a man pours out his soul, you must be sure to listen."

Foreign influences are even more apparent in the realm of customs, folk remedies, and incantations. Among the Jewish masses there was great trust in gentile sorcerers, witches, and especially in the Tatars. In the stock of Yiddish magic formulae against the evil eye and other misfortunes, there are many recipes taken directly from gentiles.

It is only logical that if Christian practices had such an

influence on Jews, Jewish customs were often equally important to Christian culture.

In Lite and also Volin, especially in the *shtetlekh*, there were a good many gentiles who spoke Yiddish well and used Yiddish even among themselves. There were even some who know so much about Jewish matters that if not for their gentile appearance, they would be mistaken for Jews. I once met an old peasant woman who worked for many years in a Jewish home. Each morning she would recite the *"Moyde ani"* prayer with the children, pronounce the blessing over *tsitses*, and make sure that they kept all the rules and regulations of Jewish law. Whenever a child did something forbidden, such as take off his hat or break something on *shabes*, she would scold him and shout:

"Goy! You'll be thrashed with iron rods!"

In the shtetl Derazhne, I met an elderly peasant who had been employed as a *shul-goy* for thirty-odd years and even lived in a room adjacent to the *shul*. Not only did he speak a good Yiddish but he also told me many khasidic tales about *tsadikim* in whom he had absolute faith. He referred to the Besht as "the saintly Bal Shem" and was proud of the fact that the Besht's wagon driver was a peasant named Alexei.

In many places the village peasants believed in the powers of the khasidic *rebe* and there are many cases of peasants coming to a *rebe* with a gift of money and with a request. In one shtetl I was introduced to a seventy-year-old shepherd who was known as Mikhaylo the Rebe's. His childless parents had asked a *rebe* to pray for them.

"Lord of the universe," the *rebe* said, "You have so many *goyim* in the world. What do You care if You have one more?"

And so, Mikhaylo was born. But Mikhaylo himself was not destined to have any children.

In the shtetl Teofipol I was shown a stream which the

Besht was said to have drawn out of the earth. Its waters provided cures for many illnesses. In time the stream was covered. Along came the peasants from the nearby village, dug it up, cleared it and began using its waters for medicine. They claimed that the Besht had appeared to one of the peasants in a dream and ordered him to dig up the stream.

The peasant population in many cases considers Jewish sacred objects to have the same magic powers as their own. In many *shtetlekh* in Volin, peasant women bring candles to the *shul* for *shabes*. They consider this a remedy for all sorts of illnesses. In the shtetl Pogrebishtshe there is a stone in the middle of the marketplace. According to Jewish legend a martyr is buried underneath it. There is a custom in the shtetl for a bride and groom to dance around the stone following the wedding ceremony. The local gentile population took over the custom. They also had newlyweds dance around the stone. They had no idea why they did it. Their explanation was simply that if Jews dance around the stone at a wedding, they should do it too.

In a village not far from Zvihil I was shown a half-finished, burnt church and was told the following story. On the grounds where the church stands there was once an inn which was run for many years by a Jew. One day the clergy decided that the spot where the inn stood was the most appropriate site for their new church. The Jew was expelled, the inn demolished, and the building begun. The innkeeper died of anguish. When the church was half built it was set on fire by a lightning storm. The peasants raised a great shout:

"Yankl the Innkeeper's tears are burning!" and they absolutely refused to rebuild the burned church.

Sh. Anski.

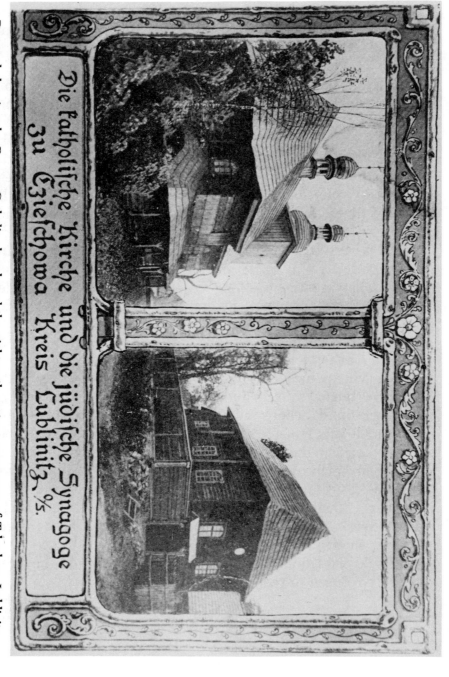

Postcard showing the Roman Catholic church and the eighteenth-century synagogue of Tsheshev, Lublinits county. Both buildings were made of wood and have certain architectural similarities. Until 1922, this town belonged to Prussia, which explains the German writing.

Die katholische Kirche und die jüdische Synagoge zu Czieschowa Kreis Lublinitz %.

80

10. THE PROCESSION

Just over the Old Bridge the nobleman's fields begin. They stretch as far as the lonely hill with the strange, imported crucifix on top. All the crosses in our region are made of wood with "that man" nailed to each one of them in shameless nudity. A little lower down hangs the knitted apron which the rain and sun have faded and turned into a tattered rag with gray and yellow smears. On both sides of the rotting wood hang the instruments of his martyrdom: a pair of tongs now covered with rust, a hammer, a spear, and a tiny ladder which is only loosely attached. That's what the local crucifixes look like, the ones in all the villages and at all the crossroads.

But not the cross on the lonely hill. You can tell at first glance that it isn't a local product: woven of thin iron like a wreath with prickly edges, it towers over the region, tall and gray. It always seems to be on the verge of collapsing, but it never does.

According to the town records, this cross marks the burial ground of the Swedish soldiers who fell here while serving their king, Charles X. It happened in the year 1655 when, after the Russian armies invaded Poland, Sweden attacked with 17,000 soldiers. In a matter of three months, they conquered most of Poland. But it was right here in Tishevits that the tide turned in Poland's favor. On December 29, leading generals and princes convened in Tishevits and took an oath that they would fight until the Swedes retreated from the country they had taken so easily.

All winter long the cross stands alone and barely braves the fierce winds. But with the coming of spring the hill attracts long rows of gaily dressed, slim girls in white bonnets. The icons they carry sway to the melancholy tune they sing. The colored shawls on their shoulders flutter in the wind. They wear brightly colored pleated skirts embroidered with gold and silver threads and bright purple. The

Catholic priest, dressed in white satin, walks under a white silk canopy with a red covering and gold tassels. The pungent odors of the meadow mix with the incense that rises out of copper pans. The chorus of young female voices grows louder and louder.

A shiver runs through the entire shtetl on the other side of the bridge. Shutters close with a bang. Children playing out of doors stop short in the middle of their game and block their ears with their thumbs. "The *goyim* are bleating again." The correct formula for just such a time is: "The Lord will answer you in time of stress." Anyone who can't remember this time-tested remedy mutters any old passage from Psalms he can remember. Then he hurries into a Jewish home to be under the protection of a *mezuze* and a holy book.

Those children whom the singing catches playing behind the *shul* run fearfully into the nearby *besmedresh*. As they wash their hands they cannot help but glance at the high windows in the southern wall, the wall facing "the hill." The singing cannot be heard from here but the light—tons of light—glimmers and glows from afar. "The *goyim* are setting fire to the outside!" they think with trembling hearts. They sing the afternoon prayers at the top of their lungs.

A strong sensation overcomes them. Isn't this precisely what the prophets of old warned against? With angry words the prophets pleaded with them not to visit the holy mounds, not to burn incense under the linden trees. But they are stricken with blindness, and their ears are blocked up. "Almighty God," the children plead with eyes tightly shut, "let us not suffer on account of their sins! May our present fears be the atonement that will bring forgiveness."

Jacob Zipper, pp. 19–23.

11. JEWISH-GENTILE LAWSUITS

This story happened in the shtetl of Zaslav between *yon-kiper* and *sukes*. The Police Chief was out walking in the market when he noticed Jews building *sukes* next to their houses. This man was a real Jew-hater, a Haman, who always tried to make trouble. He went up to the Jews and asked them if they had a building permit.

The Jews burst out laughing. "Who needs a building permit to make a *suke?*" they said. The *goy* went away angry, pouting: "Those kikes! Building without a permit!"

And off he went to write a report on each one of them. A few days later, on the second day of *sukes*, the Jews were brought to trial. The judge heard the case and asked the Jews what they had to say for themselves. The defendants did not deny the charges. It was true that they had built without a permit. But they explained that this was all part of a holiday in which booths are built and Jews eat their meals there for eight days. In this way they commemorate the time when Jews were delivered out of Egypt and lived in makeshift huts while wandering through the desert.

The judge, a pretty smart man, understood it all. But since he didn't want to put the Chief of Police to shame, he fined each Jew half a ruble for building without a permit. He also ordered that at the end of eight days the *sukes* had to be disbanded.

When *yontef* was over, the Jews still had two days in which to dismantle the booths.

Naftoli Gross, pp. 156–157.

12. THE DINTOYRE

Pelte was on good terms with Reb Dovid *dayen* until it came to the *dintoyre*. From the case Pelte and his partner pleaded before him, Reb Dovid discovered their crooked dealings. First, they deliberately doctored the accounts they had with peasants; second, they charged exorbitant interest rates, and third, they cheated the peasants in weighing the produce and counting the furs with which the peasants made their payments. It was no wonder the peasants were screaming for justice.

"I regret to inform you that I am in no position to decide on your case." Reb Dovid said this with his usual calm though inside he was raging with anger. He cringed at the sight of each account with its figures falsified in both columns. "However, the transaction with them is still binding," he went on. "In my opinion, you ought to pay a visit to the *rebe* and accept his decision on the matter."

"What do you mean?" the two partners asked as they both jumped from their seats.

"I mean, that before I can issue a rabbinical decision, you must first repent for your deeds which are outright robbery. You are endangering not only yourself, but also the entire Jewish community."

"So you're agreeing with that filthy peasant who tried to shoot me after I showed him the bill?" The partner was red in the face. "It's none of your business what we do. I don't owe you any kickback from what I earn by risking my neck. To hell with your *dintoyre!*"

Pelte tried a different tactic. "You've got to take into account the risks of our trade. It's no easy business lending money to peasants these days. Your hair turns gray before you see the first penny. A man's gotta make up for the losses."

"And I repeat what I said before, that you're bringing disaster upon yourself and upon all of us!" Now it was Reb Dovid's turn to lose his temper. "Haven't we paid enough with our blood already? Now you want us to pay for your sins too. We weren't given the Torah so that you could straighten out your crooked dealings." He threw the accounts back at them. "Only if you promise to return the theft will the Torah straighten you out." Reb Dovid moved to the door, blocking their exit. "Jews, you're playing with fire! How dare you do such a thing. Pelte, your father of blessed memory, risked his life to save Jews during the cholera epidemic. How do you expect him to find rest in the grave? Pelte, think it over!" By now, Reb Dovid's voice was choked with tears.

"I promise, I promise, Reb Dovid!" Pelte stammered back at him. "Don't worry, we'll straighten the whole matter out." He grabbed for his wallet as if intending to pay the required fee.

"You'd do better giving it to the poor," said Reb Dovid in a softer tone of voice. He moved away from the door to see them out. "The way of return is open to the one who gives charity. And the highest rung of charity is the secret donation. You'll find a way of doing it and no one need ever discover why you've done it. . . ."

Jacob Zipper, pp. 347–348.

13. A BLOOD LIBEL AND A SHABES-GOY

Among the *goyim* who spent time around Jews were two Swabian brothers named Schmidt. They were impoverished members of a nearby German colony. These two brothers were locked in fierce competition for the position of *shabes-goy*. Each wanted the job of taking down candlesticks, heating the ovens, as well as chopping firewood for the more affluent Jewish households on *shabes*, when Jews are not permitted to light a match or to work. But all the jobs went to the elder brother, a giant of a man with a foot eternally swollen like a mountain, who would not leave so much as a groschen's work for his younger brother. The Jews preferred the elder Schmidt because he did not speak Swabian, as did the other settlers, but Yiddish, like any Jew. He knew all the Jewish customs and holidays and would recite the Jewish prayer over every glass of whiskey offered him. He was also aware of the law that forbids Jews from drinking wine that has been touched by a gentile, and would inform housewives of his presence so that they might remove the *kidesh* wine before he made it impure.

"Put the wine away, women," he would warn them from the other side of the door. "A *goy* is coming. . . ."

The younger brother resented the community that deprived him of a livelihood, and he spread a story among the gentiles that the Jews had lured a Christian child to the bathhouse where Reb Itshe, the *shoykhet*, had killed it with his knife; and that Eber had then carried the Christian blood in a pail to Khaskl the baker, who in turn had mixed it with the holy water and kneaded it into the *matses*. He carried this tale not only to the Swabian colony but to the Polish settlements as well, and the rumor flew from village to village. Since it was close to Easter when gentiles are generally incensed against the Jews for crucifying their Lord, the peasants' blood began to seethe. Soon professional female witnesses turned up who swore to have personally seen the Christian child being enticed to its death. One day, Yekl the peddler, who rode through the villages buying up hogs' bristles, came back to town with a split scalp. It turned out that he had been waylaid by peasants, who had repaid him for spilling Christian blood. Then Leybush the baker rode out with a wagonload of bread; he was pelted with stones. Reb Itshe, the slaughterer was afraid to show his face in the villages when he was summoned by Jewish farmers to slaughter a calf or a fowl. The *goyim* threatened to come armed with knives to the fair that fell before *peysekh*, and to murder the Jews who dared drink Christian blood.

The Jews lived in dreadful fear. Gates and doors were bolted at night. The town's prominent citizens called on the *porets* Christowski to beg his protection. The *porets*, who was also the district judge, scoffed at the accusation. A heretic who never attended church, he used to tell the Jews that the reason Jesus did not want money like everyone else was because his hands were nailed to the cross. But in his capacity as judge he wanted to know if any Christian children had been reported missing. It turned out that none were. Still, the *goyim* clung to their contention that the Jews murdered a Christian child, and the situation remained fraught with danger. Whereupon Reb Joshua, the lumber merchant, who was also the town *gvir*, had his coach and team harnessed, put on his finest coat with a hood, and drove to Sokhatshev to see the Russian official there and ask him to come back with him to Lentshin with a detachment of constables and protect the Jews from the mob.

The red-bearded official refused to be hurried, but he quickly grew more amenable when Reb Joshua slipped him a juicy bribe. He climbed into Reb Joshua's carriage, ordered ten of his men into a wagon, and set out for Lentshin. They arrived on the eve of the fair. Bands of peasants had already gathered in town. The official went to the bathhouse, where a mob of gentiles had assembled. All the Jews were there too, their hats off to the official. The younger Schmidt brother was brought forward; the investigation began.

Speaking glibly and supplying all the details, the Swabian described how he had personally seen Eber carrying a pail filled with a red liquid.

"Where is this pail?" the official asked sternly.

"Here it is, illustrious Sire," Eber said, bringing the pail stained with the red paint that had been used on the bathhouse windows. The official laughingly held the pail up for the crowd to see.

"Is this blood or paint, peasants?" he asked.

"Paint, illustrious Sire," the peasants said.

"Is any of you missing a child, peasants?" he asked further.

Local officials posing in front of Kolbushov Town Hall, 1929. At the left, Mr. Przywara, the secretary, and in the center Mr. Osiniak the mayor (a wealthy manufacturer). Courtesy of David Salz.

"No, no one, illustrious Sire," they replied in a chorus.

"Then how could a child have been killed when everyone is alive and well?" he demanded.

"We don't know, illustrious Sire," the frightened peasants replied, "but the Swabian told us he saw with his own eyes how the Jews killed a Christian child in the bathhouse. . . ."

The official seized the tall, thin German by the lapels of his oversized jacket and shook him. "What did you see, you son-of-a-bitch? When did you see this? What did you see?"

The man promptly began to sputter and the official hit him so hard that he turned a somersault.

"I'll slice strips from your hide, you son-of-a-bitch, if you don't tell the truth!" he roared.

The German sank to his knees and began to beat his breast. "I made it all up, illustrious Sire," he blubbered, "because they wouldn't give me work, these Jews. . . . They give it all to my brother and let me starve to death. . . ."

The official thrust out a chest blazing with medals. "I'll send you to Siberia for stirring up the people!" he cried. "You'll rot in chains, you son-of-a-bitch!"

The policemen fingered ropes, ready to bind the kneeling German, but the official told them to put them away.

"Turn the son-of-a-bitch over and give him a dozen across his bare ass," he ordered. "Then he can go."

Before we knew what was happening, the tall gentile lay with his lean buttocks exposed for all to see.

"Jesus!" he shrieked in German.

The policemen eagerly brought their whips down on his bony behind and counted the strokes off slowly.

And with each stroke the official preached anew, "That's what I'll give anyone who spreads lies and stirs up the people," he threatened. "In my district order will prevail, peasants."

I. J. Singer, pp. 49–53.

14. POGROM

"Pogrom" is a Russian word for a mob attack including looting and bloodshed. In modern history, pogrom has come to mean the specific attacks of Christians on Russian and Polish Jewry with the consent or the full knowledge of the local police and civic leaders. Three waves of pogroms occurred in Russia, each worse and broader than the previous wave: 1881–1884, 1903–1906, 1917–1921.

What can explain these mob attacks on the impoverished Jewish communities? One, there was a tradition of anti-Jewish hatred which dated back to the seventeenth and eighteenth centuries; two, thousands of homeless seasonal Russian workers regarded the Jews as rivals; three, extremist revolutionary groups went to any length to secure power over a mass of Russian peasants. Four, a backward, feudal and war-torn Russian Empire encouraged such mob action to divert the attention of poor, discontented peasants.

On *peysekh*, 1903, a mob of Christians, encouraged by the Russian Minister of Interior, attacked the Jews of Kishinev. Forty-five persons were killed, their bodies mutilated. Hundreds of Jews were injured. Fifteen-hundred homes and shops were destroyed. At about the same time 300 Jews were killed in Odessa.

These mass murders caused protests in many parts of the world. Armed Jewish defense groups were organized for the first time in Russia and succeeded in protecting many Jewish lives and Jewish property. Almost a million Jews decided to leave Russia. Those who stayed behind began to take their lives into their own hands by establishing educational institutions, literary societies, Zionist groups and socialist-revolutionary organizations.

15. NEWS OF A POGROM

One day a revolt did erupt in Lentshin. A peasant named Mikhalastshak, who had worked in a factory in Warsaw, began to sing a ditty mocking the tsar. The two policemen on duty at the marketplace tried to arrest Mikhalastshak for sedition, but he was a giant of a man and he tore off the policemen's medals and beat them up. When one of the policemen drew his sword, Mikhalastshak took it away from him and sent them both running. His hands cut and bleeding, Mikhalastshak ran into the courthouse and tore down the tsar's portrait and the plaque of the imperial eagle. He dragged the portrait out into the street and urinated over it, then called on his fellow Poles to seize pitchforks and drive the Russians out of Poland.

The Jews quickly gathered up their goods and locked themselves behind closed doors and shutters. Mikhalastshak urged them not to be afraid and proposed a united front against the Russians. But bitter experience had taught the Jews not to become involved with gentiles, and they remained behind their barricades. The two policemen hid in the attic of a Jewish home. That night they disguised themselves in long coats, bound handkerchiefs around their faces, and fled to Sochaczew.

Three days later the Russian police drove up with several wagons of armed men, rounded up some peasants, and bound them with ropes. The police personally flogged the Polish peasants in front of the whole town.

"You'll rot in chains!" roared the captain, stomping his gleaming boots. "I will have order in my region."

For a while there was no further trouble. One day, however, Yosele Royskes learned from the Hebrew newspaper to which he subscribed and which came a week late that a pogrom had taken place in Bialestok.

No one in Lentshin knew just where Bialestok was; it was generally believed to be inhabited by Litvaks. Still, the accounts in the newspaper were terrifying. Yosele translated into Yiddish the report of the atrocities committed against babies, about old men who had been hacked to death

91

Victims of the Bialestok pogrom in 1906 lying in the garden of the Jewish hospital. An attempt is being made to identify the bodies.

with axes and about pregnant women whose bellies had been slit open. The people in the *shul* were left pale and shaken. I was so disturbed by the news, I couldn't eat. I lay down on a green trunk that stood in our house and raged inwardly against a God who would permit such outrages. My parents, who were just as distressed as I, claimed that the massacre had come about as a result of sins committed by Jews. I wouldn't accept such a simplistic explanation.

"It's God's fault!" I cried. "He is evil, evil." My parents clapped hands over their ears to shut out the blasphemous outburst.

The terrifying reports began to drift in from other places with greater frequency. They were brought in by local men who went to Warsaw to buy goods. Father even began reading the forbidden Hebrew newspaper. During services, the Jews gathered in tight clusters, like sheep seeking protection from a wolf, and spoke about the danger and suffering of Jews.

Jews from the country spoke of the unrest in the rural areas. Others said that a band of Russians had been imported especially to pillage the town. All kinds of horrible rumors began to circulate.

One day, during morning prayers, when the Torah was taken out of the ark it was discovered that the small Torah with the brass handles, usually read on weekdays, was missing.

A great commotion broke out in the *shul* and everyone felt that something evil had happened. After hours of searching, someone noticed the tip of a brass handle sticking out of the pond near the *besmedresh* in which ducks swam and hogs cooled their great steaming bodies in the heat of the day.

The Jews raced to remove the scroll as if it were the body of a murder victim. With trembling hands Father picked up the soggy scroll and laid it across a *tales* on the reader's stand. The parchment was soaked and stank. Father recited: "Blessed be the true judge!" over the scroll—the same prayer that is said after hearing about the death of a person. Father ordered that the scroll be buried in the Zakrotshin cemetery. On the day of the burial everyone fasted and prayers of forgiveness and other prayers were recited in the *shul*.

Soon it came out that the foul deed had been done by the son of the peasant Gruski, a swineherd who grazed his abominations near the *besmedresh*. But the Jews did nothing in fear of arousing the peasants. They only made a complaint to the parish priest, who promised to correct the youth during the catechism lesson in church.

In the *shul* talk started that the coming of the Messiah must certainly be near at hand.

I. J. Singer, pp. 222–225.

16. THE POGROM IN LEGEND

In 1917–1918 during the pogroms in the Ukraine, a friend of mine who recorded these events was struck by the fact that a certain town directly in the path of the passing hordes had always been skipped over in the massacres. My friend expressed his surprise to a resident of the town who offered the following explanation: "We had been promised safety. Centuries ago there lived in our town a great saint. It came to pass that on a certain Friday he had to go, for the sake of a *mitsve*, to a neighboring town. The saint hesitated for a while. Why set out on a journey just before *shabes*? But the distance was short, the trip urgent, and he went. Unfortunately, the journey took much longer than he had expected. Finally, when he arrived in the town, the *shabes* candles were gleaming in Jewish homes. The saint was angry with God that he had done this to him. In his anger he refused to say *kidesh*—the blessing over the wine.

The heavenly spheres were, of course, quite impressed with the saint's protest. But the saint didn't give up easily, not until he was promised that there would never be a pogrom in his town. Only then did he agree to welcome *shabes* into his home.

Abraham Joshua Heschel.

17. A SONG OF THE BALTA POGROM (1882)

I.

a. Umglik, shrek un moyres
Mir veysn nit fun vanen,
Oykh haynt vi in ale doyres,
Zaynen mir oysgeshtanen.
Shrayt yidn, shrayt aroyf.
Shrayt hekher ahin dort;
Vekt ir dem altn oyf—
Vos shloft er kloymersht dort?
Vemen vil er gor gevinen?
Vos zaynen mir—a flig?
Loz er undz a zkhus gefinen
Oy, es zol shoyn zayn genug!

b. Tseshlogn, tseharget ales,
Tsevorfn yedes bazunder,
Fun khasanim—kales,
Fun muters—kleyne kinder
Shrayt, kinder, shrayt aroyf.
Shrayt hekher ahin dort;
Vekt ir dem tatn oyf—
Vos shloft er kloymersht dort?
Far dir herstu veynen, klogn
Kinder fun der vig
Zey betn dikh, du zolst zey zogn:
Oy, es zol shoyn zayn genug!

c. Ales iz tserisn:
Kales, khupes, kleyder,
Fun betgevant un kishn
Nit gelozt keyn feder.
Flit, feder, flit aroyf;
Flit hekher ahin dort;
Vekt ir dem altn oyf—
Vos shloft er kloymersht dort?
Tsebrokhn iz ales af sakones
Bizn letstn krug.
Nu, hob shoyn du aleyn rakhmones,
Oy, es zol shoyn zayn genug!

II.

a. Misfortune, fear and terror
Have always been our lot
Now and in all ages past,
We know not where they
come from.
Shout Jews, shout loud and clear;
Shout higher for up there to hear.
You can wake the Old Man up.
His sleep is just a lie.
Why's he trying to pretend?
What are we—a fly?
Is there nothing in our favor?
Enough! It's got to end!

b. All of us beaten and bruised.
Our belongings thrown asunder.
Brides taken from their grooms.
Children from their mothers.
Shout, children, shout loud and clear;
Shout higher for up there to hear.
You can wake your Father up,
As if He were asleep for real.
Listen, and You'll hear the cries.
Of children in their cribs.
They plead with You that You might say:
Enough! It's got to end!

c. Everything is torn to pieces,
Brides, canopies and clothes.
Of bedding and pillows
Not even a feather was left.
Fly you feathers, fly aloft,
Fly higher to the One Above;
You can wake the Old Man up.
As if He were asleep for real.
All we own is smashed to bits.
To the last bowl and cup.
It's time You Yourself took pity.
Enough! It's got to end!

d. Farshraybt af lange doyres
Di retsikhes un di eymes.
Tserisn seyfer-toyres,
Tseshmutst di reyne sheymes.
Flit sheymes, flit aroyf.
Flit hekher ahin dort;
Vekt ir Moyshe Rabeynu oyf—
Vos shloft er kloymersht dort?
Mir hobn zey nit gekent farhitn,
Ver ken zayn azoy klug?
Loz er baym tatn poyln mit gutn
Oy, es zol shoyn zayn genug!

d. Record it for the time to come,
The murder and the fright.
Torah scrolls were desecrated.
The sacred parchment—defiled.
Fly you parchments, fly aloft,
Fly higher to the One Above;
You can wake Old Moses up.
As if he were asleep for real.
We weren't able to protect them,
Who could have known what would descend?
Enough! It's got to end!

Heard in Russia in the 1880s.

Bine Silverman-Weinreich (1949).

96

UNIT FOUR
WORKADAY JEWS

A woman picking feathers in Lipkza, Bessarabia.

1. KAHAL AND THE DRAFT LAW

It all began in 1827 when Tsar Nicholas I decided to draft Jews into the army. Until then only the peasants had to face the 25-year army service. Now Jewish men aged 18–25 would be called up for regular service, and younger recruits, aged 12–18, would be given preparatory military training. These teen-age Jewish soldiers were known as Cantonists.

The draft quota went as high as 30 boys for every thousand Jews. The people responsible for filling the quota were the members of kahal, the Jewish community council. The results were disastrous both for the Cantonists — who either died of starvation or were forced to convert to Christianity, disappearing from home for twenty-five years— and for those Jews who stayed behind, full of fear and anger. As far as the tsar was concerned, the aim of the Cantonist system, which applied to Jews for twenty-nine years and involved almost 40,000 Jewish boys, was conversion and assimilation. As far as kahal was concerned, this was their chance to assert absolute power over the community.

According to the new draft law, kahal was allowed to use the draft as punishment of Jews who failed to pay their taxes. Jews caught without a passport were drafted.

Never before in the history of Polish-Russian Jewry was the split between rich and poor as deep and painful as it now became. Never again would the Jewish community be seen as "one big happy family."

CANDIDATES FOR THE DRAFT
The Jewish Community of Minsk
1827

NAME	AGE	FAMILY	HOME OWNER	WORK	TAXES PAID	RESIDENCE
Itsik Volman	24	Parents, Brothers	No	Handyman	No	Minsk
Benyomen Gertik	13	Parents, Brother/ Sister	No	None	No	Minsk
Grishe Meyerov	22	None	No	None	No	Minsk
Kiva Grayever	17	None	No	Beggar	No	Minsk
Faybush Tshertov	24	Lives by himself	No	Tailor	No	No Passport
Avrom Pertsov	19	None	No	Unemployed Cardplayer	No	Minsk
Aron Kalkov	23	Mother, Wife	No	Rendar	No	Villager
Itsik Movshov	19	Lives by himself	No	Glassworker	No	Minsk
Leyb Nigin	19	Parents	No	Tavern	No	Villager

O. Margolis, pp. 330-33.
Document 88.

From: The Community of Chichelnik in the Providence of Podolia
To: The Minister of the Interior, the Right Honorable Bibikov

Things are so bad with us poor people, sir, that we ain't got no choice but to bring our case before you. We write you with our tears. Those rich people are to blame. We've already given two recruits each, but our money and our souls are being wiped out. You should know that we're poor, so we can't do nothing to stop them. All of them break the laws against our lord and master, the Tsar, may his glory soar. Them rich people don't pay no taxes and the little bit that's squeezed out of us poor folks isn't even handed over. No sir, they spend it all on their crooked payoffs, on

100

whiskey, and the best proof is that for a whole year the tax bureau hasn't made a penny. The richest guys in Chichelnik, namely Ber Marakhaver, Moyshe-Eliezer Lekhter, Herts Drabetske, Borukh Solts and the rest of them, all have big families, with three or four working members in each. But what happens when there's a draft call? Then they all get together and choose Ber Marakhaver as tax-collector and he helps them out with their malpractices.

Oh, that Marakhaver, he sees the name of the Khalef family on the draft list and tips them off (they're his relatives). Sure enough they ran away. Once the heat was off he personally got them forged passports, not only for them, but for other relatives also. And that's not all—during the last call-up he gave the name of Arn Roykhvarger who doesn't even live here anymore! If you don't believe us, you can check in the register. He also forges the names of Chichelnik families on official documents of the town council so that the families listed on the draft register won't have to be drafted.

There's nothing we can do because all the rich people are in cahoots with him. Marakhaver even gets to pocket the measly bit of taxes he squeezes out of us poor folk. He spends it any way he pleases. In 1852 there was a call-up, so this Marakhaver collected so much tax money and pay-offs that he married off his son which cost him 1,000 rubles.

Now Moyshe-Eliezer Lekhter is the richest man in town. He and his two sons pay less in taxes than the poorest one of us. Besides, one of his sons should have been drafted a long time ago, but he had his younger son listed on the census as being much younger than he is and now he had the other son cut off his toe so that he don't have to go. And even though we reported this right away to the bailiff, he too is on their payroll and he hushed the whole thing up. Thank God he didn't know it was us who reported it, cause he would have eaten us up!

So in the last call-up of 1852, Ber Marakhaver, Borukh Solts and the rest of them took recruits from families that had already given a recruit. What's more, they called up only-sons who weren't even on the draft list, and lied that these only-sons have brothers and that they themselves are 12 years old. But we can prove that there were no brothers to speak of and that these boys aren't older than seven or eight. They were all drafted for nothing.

Please! Take pity on us. Read our words carefully and be sure to report it all to Kamenets and Kiev. And see that we aren't punished for writing you all this. We hope and pray that you, right honorable minister, will grant us a speedy reply.

May 3, 1852, here in Chichelnik.

O. Margolis, pp. 353–58.
Document 94.

A "professional" kidnapper came into being among Jews, the *khaper*. Often with the support of the kahal the *khaper* would use all means possible to supply Jewish boys for the army. *Khapers* promised rewards for finding boys in hiding; they urged Jews to turn each other in for a price.

The experiences of the Cantonist period were not easily forgotten by the Jews of Russia. The corruption of the kahal against their own people, the despised *khaper* and the pain of separated families found expression in folksongs remembered and sung until the twentieth century.

102

(a) Tsvantsik mayl bin ikh gelofn
    Hob ikh a shtibl ongetrofn.
(b) Balebos! Git mir a shtikl broyt;
    Zet mayn ponem, vi bleykh un toyt.
(c) Tsu broyt, tsu broyt shnel geyt zikh vasn [vashn].
    Men geyt do arum fregn far pasn.
(d) Af broyt, af broyt, makht men hamoytse—
    Un zen shpeter vet men an eytse.
(e) Nokh broyt, nokh broyt tut men bentshn,
    Do geyen arum khapermentshn.
(f) Ikh hob zikh gevashn un gebentsht,
    Iz arayn a khapermentsh.
(g) Fregt er mir: "Vu tu ikh forn?"
    Zog ikh im: "Nokh veyts un korn . . ."
(h) "Neyn! Nit nokh dem tustu forn,
    Du antloyfst fun dayne yorn."
(i) Un in prisutstve mikh firt men avek.
    Es lozn ale arunter di kep.
(j) Mikh shteln vet men untern mos—
    Un oysrufn: "Soldat khorosh."

Translation:

(a) I ran and ran for twenty miles.
    Until I came upon a house.
(b) Sir! Give me a piece of bread;
    Look at me: I'm pale and dead.
(c) Quick, get washed before eating the bread.
    They're checking for passes all around.
(d) On bread, on bread, I make a blessing—
    Later I'll figure out what to do.
(e) After the bread one must say Grace
    Here snatchers are going all about.
(f) I had already washed and said the blessing
    When the snatcher walked right in.
(g) Says he: "Where are you going?"
    Say I: "To buy wheat and corn."
(h) "No, that's not why you're on your way,
    You're trying to escape from your age in life."
(i) They drag me off to the draft board.
    Everyone lowers their head in shame.
(j) They put me through the physical test—
    And announce: "A soldier, one of the best!"

Eleanor Gordon Mlotek.

2. THE SHTETL CRAFTSMAN AND HIS APPRENTICE

Kahal kept the artisans in fear, divided from well-to-do Jews. On *shabes*, an artisan was not allowed to wear a silk *kapote* or a *shtrayml* on his head. In the *besmedresh* or small prayer house his place was always on the last bench. He never set foot into meetings where the big shots got together to discuss town business; no one asked his opinion. For showing disrespect or some other infraction he could be scolded, slapped, and sometimes even beaten in the assembly hall. His children were kidnapped and turned over to the army in place of the children of the *besmedresh* bench-warmers. Often the names of imaginary brothers were listed on the draft register next to the names of well-to-do children. These "brothers" were drafted in their stead. They were poor children, total strangers, and not related at all.

In those days, alas, the Jewish artisans themselves were down and out. From the start, the teaching of crafts was poorly managed and resulted in many bad products. An apprentice spent years working for the average craftsman carrying out the sloptub, helping out the housewife in the kitchen, and receiving blows galore. And since he barely had a chance to learn the skills, he barely knew them. He later became a bunglar, a sour wretched person who looked to the bottle for solace. His hand was always ready to deliver a blow, sometimes he even gave his own wife the honor. Pity the apprentices who, when the time came, fell into his hands. And who, pray tell, were these boys who ended up with someone like him to teach them the trade? Orphans, paupers, abandoned children, who never studied in a *kheyder*, couldn't read—total boors.

Mendele Moykher Sforim (1929).

This Jew has a wife, one son and two daughters. Here is a list of his average yearly expenses:

Rent per year	16 rubles
Taxes, membership dues in the tailors' guild	6 rubles, 15 kopeks
Food, averaging 30 kopeks a day	100 rubles
Expenses for *shabes* over and above the daily average	15 rubles
Light, wood, etc.	10 rubles
Expenses for *sukes, peysekh* and other holidays	6 rubles
	153 rubles 15 kopeks

In other words, a Jew spends about 160 rubles a year just to feed a family of five. Not counting clothes, he has to spend around 9 silver kopeks per day per person. This tailor charges 75 silver kopeks for sewing a *kapote*. In any given week he earns anywhere from 1½ to 3 rubles. In a year, not counting the days he doesn't work—because of holidays or sickness—the tailor earns no more than 100, maximum 120, rubles.

His wife makes up the deficit by working as a petty merchant. She spends the entire day in the marketplace and leaves the three little children with her husband. No matter how good or energetic a businesswoman she might be, her efforts earn her no more than 60 kopeks, rarely more than one ruble per week. With luck, then, she earns barely a quarter of what her husband does. All in all, both husband and wife hardly earn more than their expenses for food alone.

In a good year the tailor can have maybe 20 or 30 rubles left over for clothes, including underwear, shoes, and the like. But just consider his working conditions: He slaves away all day in a tiny, poorly ventilated room; the air is bad both from the smoke inside and the smells outside. So what

A Jewish tailor working at home in Kinev, Kelts province.

does he do in a bad year, in cases of accident or illness? How will the children have anything to eat when the wife has to take care of her sick husband? You can tell from their faces which of them would have been better off had they not been born at all. For weeks on end they must subsist just on water, bread, and onions.

This, by Jewish standards, is not considered a poor family.

O. Margolis. Document 36.

3. ARN-MOYSHE'S STATION HOUSE

The sun has barely risen and Moyshe *shames* is already on the beat. He raps his special hammer on all the shutters of the sleeping market and his rasping, melancholy voice pleads with the population: "Awake, O Jews to serve the Lord! Get up, dear Jews, the *besmedresh* is waiting. Get up now to recite the Psalms!"

The first response to his call comes from Arn-Moyshe's station house at the very edge of the market. The huge front gates open with a crashing sound. Here the wagons bringing merchandise from the larger towns pull to a stop.

The long building is still hidden in heavy shadows when the first panting horses pull in at the open gates. The weary, dusty wagon driver climbs down from the coach box, gives the horses a friendly pat and leads them through the gates.

"What's the matter?" he asks the horses. "You haven't said your morning prayers yet? Get a move on!"

The porters, with heavy ropes over their *kapotes*, are ready and waiting with cries and curses. The old-timers have tangled beards and the build of an ox while the younger ones are cleanshaven. The porters attack the wagons and packs start flying into the corners of the yard.

"Hey, fatso, shake a leg!"

"Grab him by the tail, you slob!"

"Watch out, those are Khayim Rupture's packs!" The

107

shouts bombard the open window of Arn-Moyshe's office where there's always a lamp burning, day and night. The wagon driver is now inside delivering the bill of goods to Arn-Moyshe himself. As he hears each box hit the floor with a thud, the boss's heart skips a beat.

"They'll run me into the poorhouse at the rate they're going," he moans.

The driver goes outside to offer the porters a bit of advice: "Shut your traps!" he roars.

It doesn't do any good.

"They've gone wild!" he says as the thudding and banging starts working on him too. The sudden crack of his whip brings everyone to their senses.

Now it's Arn-Moyshe's turn to give them a piece of his mind: "There's a fortune lying there in those boxes. You'll ruin everything!"

"Then we'll all go hungry, a plague in your bones," the driver says, to complete the thought.

"I have to prepare for *shabes*," one of the older porters complains.

"So go tell your gripes to the rabbi," another porter yells at him. But things quiet down and the work continues at a slower pace under Arn-Moyshe's supervision. The goods get sorted in different corners. At each heap a porter stands ready to carry the goods to the proper customer. Soon, walking crates and sacks can be seen moving out of the front and rear entrances. Arn-Moyshe rushes from one gate to the other, throwing a quick glance at the list as he takes stock of each item:

"This sack of sugar goes to Khayim Moysheles," he calls to one of the porters and the latter shouts back:

"To Khayim Rupture? Sure enough!"

"A sack of salt to Khantshe Braynes!"

"I know, the *gabe's* wife has been waiting for it," says the porter as he sets out on his way.

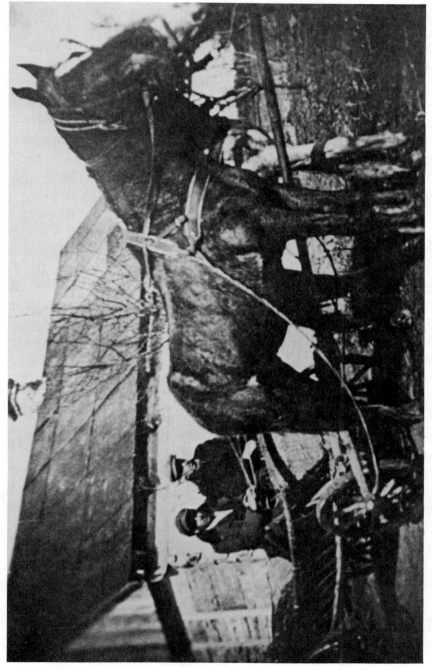

Two Jewish farmers and a wagon in the village of Azdititsh, Volin province.

"A box of yeast for Borukh the Baker!" comes the next order from Arn-Moyshe.

One by one, the porters set out for various points in the shtetl. Those who take the back exit pass by Arn-Moyshe's little *shul* where porters and drivers catch a quick afternoon or evening prayer during the week. On *shabes* and holidays it's an altogether different story. Then they sit quietly around the long tables and watch their language in the presence of the holy scroll. And if there happens to be a khasidic *rebe* visiting their *shul* on that particular *shabes*, then they're on their best behavior. Their bodies tensed, they try to catch every sound and movement the *rebe* makes. They even wear their *taleysim* differently—covering their entire head and most of their face—and each of them is visibly proud to be on equal footing with the rest of the Jews on this day.

Naturally, Arn-Moyshe, the warden and supporter of the *shul*, is proudest of all. On that *shabes* his little *shul* is packed even during the Torah reading and, as soon as the prayers and the *kidesh* [kiddush] are over, the men rush home to eat and come right back with their wives and children to watch the *rebe* at his "table." It's *their shabes* then, and with heads raised they exchange greetings with the Jewish merchants and *khasidim* they meet along the way or who have come along to see Arn-Moyshe's little *rebe*. In their great joy they pretend not to notice that most of the well-to-do *khasidim* are only there to have something to laugh about later. As long as the "beautiful Jews" feel obliged to visit their *shul* once in a while, that's all that really matters.

A *rebe* whose followers have their own *shtibl* in town or even a descendant of a famous khasidic court will hardly celebrate the Sabbath at their *shul*. But, whenever a *rebe* shows up who doesn't come from khasidic royalty, he ends up wandering around town with his manager like a blind sheep. He doesn't stand a chance at the *shtiblekh*. The

Radziner *khasidim* won't beat around the bush. They'll come right out and say:

"Listen mister, you're wasting your time."

The Rizhiner *khasidim* will give it to him in simple language: "Look, if it's charity you're after, fine. But don't come here to play the part of a *rebe*."

The other *shtiblekh* will ignore him altogether. As far as the *besmedresh* crowd is concerned, he won't go anywere near them. There, to top it all off, he'd have to pay his respects to the rabbi as well. Only the most famous *tsadikim* end up spending *shabes* in the *besmedresh*.

Thus a *rebe* of his rank ends up in Arn-Moyshe's little *shul*. There he'll enjoy a sumptuous *kidesh* and Saturday night meal. True, he won't make much on donations—they're poor Jews after all—but he'll be surrounded with glowing faces who are honored to have such a "saintly man" in their presence.

Since it isn't polite for him to drive right up to Arn-Moyshe's inn, he spends half a day at another inn. Sure enough, as soon as Arn-Moyshe finds out from the driver that a *rebe* is in town, his manner changes completely. His hard figure and angry tongue soften up. He gets the wagon unloaded in double time and pushes the porters with subtle hints:

"C'mon fellows, hurry up. There's someone I want to meet in town." They get the message. Now's not the time to fool with Arn-Moyshe. He's got to run off and inform Beyle to clean up the front room and den in honor of the guest. Someone else may come along and grab the *rebe* from under his fingers. The butchers are just itching for a bit of khasidic honor. Their *gabe*, Hersh Trelbakh, has been waiting for a chance to depose Arn-Moyshe from his pedestal.

"Listen," says the driver all out of breath, "Hersh Trelbakh's been sniffing around the inn. At the sight of the *shtrayml* he closed his butcher shop."

"Don't worry, he'll be *my* guest," says Arn-Moyshe with determination as he directs the porters every which way.

"You should see his manager!" says the driver. "Doesn't take his eyes off him. Must be a real important guy!"

As soon as the goods are dispatched, Arn-Moyshe bangs the gates shut and rushes home to change into his cloth gaberdine and satin hat. Decked out in his Sabbath attire he hurries off to Meyer's Inn where all the *rebeim* and their managers stay.

This time Hersh Trelbakh has in fact beaten him to it. Arn-Moyshe doesn't want to start up with him. He'll get his way using the polite approach. Meanwhile he forgets the stranger standing next to Hersh and starts right in:

"Hersh, you know our *shul* has first claim and my Beyle's already prepared the front room and den. Are you listening? Look, we aren't playing games, you know. I couldn't get away any sooner."

The stranger stares at him and doesn't seem to grasp what's going on. Then he understands and tries at once to work out a compromise:

"First of all, how do you do, Reb . . ."

"Arn-Moyshe," both men call out together.

"Very fine, very fine of you Reb Arn-Moyshe. But as far as a *shul* is concerned, Reb Hersh has already offered—"

But Arn-Moyshe cuts him short. He would have liked to give Hersh a piece of his mind but controls the urge and weighs his words carefully:

"It's my right to entertain the guest. The house is empty. You know that, Hersh."

Instead of answering, Hersh stands there playing with the tassels of his belt.

"All right," Arn-Moyshe yields a bit, "let him stay at your place. But Friday night must be ours."

The manager is apparently pleased to see two Jews arguing over his *rebe* and in such a gentlemanly manner. Stroking his grayish beard he addresses them in an even milder tone:

"God willing, there'll be one Friday night with you and one with them."

"No," says Hersh firmly as he stares Arn-Moyshe right in the eye. "He spends all of *shabes* with us. There's no other way."

"But I get Saturday night!"

"Sure," says the manager, "when the afternoon prayers are over and the *rebe* has had his say."

"Well, I guess that's the way it'll be," says Arn-Moyshe giving in completely, though he knows full well that his men will hold it against him through all of *shabes* for letting Hersh get away with it. And it's all out of sheer spite as Hersh himself is the first to admit as soon as he gets a little bit tipsy in Baneshe's Tavern. That's where all butchers and artisans get together on Monday and Wednesday nights. Then Hersh starts bragging about how he cheated Arn-Moyshe out of his *rebe*:

"There I was biding my time with that manager who was the finest of the fine, you can be sure. I made him no definite offer. After all, our place is in the synagogue—we're not even *khasidim*. Then along comes Arn-Moyshe in his cotton gaberdine and his satin hat, a real honest-to-goodness *khosed*. He takes one look at me and nearly faints dead away. Well, well, I think to myself. Fell right into my hands. In that case I won't budge an inch. The first *shabes* is mine and let him know it."

Sometimes this bragging ends in a fist fight and the two Jews won't speak to each other until the next *rebe* comes to town.

Jacob Zipper, pp. 78–85.

4. THE WORK WEEK

The first sign of morning is greeted each day of the week by another household. The first fire is lit before the sun has actually risen. The real signal though is the hoarse voice of the *shames* that accompanies his rap on the shutters: "Dear Jews, awake to recite the Psalms!" He never gets as far as the Narrow Street but his echo can be heard even here, on the far side of the market.

Sunday morning, the first fire appears in Yoyne the Peddler's attic. Soon he can be seen hurrying through the street like a long shadow, with the bottom half of his *kapote* tucked into the rope around his waist. His sack, still empty, bounces on his small back as he tries to be the first one out of town. He leaves even before morning prayers which he catches in the home of Moyshe Presper, the only Jew who lives at the very edge of the gentile suburb, near the forest which marks the outer limits of the *porets's* estate. If he is in fact the first to arrive in the village, he can start the week off with a real bargain (why else would Moyshe Presper choose to live among the *goyim?*). Yoyne claims that the night after *shabes* brings good luck but it's only on the following Friday, when he returns with a full sack, that his luck can actually be tested.

"The bargain's arrived," the Narrow Street will say, half in jest and half in anticipation. "Time to light the candles, then," one woman will say to her neighbor as they both lose sight of tired Yoyne who disappears into the large door that leads to his attic. Soon a strange voice will shout: "A bargain!" That is his crazy daughter greeting him, the one who still hasn't found a husband and sits home all day.

Early Monday morning the first light appears in Meyertshe Carpenter's yard. The light is accompanied by the old man's shouts to his sons:

"Hey slobs, don't forget the saws!"

"Shike, watch out for the ax! What d'ya do with the chisel?"

114

Their shouts and preparations as they set out for the nearby villages wake up everyone in the street including Khayim Tinsmith. The latter then proceeds to drag his apprentice out of bed: "Get up already! We've gotta roof the whole church this week!" He is the chief tinsmith in the region who can claim responsibility for every roof on the *porets*'s estate and every church dome. He is proud of his craft and often brags to the carpenters:

"Who ever sees your carpentry? It's painted over and covered. I get to sit up high. I see the world and the world sees me."

He joins forces with the carpenters only in the summertime. That's when they build houses and he does the roofing. Wintertime, he sits at home and makes things that can't even be bought in Lublin: pots and pans, candelabras and what-not. He's a craftsman, all right. But his real skill only comes out when there's a holy place to be roofed. On such days he can barely wait to climb up onto the roof. Each bang of his hammer is accompanied by a melody or a part of the prayer service. Working on the dome of a church gives him no less satisfaction. Suspended on a rope, he works almost flat on his stomach, and he seems to be holding on to the dome with special pleasure.

The first time he sensed how much he enjoyed it, he went off to consult the rabbi to find out whether or not a Jew can decorate a church. When the rabbi was slow to answer, Moyshe tried to find excuses:

"Rabbi, I buy food for *shabes* with that money, my little Avreml studies in Reb Lozer's *kheyder* and as for myself, I sing only Jewish tunes when I'm up there."

"But what about 'that one' on the tip of the dome?" The rabbi cuts him short.

"Oh, I don't even have that in mind, rabbi. I only look at my tin plate and at the world. If you could only see what it looks like from up there. I tell you, the Lord has created a beautiful world!"

Woodcutters in Sighet, Hungary.

"If that's the case, sing as much as you want. But it's not worth uttering any words in the sacred tongue."

Despite the rabbi's approval, each time Moyshe is hired to work on a church, he refuses to tell anyone where he's going. He sneaks out of town and disappears for a whole week. Even his older son Big Leyzer, who helps on every job, can barely get permission to go along. "You leave me alone," says Moyshe. "It's too high for a sissy like you. Besides, you'll get enough practice in this lousy profession."

On the other days of the week, before sunrise, the lamp in Leybush Water-carrier's hut is the first to light up. He lives right on top of the town dump and the unmistakable smells stick to him as he trods along under the heavy weight of the full buckets hanging from the yoke on his shoulders. Slowly, with measured steps, he makes his way from house to house of the rich merchants who live in the market. His broad red beard, straight as a ruler, leads the way. Before morning prayers he sets out with dry buckets to bring the first water for Khayim-Yoyne the Miller's samovar. His studded boots resound on the boardwalk informing the whole street that Leybush is on his way to the spring up there in the hills, past the white church, to draw fresh water for the richest man in town. Though the miller has his own well in the yard, he insists on having spring water for his morning samovar. Thus Leybush earns his first fees on an empty stomach. He says morning prayers in the miller's house and gets a bite to eat there, and if the maid is in good spirits, he can bring home a snack for later too. Only on leaving the miller's house does Leybush start his regular route of bringing ordinary pump water to various households.

On Thursday and Friday mornings Leybush is forced to abandon his leisurely pace. No matter how fast he moves he still can't avoid the impatient calls of the housewives: "Reb Leybush, me first. I have to rinse the meat. Because of you I'll end up working into the Sabbath, God forbid."

A water-carrier and his son at the pump, Navaredok, Belorussia.

Leybush does his best. His red beard jerks every which way and the tails of his *kapote* are completely soaked. You can hear them slapping against his boots. He obviously wants to serve each customer first, but once the shouts reach an almost hysterical pitch and some housewives even try to drag him into their house, that's when Leybush loses his calm. He stops dead in his tracks, lets the buckets down, detaches the yoke and says:

"Take a look will ya? You're runnin' me ragged and I don't have nothin' for *shabes* yet."

Having made his statement he remains standing in exhaustion and finally hooks up the buckets again, slowly, having regained his usual pace.

"Don't worry. You'll all get your water for *shabes*. There's still plenty of time."

Gdalye Shoemaker, who is also a bagel baker a few days in the week, is another one of the early risers. He lives on the top floor of the ramshackle building that also houses Leybush Water-carrier. The neighbors claim that Gdalye begrudges the roosters and makes it a point to get up before they even take their positions on the rooftops. Lest the neighbors suspect him of having slipped a little, he immediately opens his window wide and sings loud and clear, to the accompaniment of his hammer on the shoemaking days, or as he heats the oven on the days he bakes thin flat rolls or crispy bagels whose aroma quickly reaches the well-to-do houses on the street and nearby market.

Summer and winter his window is "open to the world." His clear, melodious voice carries through the air with his constant practice of the traditional Torah melody. For Gdalye is the Torah reader in the artisans' *shul*, and all week long he lives for the pleasure of his Sabbath performance. His chanting is so pleasant that no one leaves the *shul* during the Torah reading, even on the hottest summer day. The congregants sit still, totally absorbed in the drawn-out chant of Balak's sinister words to Balaam: "So then, now go, curse this people for me, for it is too mighty for me." But the same voice that evokes the eternal hatred for the People of Israel also puts that arrogant Balak in his place. In the winter months the voice resounds with the eternal pride of Israel: "Now these are the ordinances which you shall set before them. If you buy a Hebrew servant, he shall serve six years and in the seventh he shall go free for nothing."

Gdalye is the pride and joy of the workaday Jews. Even though he's only an artisan, he's almost considered one of the aristocracy. No one begrudges him his satin hat on *shabes* and his silk *kapote* on *yontef*. The *khasidim* and top men of town don't stop their sons, who bring the *tsholnt* up to his house on Friday afternoon, from staying over and practicing the next day's Torah reading with all the "simpletons" of the neighborhood.

His room which serves as a workshop, bedroom, and dining room is tidied up by then. The large, flat kneading table has been cleared of dough. His shoemakers' bench and tools in the corner of the room are covered with a heavy, thick cloth and his wife is busy whitewashing the black edges of the oven to prepare it for *shabes*. Now, on Friday afternoon, the room becomes a *kheyder* filled with the age-old melody led by Reb Gdalye's clear voice.

He never took payment for teaching the boys how to chant the weekly Torah portion, but well-to-do fathers considered it a ritual during *khanike* and *purim* when the *rov*, *khazn*, *shames*, and *melamed* were sent money, to include something for Gdalye's benefit. On those days he would be seated at his table, like one of the religious functionaries, wearing his satin hat. Each time a lad would come up the snow-covered steps, Gdalye would greet him in a sing-song voice: "Wonderful, wonderful. May you be privileged to greet the Messiah with bread and salt." Then he would hand the bashful lad a freshly baked flat-roll.

Gdalye was always thankful to God for providing him, not only with a beautiful voice, but also with a profession so that he could sing whenever he wished and not have to live off his musical talent. His day began very early and was well divided between sacred and secular functions. As soon as the baking was done, he would hurry off to the *besmedresh* for morning prayers leaving his wife with the job of selling the crackers and rolls in the market.

"I'm an artisan, not a salesman," he would argue whenever she put up a fight about having to stand on her feet with the baked goods all day. "And second of all, it's only a few mornings a week and a Jew has to pray with a *minyen* every day."

He baked only on Tuesday, Wednesday, and Thursday mornings. Sunday and Monday weren't good days for bagels and rolls because there was still leftover *khale* from *shabes*, and on Friday housewives did their own baking. On the non-baking mornings he made shoes until sunrise and then went off to the khasidic *shtibl* where he stayed until well in the morning.

"You can't spend a whole day fixing shoes, you know," he would explain to his wife. "The old shoes won't run away."

"And how, pray tell, will we have something to prepare for *shabes*, if the shoes keep on gathering dust?"

His wife still hadn't settled her accounts with the shoemaker's trade. She was convinced that all the sorrow in her life stemmed from the changing fashions in shoes. Who could keep up with the imports from Warsaw? And wasn't it because of the new styles that their eldest son Avreml had picked up one day and set off for the big city? His fireman's helmet has been hanging on the wall for years now. It served as a constant reminder of the Wednesday evenings when Avreml would get all dressed up, put on his helmet and step out onto the porch to sound the alarm. At the blast of his trumpet all the volunteer firemen would come running to their house from all sides carrying axes, buckets, and hooks. Together they would rush to the pump in the middle of the market, right next to the fire bell that would be rung in case of a real fire.

When the first photo arrived no one could recognize him. Clean-shaven, hatless, and with his hair parted in the middle. A portrait on glossy paper. She felt that her own son had become estranged from her forevermore. She stuck the photo into the frame of the *mizrekh* and tried not to look at it. But the other children couldn't tear their eyes from the photo and one by one each of them set out for that unknown place where Avreml sat and repaired shoes.

Jacob Zipper, pp. 223–236.

5. WOMEN AT WORK

These are some women's professions that I remember from the shtetl Sonik in Galicia.

1. Matchmaker.
2. A medic—who healed with leeches and other folk remedies.
3. A bathhouse attendant—who cut toenails and helped women bathe.
4. An *opshprekherin*—a woman who gave advice and remedies to people who were convinced that they had been cursed by the evil eye.
5. Chicken feeders and chicken sellers.
6. Cap-makers and pearl-stringers.
7. A syrup maker.
8. A baker.
9. Pretzel-baker and peddler.
10. Knitters; socks, gloves, shawls.
11. Girdle-maker.
12. Sausage-maker.

Esther the beltmaker. Porisov, Lublin province.

13. A yeast seller.
14. Pickle vendor.
15. Herb vendor.
16. A woman who resold used clothing—real rags.
17. A woman who sold honey and dates.
18. A cracker-maker and vendor.
19. A goose-fat seller.
20. A sponge vendor.
21. And, finally, "the Holy one." She was a woman who sold crosses, prayer beads, and Christian portraits—so everyone called her "the Holy one."

Berl Rabakh.

6. SAYINGS FROM WORK

געלט האַלט זיך נאָר אין אַ גראָבן זאַק.

Gelt halt zikh nor in a grobn zak.
Literally: Money stays only in a thick sack.
Compare with: The rich get richer.

ווי מען בראָקט זיך איַן די פֿאַרפֿל, אַזוי עסט מען זיי אויף.

Vi men brokt zikh ayn di farfl, azoy est men zey oyf.
Literally: The way your *farfl* is cut, that's how you'll eat it.
Compare with: You made your bed, now you'll lie in it.

אַז אַן אָרעמאַן עסט הון איז ער קראַנק אָדער די הון.

Az an oreman est hun, iz er krank oder di hun.
Literally: If a poor man eats a chicken, one of them must be sick.

אַ סך מלאכות און ווייניק ברכות.

A sakh melokhes un veynik brokhes.
Literally: Many trades and little profit.
Compare with: You'll work all day for a wisp of hay.

124

אַז מען גיט אַ קלאַפ אין טיש, רופֿט זיך אָפּ די שער.

Az me git a klap in tish ruft zikh op di sher.

Literally: If you knock on the table, the scissors answers.

Compare with: Speak to the walls.

אויף אַ פֿרעמדער באָרד איז זיך גוט צו לערנען שערן.

Oyf a fremder bord iz zikh gut tsu lernen shern.

Literally: It's good to learn barbering on someone else's beard.

אַלע שוסטערס גייען באָרוועס.

Ale shusters geyen borves.

Literally: All shoemakers go barefoot.

ער לינט אין דער ערד און באַקט בײגל.

Er ligt in der erd un bakt beygl.

Literally: He lies in the ground and bakes bagels.

Compare with: The fellow is "down in the dumps."

7. NICKNAMES IN A SHTETL

Anything at all out of the ordinary aroused immediate interest among the shtetl population. All a Jew had to do was to eat lunch at the same time every day for him to be called "Count" or "Prince." And if the house was kept clean and underwear was changed at least once a week, the whole family soon came to be known as the "Tsar's Household." In all honesty, though, the shtetl often had a keen and accurate eye for summing up a person. Here are some examples:

"Leybe the Head" was the name of a blind Jew with a big head. He sat at home all day and gossiped about everyone in town.

"Sholem the Jacket"—a small Jew who walked around in a cotton jacket. He was in his seventies, but young and old alike called him by that name. He wouldn't even get insulted anymore.

A group of brothers all had long noses. On any community matter they always supported each other to the bitter end. "Oh, the Noses," people would say and it was obvious whom they meant.

"Kaiser" was a poor Jewish peddler who was cross-eyed. He had a "cunning stern look." According to shtetl notions, only a king looked that way. His son was called "the Successor," his wife was "Her Royal Highness," and his daughter, "Little Princess." Even *goyim* called him "King." No more ironic nickname could ever be imagined.

Once a Jew built a house with a glass-enclosed balcony and rented it out to a shoemaker who was very sharp and an established liar. Eventually his given name was forgotten for it was replaced by the nickname "Balcony." Whenever a customer wanted to get back at him for not having the work ready on time, he would say: "A plague on the Balcony!"

A tailor and his wife who didn't weigh 200 pounds between them were called "The Gang." While their rickety, crippled children were known as "The Cossacks."

The favorite victims were sons-in-law who were being supported by their wives' parents. A mere remark on the parents' part could stick with the young man for the rest of his life. A father boasted that he had finally found a groom, a real "winner." Thus the son-in-law was called "The Winner" forever after.

"Professor" was the name given to a son-in-law who wore glasses. A quiet fellow who wasn't quite mature yet was known as "The Little Donkey." Someone else, who kept his mouth open more than was necessary was named "The Crow."

The shtetl knew the most intimate secrets of everyone's life. One poor fellow had the misfortune to become the father of a son three months after his marriage. That earned him the nickname of "The Hero."

The first tailor who stopped taking measurements with a string and used a tape measure was called "The Tape Measure." Other nicknames were "Canary" for a tailor who sang at work, "Sparrow" for a little shoemaker with a high-pitched voice, "Itshe Potato" for a stutterer and "Swallow," "Fox" and "Piggy" for other idiosyncrasies.

A person who was universally respected was never given a nickname, but, actually, there weren't too many people in that category. The tendency to ridicule was very strong in the shtetl and a new person would be scrutinized from every angle until a single word could be found to characterize his strangeness.

From the shtetl Visoki-Dvor, in 1925.
Hirsz Abramowicz.

8. TAILORS' STREET

Their street was on the edge of town, they had their own *shul* and grocery store. Years would go by and no one would hear from them. Day and night they sat and sewed. No one mixed with them. You see, if a girl was born to a tailor's family, soon enough a boy would be born to another tailor. The girl and boy grew up together until they got married, had children and raised more tailors. They worked, ate, made arrangements, fell in love and picked fights all in the same place. Here a father taught his children how to get along in the world. Here a mother taught her daughter how to be a mother. Here they all slept together in one heap.

Two zigzag rows of houses—this was the Tailors' Street. Either because the street was so crooked or because children played in the middle of it and sometimes fell asleep on the

Children learning to be tailors in a Jewish vocational training school during the 1920s.

spot, whatever the reason, no one used the street as a thoroughfare. In the winter the street was unusable because of the ice; in spring and autumn—because of the mud. Summer, everyone—old men, women and children—literally sat out on the street to take in the sun. But maybe the real reason no one drove through the Tailors' Street was because they simply forgot that the street existed. That is to say, the shtetl surely knew that there were tailors but it simply didn't bother about them.

The tailors of the shtetl were divided into several classes: First, the tailors who made the rounds of the villages doing on-the-spot work. They would get up early Sunday morning and set out for the villages, returning Friday before sunset. Second, tailors who worked on second-hand clothes for the shtetl stores and third, tailors who were the big shots of the street because they made clothes to order for the well-to-do citizens of the town.

Every tailor lived on this street. It was part of their tradition not to mix with the other Jews and besides, the rest of the town probably didn't want them. That's not to say that the ordinary townsfolk were any more honest or God-fearing than the tailors. Nevertheless, the tailors, especially the apprentices, were considered a good-for-nothing, rowdy bunch.

The young tailors were clean-shaven and ran around with girls. A tailor was always busy at work except for Saturday night when he went out for a good time. Having a good time meant drinking lots of wine, singing, kissing girls, and getting into fights. But even on that one night of the week, a tailor never managed to do all four things at once. Cursed be the day he was born!

Why didn't the Creator of the world make him into a merchant and make the merchants—tailors? Why do they, the big-shots, curse their children by shouting: "You're nothing but a tailor" or "Watch out, you're becoming like one of the tailors"?

The tailors, in turn, curse their own children by yelling: "What'll become of you—a scholar, a bench-warmer!" or "You hold the needle just like a *rebetsn!*" They don't even mind that no one drives through their street. Maybe it's not a street after all, but their own empire and the rest of the town can go to—.

Their children don't know how to pray. A tailor has no need for prayers. Besides, who's got the time? Whatever the kids have to know—they learn. Lucky is the tailor who has girls for children and woe to the tailor whose children are boys. Girls handle a needle better. At age twelve a girl knows how to sew, but a boy can't sew until his fingers bend into place. Years go by before a boy can handle a needle properly.

And so the place is flooded with second-hand tailors, tailors who do the rounds of the villages, while the refined type of tailors are few and far between.

A. Raboy.

9. GREBLYE STREET

The arcade on Greblye Street is on two levels. From the bottom level which is public property the street looks like one undivided block. But from the upper level each house looks different, each with a separate driveway to the back-yard, each with its own pail for rainwater and each with different odds and ends lying about. It's easy enough to tell which house belongs to someone who just happens to live there and which—to the *real* Greblye crowd: the Leyzer-Ayzik and Bere-Aba families who are butchers, oxen and horse dealers. Their yards are always crowded with animals, horses, and wagons.

Public opinion has it that their main income is from opening other people's stables and transporting the contents over the border. This explains the nickname they've all inherited: The Society of Sitters. Either they sit it out in jail or they're sitting on the backs of stolen horses.

They mark their bridles and whips with a red mark. The moment a peasant catches sight of that mark on market day he quickly crosses himself and pulls off his hat:

"Of course I'm ready to sell," he says to the bearer of the mark. "Wait just a minute, sire, and I'll show you what a winner this is." He gives the horse a slap on the hump or tugs at the cow's udder. The peasant knows full well that if he dares to hesitate, sooner or later his own stable will be found open and no one will help to find the thief.

"You can't just accuse someone out of the blue," the sheriff will explain to him. "You bring me an eye-witness and I'll have him sent off in chains." The peasant, not quite sure *who* will be sent off in chains, leaves with empty hands.

Not so when the stable in question belongs to a *porets*. Then foreign police show up and accompanied by the local police they go from stable to stable on Greblye Street and measure the combed manes of all the horses. The search usually ends with one of the houses lit up with lights and filled with snacks and bottles of whiskey from the nearby tavern. The party goes on till late at night, for, as the owners explain: Give the stray dog a bone and he'll stop barking. Sometimes, though, the party never takes place. The police cannot be bought off, in which case, one member of Greblye Street is called upon to perform the commandment of "sitting."

The Bere-Aba's are only a small bunch now, only Dudye, his sons and sons-in-law. They all have short red beards and flaming eyes. Where did he ever find sons- and daughters-in-law to look just like him? The men—tall and ruddy, the women—black-haired and slim. Dudye is a generous man. When he throws a wedding, the whole town is invited. To be sure he swears a lot and pokes fun at the "bench-warmers", but in his own way he shows respect for the *khasidim* and the learned class. In fact he even prays in a khasidic *shtibl* though the service lasts much too long as far as he is concerned.

Dudye may be a horse dealer, but he's proud of his *yikhes*. No one will ever dare offend him when it comes to his great-grandfather who was supposedly the first Jew permitted to live in Tishevits. The old king brought him here especially from another country to develop local trade. According to Dudye, this great-grandfather got permission for Jews to build houses as high as those of the gentiles and to learn weaponry for times of danger. All this is recorded in an old book. Dudye was fond of telling about his great-grandfather's exploits, of how he led a group of his men against the Cossacks who captured and destroyed the town during the Khmelnitski massacres.

Dudye would look into this family heirloom only during important family events or before undertaking a large business venture. The book was kept locked up in an old oak trunk on wheels which he kept in his bedroom. He wouldn't trust anyone, even his wife, with the key. It was known that whenever he married off a daughter she would carry the book with her for good luck. But Dudye hid the book so well among the folds of her wedding dress that no one ever saw it. Or perhaps since he led her by the arm to the *khupe* he had the book hidden in his own wide pockets all along. No one would dare ask.

And so the shtetl watches the wedding procession go by and is amazed to see that yet another son-in-law looks exactly like Dudye. The boardwalk trembles under the groom. Dudye and daughter walk behind, she—dressed in fabulous veils that are also a family heirloom. They barely cover her thick, black hair that Dudye is most anxious to hide from the eyes of the pious. (A special hairdresser from Warsaw worked all day to make her hair look like a wig.) Dudye even paid the *mikve* lady the special haircut fee though only the tip of one braid was actually cut off—to be kept in the pages of the book as a souvenir. Yes, the book which the very first Bere-Aba kept with him as he lay in the sands outside Tishevits with a band of Jews waiting to ambush Khmelnitski's army.

Jacob Zipper, pp. 156–163.

10. LEGENDS OF THE WORKADAY JEW: THE LAMEDVOVNIK

I'll tell you a story I once heard from Fishl about a *lamedvovnik*. You know what a *lamedvovnik* is? He's one of the thirty-six persons the sages say have to be alive in each generation in order for the world to continue to exist. If there were just one less, then the world could not go on. Thirty-six just men. Now the essence of the *lamedvovnik* is that no one can discover that he is one of these thirty-six. The minute he is discovered, he must die. A *lamedvovnik* can be in various forms. He can be a woodcutter, or a water-carrier. He can be rich or poor.

Fishl told me this story that he heard from his rabbi. Who knows if it's true or not? In a particular city, not a small town but a medium-sized city, there lived a man that everybody used to hate. Everything that he did, he did for money.

There used to be an abandoned woman in the city—her husband had disappeared. He left her and she had no way of supporting herself. So this man found out that she was alone. All of a sudden, he went away to another city. He came back and told her, "I met your husband, and I told him that you're suffering. He sent you some money. I'll deliver the money every week, but I want half of it." So he gave her twenty rubles a week and said, "The other twenty rubles I'm keeping for myself, for doing this service for you."

The city found out and the people were so furious at him they wanted to kill him. His name was Moyshe. "Moyshe! Moyshe!" They wouldn't call him up to the Torah in *shul*.

133

Young leather workers in Gombyn, Warsaw province, 1909. Each one demonstrates another phase of the work.

They gave him a seat at the very back. And they told him that when he dies they're *never* going to bury him, or they'll bury him next to the cemetery fence!

"How can you take twenty rubles away?" pleaded the woman.

"Otherwise," he answered, "I'm not doing you any favors." She had no other alternative, so she accepted.

Another man, also a very, very poor man, told Moyshe that he had received a letter from his daughter in America. Moyshe offered to help him write a letter to the daughter asking for money. But for the work, he again wanted half of all the money that arrived. The city was so angry at him—they wanted to kill him. But he wouldn't budge. "I don't do anything for free," he said. Before long he was doing this for several people, and each time he took a heavy share of the profit for himself.

One day this Moyshe died and the people of the city said this is the time to get even with him. They made him a funeral fit for the worst pauper in the city. They carried him to the cemetery at night. Nobody knew about it. They buried him without a shroud. They just threw him in the grave and put up a marker saying, "Here lies Moyshe Goy" —Moyshe the gentile.

Time passed and the abandoned woman stopped receiving money altogether. The poor man stopped receiving money from his daughter. The other water-carriers and wood-cutters, everybody, stopped receiving money. When they started an investigation, the woman's husband was never found. The daughter was never found. People realized that Moyshe had actually been the sole supporter of these people, but in order to keep his identity, his *lamedvovnik* identity, hidden, he purposely made himself seem so vicious that no one could ever guess what he was doing.

The city began seven days of mourning and cried over this saint who died as far as they were concerned, in such an obnoxious way. They went to the Rabbi and asked him what to do. They took out his body, covered it and gave him a really fancy funeral. As for the marker that read "Moyshe Goy," the Rabbi said, "Leave this. Only add one word. After *goy*, write, *kodesh*, holy."

Goy kodesh has two meanings. Moyshe Goy by itself means Moyshe the gentile. But Moyshe *goy kodesh* means Moyshe the holy man of his nation. *Goy* can also mean nation.

So this is the story that I remember from Fishl.

From 1929 to 1934 Jack Starkman was apprenticed to an old furrier named Fishl, in Lodz, Poland. Fishl used to sing and tell tales by the hour. In 1929, when Jack was fourteen years old, Fishl told Jack this legend.

Barbara Kirshenblatt-Gimblett.

11. THE LEGEND OF ZHAMELE'S YARD

Zhamele's Yard in Tishevits clung to the top of the hill: a row of dilapidated cottages in a cluster. Parts of harnesses and balls of combed flax lay strewn in the alleys between the buildings.

On sunny days the rope-spinners stand at their looms turning the cranks of the wooden wheels that weave the threads of flax into thick and thin ropes. The wheels creak as the balls of flax attached to a log sticking out of a wall whirr and hum as if they were in no particular hurry to leave their cuddly warmth. The rope-spinner does several things simultaneously: one hand turns the crank while the other adjusts the spindle to produce the proper width of rope. At the same time he keeps an eye on the thin thread coming from the second ball of flax suspended from his neck to make sure it doesn't tangle with the main thread. It looks as if the thread were unwinding from his belly button.

You have to be stronger than iron to sit still in Yankev Yoshe's translation *kheyder* and not want to join the rope-spinners in their work. An added distraction is the constant singing coming from the cobbler apprentices who work in Zhamele's yard. In one of those cottages, many years ago, there lived Zhame the peddler and tailor. Not a tailor exactly, but a mender of old clothes. His overgrown tombstone stands in the old cemetery, hiding within it the secret light that shone from his cottage over the river and meadow and reached as far as the city of Safed in the Land of Israel.

But while Zhame lived, no one noticed the light, in fact no one bothered with him altogether. In summer and winter, when all the roads are open, he would make the rounds of the nearby villages or would serve as a messenger for kahal to other *shtetlekh*. In autumn and spring, when the mud and floods cut off the town from the rest of the world, he sat at home mending clothes day and night. In the *besmedresh* nearby, his place was behind the oven. So no one noticed and no one knew what Zhamele did after midnight when the entire shtetl was asleep, covered by the thick fog that rose from the river.

Only Rabbi Isaac Luria, the "ARI" of Safed was not asleep. With an open eye he kept watch over all the communities of Israel in search of someone who was worthy of being the messiah of his generation. Every midnight he searched through the darkness of the world until, one night, a light broke through the fog revealing the old, tottering Pasture Bridge in Tishevits. And just opposite the bridge, coming from an open window he could hear an anxious voice call out:

"Watchman, what of the night?"

The "ARI" immediately sent two of his students to follow the man's voice. His instructions were that if they found him at home and if they would be able to look straight into his eyes, then the time of redemption would be near.

137

A woodcutter in Marmerush, Hungary.

Alas, the time had not yet come, for the wall of sins blocked the sound of his voice and the sight of his light. The holy messengers lost their way in the forests and swamps around town and they stumbled and wandered until the sound of morning prayers broke through the wall of silence and sent new light for their searching eyes. They arrived at Zhamele's house on Friday after twelve noon. Sure enough, the door was open, but when they entered, all they found was the tailor's wife whitewashing the oven door for *shabes*. Before they had even had a chance to look around, they heard the door creak and then noticed someone bending over a bed that stood in the corner. The next thing they knew the figure removed some straw from the mattress, spread it out over the floor, and lay down with his feet facing the door. They could only make out the dying man's last sigh, but try as they might, they couldn't see his face through the heavy mist and darkness that descended upon them.

Soon the men of the *khevre kedishe* [burial society] arrived and rushed him off to the cemetery so that he could be buried before candlelighting. During *shabes* a nut tree sprouted over his grave and casts its shadow until this very day. Only on *tishebov* [Tisha b'Av] and during a crisis do people visit the grave in their stocking feet and stand at the outer limits of the tree's shadow. The tombstone is bent and covered with moss, and beneath it burns the hidden light.

Jacob Zipper, pp. 394–96.

A yishuvnik or village Jew at the Kolbushov market, 1929. Courtesy of David Salz.

UNIT FIVE
GROWING UP IN THE SHTETL

Leyzer Segal's kheyder in Dlugeshedle, Grodne province. The melamed's father is sitting on the left.

1. WATCH NIGHT

In olden days, the Watch Night was a far more solemn occasion than it is today. People kept a close watch for Lilith who was known to steal newborn children from their mothers during the first eight days after birth, and especially on the last night known as Watch Night.

On this last night Lilith reigned supreme. Like a cuckoo bird she either exchanged the child for one belonging to demons (this is how all evildoers are born into the world) or she killed him outright. For protection, mothers pasted up a sign on the wall on which was written: *Lilith and Her Band — Stay Out*. Also, *belfers* brought their *kheyder-yinglekh* to read the "Sh'ma" prayer every evening at the home of a newborn boy until he was circumcised. On the last night before the *bris* candles were lit and poor Jews who were very learned recited Psalms and studied all night. A special dinner was made for them and charity was given out.

In an out-of-the-way village called Roznoy there lived a learned and very pious Jew named Reb Henekh Reydzisker. It was his great misfortune that each of his children died after birth. They were all born healthy and beautiful but on Watch Night would be snatched away. He was still young then, his wife younger still and quite wealthy at that, so they spared no efforts. To no avail. Six children already lay buried and now a seventh was on its way. They were very worried.

Unfortunately, our Lite was still a wasteland in those days. There were no *khasidim* and no khasidic *rebeim*. In such cases, there was no other choice than to seek the help of magicians and sorcerers who knew far less than the Tatars of today.

Luckily, there arrived at the Zelver Fair none other than the world-famous Reb Yoel Bal Shem (Master of the Name), author of the book *The Deeds of God*. Reb Henekh and his wife appealed to him for help offering a huge sum of money, and Reb Yoel accepted. They happily received him into their home a full month before she was expecting; they gave him a separate room with all conveniences. He stayed there until she gave birth. Then Reb Yoel gave the mother a large amulet (good luck charm) and a tiny one for the child. He drew a circle in charcoal around all the walls, and above the chimney he hung a bunch of different things: a bit of hay that fell out of a horse's mouth while the moon was shining; seven different types of hair taken from seven animals; seven pieces of cloth taken from seven shirts worn by seven men.

On Watch Night he put an amulet on the maid as well. He ordered twenty poor Jews to bathe themselves and stay up all night to study. He had as many candles lit as were stars in the sky. In the house itself he forbade the chimney and the door to be opened. Despite all these precautions a cat managed to steal into the house with a terrible howl. She grew larger and larger and kept trying to break into the room where the mother and child lay. The Bal Shem sat at the door and beat back the cat with his cane that had a pointed metal tip. The cat kept lunging at him and began to spurt forth glowing sparks. The people standing round were petrified.

Finally Reb Yoel got the better of her and gouged out one of her eyes with the tip of his cane. He chased her out of the house and ran after her. The Bal Shem did not appear for quite some time. At last, panting and drenched in sweat, he returned and shouted: *"Mazltov!* We are home at last. With God's help we pulled through. Bring out the brandy and cake!"

A printed shir hamayles. Contains passages from Psalms, the
words G-D DESTROY SATAN, the names of the angels
Sani, Sansani and Samangelof; variations on the magic
formula "A witch shall not live" and the names of Adam and
Eve, Abraham and Sarah, Isaac and Rebecca, Jacob and
Leah.

Well, there was joy upon joy. Everyone sat down at the table, feasted, discussed holy matters and had a good time. The next day many friends and relatives arrived for the *bris*. All the invited and even uninvited guests came except for one person. This was the midwife. The mother was very upset.

"How can this be?" she cried. "She attended all the previous births when there was no cause to celebrate. Today, when we can finally rejoice, she is missing." She called a halt to the ceremony until the midwife be brought. While someone went out to fetch her, the Bal Shem chuckled and said to all the guests: "You can be sure that she will not appear at this *bris*." And so it was that the messenger returned to say that the midwife was sick, that one of her eyes went blind during the night. The mother was very grieved to hear this, but the Bal Shem on the contrary was as pleased as could be.

Later, when all the guests were seated at the table he revealed a great secret to all. "I want you to know," he said, addressing himself to Reb Henekh in particular, "that the midwife murdered all your previous newborn babes. She is a witch. She is in cahoots with Lilith whom she gives all the children that she delivers. In all those holy places where Lilith cannot enter, the midwife helps her out. Since I placed such a close guard last night, she could not use her usual tactics and turned herself into a cat. I gouged out one of her eyes which explains why one of her eyes went blind this very night. As for what happened outside, that I cannot tell you. From now on you should always know who your midwife is and who is the woman in attendance. This is a serious matter and much depends upon it."

Soon afterwards the midwife died and confessed beforehand that she had turned over many children to the demons. She was buried on the outside of the cemetery fence and for several years after her death she could be seen walking about in the fields and forests.

Ayzik-Meyer Dik, pp. 32–39.

2. YANKELE

Sleep, Yankele, my darling little baby,
Shut your big black eyes.
A big boy who has all his teeth,
Ought Mother sing him lullabies?

A big boy who has all his teeth,
And will go to school by and by,
And study Torah and Talmud,
Ought he, when his mother rocks him, cry?

A big boy who soon will study Talmud,
While father stands by, nodding happily.
A big boy, who's growing up a scholar,
Ought he nights not let his mother be?

A big boy growing up a scholar,
And an enterprising merchant yet.
A big boy who will make a nice girl happy,
Ought he to be lying here so wet?

Sleep then, sleep, my groom that is to be,
Right now you're in the cradle, sad but true—
It will cost much toil and many tears,
Before anything becomes of you!

Mordkhe Gebirtig.

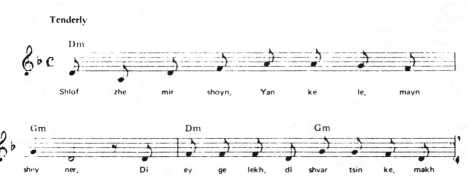

147

Shlof zhe mir shoyn, Yankele, mayn sheyner,
Di eygelekh, di shvartsinke, makh tsu;
A yingele, vos hot shoyn ale tseyndelekh,
Muz nokh di mame zingen ay-lyu-lyu.

A yingele, vos hot shoyn ale tseyndelekh
Un vet mit mazl bald in kheyder geyn,
Un lernen vet er khumesh un gemore,
Zol veynen ven di mame vigt im ayn?

A yingele, vos lernen vet gemore,
Ot shteyt der tate, kvelt un hert zikh tsu,
A yingele, vos vakst a talmed-khokhem,
Lozt gantse nekht der mamen nisht tsu ru?

A yingele, vos vakst a talmed-khokhem,
Un a geniter soykher oykh tsu glaykh,
A yingele, a kluger khosn-bokher,
Zol lign azoy nas vi in a taykh?

Nu shlof zhe mir, mayn kluger khosn-bokher,
Dervayl ligstu in vigele bay mir.
S'vet kostn nokh fil mi un mames trern
Biz vanen s'vet a mentsh aroys fun dir.

שלאָף זשע מיר שוין, יאַנקעלע, מײַן שיינער,
די אייגעלעך, די שוואַרצינקע, מאַך צו;
אַ ייִנגעלע, וואָס האָט שוין אַלע ציינדעלעך
מוז נאָך די מאַמע זינגען אײַ־ליו־ליו.

אַ ייִנגעלע, וואָס האָט שוין אַלע ציינדעלעך
און וועט מיט מזל באַלד אין הדר גיין,
און לערנען וועט ער הומש מיט גמרא,
זאָל וויינען ווען די מאַמע וויגט אים אײַן?

אַ ייִנגעלע וואָס לערנען וועט גמרא,
אָט שטייט דער טאַטע, קוועלט און הערט זיך צו,
אַ ייִנגעלע, וואָס וואַקסט אַ תּלמיד-חכם,
לאָזט גאַנצע נעכט דער מאַמען נישט צו רו?

אַ ייִנגעלע, וואָס וואַקסט אַ תּלמיד-חכם,
און אַ געניטער סוחר אויך צו גלײַך,
אַ ייִנגעלע, אַ קלוגער חתן-בחור,
זאָל ליגן אַזוי נאַס ווי אין אַ טײַך?

נו, שלאָף זשע מיר, מײַן קלוגער חתן-בחור,
דערווײַל ליגסטו אין וויגעלע בײַ מיר.
ס'וועט קאָסטן נאָך פיל מי און מאַמעס טרערן
ביז וואַנען ס'וועט אַ מענטש אַרויס פון דיר.

148

Some things in life are certain while others are not. Birth is one of those things that no one can be certain about: Will the baby live? Does it remember what it was like "up there" just seconds before birth? What kind of person will it grow up to be? The more uncertain things are, the more precautions are called for. An evil eye can harm the expectant mother, or Lilith, heaven forbid, can make off with the infant. Once the child is named, and if he happens to be a male—circumcised as well—then there is much less to be worried about. Now the child has made the first crucial steps towards becoming a Jew.

In the shtetl, one more thing is certain, that each and every Jewish child will learn to read. For how can there be a Jew who does not know how to pray, and how can he pray if he cannot read? On the uncertain side are the painful questions: what next? Will he go on to become a scholar after mastering the alphabet and prayer book? Better yet, will he combine Torah learning with a successful business? Will he find a good match? And just as the newborn infant has watchful eyes guarding him, so too does the child of school age have people to help him through the uncertainties. One such person is the *melamed* or teacher, the other is the *belfer* or assistant. The scene is the teacher's home which is transformed into an elementary school, a *kheyder*, for most of the day, six days a week.

3. GERSHN MELAMED'S KHEYDER FOR BEGINNERS IN TISHEVITS

In our shtetl, Besmedresh Street was situated behind the marketplace. For us, this street was holy from beginning to end. Opposite the *besmedresh*, on its left-hand side stood Gershn Melamed's beginner's *kheyder*. Up the hill a bit from this *kheyder* was Yankev Yoshe's translation *kheyder*. There was a path that led from Gershn Melamed's *kheyder* to the river and on this path stood two other schools: Peysekh Melamed's translation *kheyder* and three houses up

149

from him—Kalmen Dovid's beginner's *kheyder*. As a result, this area was always filled with children's voices—the voices of children playing outside the *kheyder* and of those studying inside.

The inside of my *kheyder* consisted of a large square room divided in two by a screen. Behind the screen was the teacher's bedroom and kitchen. We used to call it "the teacher's alcove." Over the opening of the alcove hung a red sheet covered with countless white dots. We would wrap ourselves in this sheet and play hide-and-seek. During the winter, at twilight, when the teacher and his helpers were in the *shul* and the boys were alone, this sheet was converted into a *tales*, and would-be magicians wrapped themselves around in it and imitated the *khazn* in the *shul*.

Through the second door one could see the dark kitchen with the rusty chimney-stove, full of dishes and kitchen furniture. The room was always full of curious children who watched the teacher's wife putter around in the kitchen.

At the west wall, between the opening to the kitchen and the hall stood a wooden alcove. It was a sort of pantry. We always watched the *melamed's* wife open and close it and almost every school boy knew every piece of kitchenware she owned.

Near the north wall stood a long wooden bench. During the winter children would draw figures on it or play *iks-miks-driks* [tic-tac-toe]. The teacher would sit on a little pillow on his bench, near the table. At the other end of this table was a helper who taught another group of children.

The *kheyder* was as noisy as a fair, especially during the winter. The children ran around from one place to another; some would sit on the ground, clap their hands and sing. Others just yelled or fought with each other and made a racket. Near the teacher on the bench there would always be a new kid, brought to school for the first day and crying bitterly. The commotion was made all the greater by the slamming of the door. The bedlam was particularly great when a beggar would come in. (The *kheyder* also served as a sort of lodging-house for wandering beggars.) The youngsters would surround him, help him unpack his bundle. From amidst the uproar one could hear several children's voices, repeating in a sweet, sorrowful chant their reading lessons or the Bible. You can imagine what went on when you consider that there were 70 or 80 children in such a *kheyder*.

Yekhiel Shtern (1950 A).

4. LEARNING TO READ

From the first day on which the *belfer* showed me the letters of the *alefbeys* set out in rows, I saw leaping forth the measured ranks of soldiers like those who at times passed in front of our house, with their drummer, rattling *tum tararum tum*, at their head. Those that most resembled this were the *alefs*, all arms swinging and legs striding, and the *gimls* with their boot moving off to the left, particularly when they had the *kibutz* vowel beneath them, its three dots like a ladder. These were real soldiers, armed head to foot. The *alefs* had their knapsacks on their backs and strode along somewhat bowed under their burden, proceeding to maneuvers, while the *gimls* stood foot out, all ready for the march. My eyes began to search the sides and flanks of the book.

All day long I day-dreamed about armies and soldiers. When I went up again, the *belfer* showed me the form of an *alef* and asked me:

"Can you see the yoke and pair of pails?"

"That's true, upon my soul; a yoke and pair of pails!"

"Well, that's an *alef*," testified the *belfer*.

"Well, that's an *alef*," I repeated after him. And the minute I went down the *alef* flew away.

The other letters also had their various aspects for me; they looked like beasts of burden and wild animals or uten-

151

Young and old at the town well. Kozhenits, Kels province.

sils, or simply like weird creatures, the likes of which I had not yet seen in this world. The *shin* was a sort of snake with three heads. The *lamed* was clearly nothing but a stork stretching out its neck and standing on one leg. The *giml* was a boot, like the one shown on the tins of shoe-polish, where a little devil with a tail polishes diligently. Meanwhile, the little *yud* looked like a tiny creature which seemed to have no shape and nothing on which to rest; nevertheless I felt more fond of it than of all the rest. It always seemed to be floating in the air.

Chayim Nachman Bialik.

5. ALEFBEYS

א	= *alef*	A water-carrier with two buckets.
ב	= *beys*	A little hut with an open wall. A *beys* has a mouth open, always ready to receive wisdom.
א-ב	= *alef-beys*	Stands for *alef binah;* to learn wisdom.
ג	= *giml*	A soldier putting his left foot forward to march.
		A man with a pocket of money at his side, always ready to aid the poor.
ד	= *daled*	A hammer with a handle.
ג-ד	= *giml-daled*	Stands for *gemol dalem;* be kind to the poor.
		The foot of the *giml* is turned to the following letter *daled* to remind one to look for the poor and to help them. *Daled's* face is turned so as not to be ashamed to receive help.
ה	= *hey*	A man crippled on one leg.
ש	= *shin*	Stands for *sheker;* falsehood. A *shin* has three branches but no root; just so, *sheker* never takes root, is never permanent.

‎פ	= *pey*	A mouth, closed shut.
‎ָ	= *komets*	A stick with a beard.
‎ֶ	= *segol*	Three true friends, always together.
‎ֹ	= *khoylem*	A soldier looking down from a brick building.

Learning to read is no easy task—especially when you are 3 or 4 years old and you *start* with a foreign language. In this case, Hebrew. Children in the shtetl only learned to read Yiddish much later, and usually outside of the classroom. To teach the alphabet, *melamdim* created dozens of descriptions, riddles and puns to help their students remember and recognize the letters. The tricks of the trade were generations old; some may even go back centuries.

After the alphabet comes reading. In Tishevits these two tasks were taught in separate schools: beginner's *kheyder* and translation *kheyder*. In other towns the two were combined in one school. The third level of learning is the Bible. Each child began the study of the Bible when he was ready for it, not when the whole class was ready. To celebrate the little boy's first Bible lessons his family and teacher made a party, and he became a *khosn toyre*, the Torah's bridegroom. At this celebration the child is "engaged" to Torah study for the rest of his life.

The following is the ritual dialogue between Motl, a 5- or 6-year-old, and his *melamed* on this occasion.

6. THE TORAH'S BRIDEGROOM

On the day of the ceremony a table was set with honey cake, brandy, nuts, and candles. Avrom Ber, as proud as can be, sat at the table. To his right sat Motl's father and all around sat the other guests. The women, including his mother, stood by the side and looked on with delight. In the very center of the table stood Motl himself, dressed in holiday clothes and wearing watches and other jewelry borrowed especially for the occasion. The *bentshers* stood next to him and placed their hands on his head. Then all three boys were covered with a *tales*.

Avrom-Ber: *Yingele, yingele,* what are father and mother doing now?

Motl: My father and mother are having a grand celebration now.

Avrom-Ber: Is it because you are beginning to study the Torah that your father and mother are making the grand celebration?

Motl: Yes, *rebe*, that is so, you guessed right.

Avrom-Ber: Would you first like to recite something from the Torah?

Motl: Of course, that is what I was created for. Although I am not fit to recite any Torah, even so, I shall say a few words: Teachers and friends. Why does the Torah start with a *beys, bereyshis,* and not with an *alef?* Because when the Lord created the world, he blessed it to have permanence. *Beys* stands for *borukh, blessed* and *alef* stands for *orur, cursed.* Had the Lord created the world with an *alef* there would have been no people of Israel.

Teachers and friends. I would like to add a few words more. Why did God give the Torah to Moses and not to Abraham?

Bentshers: Because then there were few Jews and in the days of Moses there were many Jews.

Motl: You gave the answer of the Torah. I will give you the answer for a child. There was no need to give the Torah in Abraham's time because then the generation was not bad. And also, if God had given the Torah through Abraham then the Jews would have forgotten it in Egypt.

Bentshers: Bend your head and we will bless you: You shall have a wife with twelve curls and each curl shall contain

155

A kheyder for girls. Laskarev, Lublin province.

the sanctity of the tribes. As you wear the watches on your heart and as we hold our hands on your head, so shall these blessings come true. May your life and the life of your family be as sweet as the fine fruits of a tree near a spring.

The assembled guests, silent until now, then shouted *mazltov!* The women showered candy and nuts on the boys on the table. The *bentshers* then got down from the table and Motl sat down next to Avrom-Ber before an open Bible.

Avrom-Ber: What are you studying, *yingele?*
Motl: Khumesh.
Avrom-Ber: What does *khumesh* mean?
Motl: Five.
Avrom-Ber: Five what?
Motl: Five books in the Torah.
Avrom-Ber: Which book do you study?
Motl: Vayikro.
Avrom-Ber: What is the meaning of *vayikro?*
Motl: He called.
Avrom-Ber: Who called, the rooster on top of the stove?
Motl: No, God called to Moses, to tell him the law of sacrifices.
Avrom-Ber: What is the law of sacrifices?
Motl: A lamb that has a blemish is not to be sacrificed on the altar.
Avrom-Ber: And what is a blemish?
Motl: A lamb with a blind eye or a broken leg, is said to have a blemish.
Avrom-Ber: And a lamb with a blind foot or a broken eye, is that a blemish?
Motl: No.

Yekhiel Shtern (1950 A).

7. GAMES FROM KHEYDER

First, counting out, finding out who is IT.

a. Alef   אלף   A
Beys   בית   B
Giml   גימל   C
Reysh   ריש   D
Kokh mir in   קאָך מיר אין   Cook me in
a tepl fleysh.   אַ טעפּל פֿלייש.   A pot of meat.
Nisht keyn sakh   נישט קיין סך   Not a lot
Nisht keyn bisl   נישט קיין ביסל   Not a little
Nor a fule   נאָר אַ פֿולע   But a whole
Shisl. (IT)   שיסל   bowl full. (IT)

b. Eyns, Tsvey, Dray,   איינס, צוויי, דרײַ,
Lozn, lokher-lay,   לאָזן, לאָכער־לײַ,
okn, bokn, beyner-shtokn,   אָקן, באָקן, ביינער־שטאָקן,
onk, bonk, shtonk. (IT)   אָנק, באָנק, שטאָנק.

c. "A *goy* rode off to the woods. He broke the axle of his wagon, how many nails must he have to fix the axle?" The child on whom the word "axle" comes out, has to answer with a number. Then the number is counted out among the children and the one getting the last number is "IT."

d. Avreml, Berl, Gimpl   אַבֿרהמל, בערל, גימפּל,
Dovid, Hershl, Velvl,   דוד, הערשל, וועלוול,
Zaynvl, Khaskl, Tevye,   זײַנוול, חזקל, טבֿיה,
Yidl, Kalmen, Leybl,   יידל, כּלמן, לייבל,
Moyshe, Nosn, Sandl,   משה, נתן, סאַנדל,
Arn, Peysekh, Tsadek,   עהרן, פּסח, צדוק,
Kopl, Ruvn, Shimen,   קאָפּל, ראובֿן, שמעון,
Tane. (IT)   תנא.

Kheyder children posing for the photographer in Kovne, 1934.

Rhymes and Tongue Twisters.

e. Ooter tooter   Ooter tooter
 Talmen tooter   Talmen tooter
 Tooter Talmen   Tooter Talmen
 Hersh Zalmen   Hersh Zalmen
 Zalmen Hersh   Zalmen Hersh
 Boym kersh   tree cherry
 Kersh boym   cherry tree
 Gvure shloym   strength peace
 Shloym gvure   peace strength
 Gelt ashire   money wealth
 Ashire gelt   wealth money
 Oylem feld   people field
 Feld oylem   field people
 Lemeyner goylem!   Clay fool!

 Belfer gehelfer   Rabbi's helper,
 Tseknakte kneydlekh   Smashed dumplings,
 Zay a kapore   You be the scapegoat
 Far ale meydlekh!   For all of the girls!

 Oy dem rebns spodik   Oh, the rabbi's coat's on
  brent!   fire!
 Zol er brenen vi a fayer, Let him burn like a blaze,
 Zol er visn gelt iz tayer, Let him know the worth of
          money,
 Zol er visn gelt tsu   Let him learn how to save
  shoynen,   money.
 Zol er visn mitn vayb tsu Let him learn how to live
  voynen.   with his wife!

            Ruth Rubin.

f. Fun Brisk keyn Trisk loyft a fiks un halt a biks in pisk.

[From Brisk to Trisk there runs a fox who holds a rifle
in his mouth.]

g. What any baby knows. . . .

If you look at a mirror too much during the day, the image of the mirror comes to choke you at night.

If you annoy an orphan, his deceased parents will come and drag you away to their grave at night.

Burying a coin with a potato bug in the earth will lead to buried treasure.

M. Vanvild.

8. THE BUSY BELFER

After I had finished preparing, I ran to collect the children for *kheyder*. This initiated a completely new set of activities: shining boots and shoes, pulling the soaked children out of bed, finding their clothes, buttoning their trousers, blowing the feathers off their *yarmlkes*, wiping their noses, dragging them forcefully from their houses and shoving them outside. Thus I went from house to house until I had rounded up the whole command. Then began a wild march that had to be seen to be appreciated.

Before me and behind me were running boys, jumping boys, crawling boys, all with their shirt-tails hanging from their trousers. One walked sorrowfully, his head lowered as if he were being led to slaughter; another had a piece of bread and an egg which he was in the process of eating; a third one crowed "Cock-a-doodle-doo"; a fourth imitated a goat, "Me-e-eh!" I walked importantly in their midst, my pockets and arms loaded with rolls and butter, bread and butter, crusts and herring tails, little pots of porridge, sour milk, cheese, onions, garlic, and various vegetables, and leading half a dozen boys with each hand. Some of them sobbed and sniveled. Others were stubborn and refused to go any farther. Still others walked with their heads turned back howling "Mama, mama" in high, piercing voices that could be heard all along the street.

A few hours later I went to gather the lunches for the children. I was kept busy in this way until nightfall when I took the children home. Now my students ran eagerly and jumped lustily. One had a black eye, another a bruised cheek; the ear of a third was flaming red; a fourth had clumps of hair missing from his *peyes*. But no one made any fuss over these little matters. They romped, they chased, happily and merrily—they were going home.

Mendele Moykher Sforim (1956).

9. YOSL-ZISL THE MELAMED

The dusk hour was usually set aside for story-telling. And on Saturday afternoons and holidays, Yosl-Zisl sat and talked with the boys as if they were his equals.

Not only did he tell them stories from the Midrash and Talmud and miraculous tales of the holy khasidic rabbis, but he also discussed worldly matters and explained things that puzzled them. And the children were curious and full of questions like children all over the world.

When the government opened a telegraph office in the railroad station of Khelm the pupils were puzzled. "Who needs a telegraph office and how does it work?"

Yosl-Zisl explained everything. "The government needs it. A telegraph office is a must for the tsar. The Russian Empire is big, very big, and the ruler is always afraid of rebellion and trouble. So, every morning he sends telegrams to all the stations:

"Is all well in your town?"

In olden times he had to send couriers, but now he gets an answer by wire in an hour:

"All's well."

If there's rebellion, the telegraph operator answers one word:

162

"Trouble." The operator is sparing with words because each word costs money.

"But, *rebe*, the capital is hundreds and hundreds of miles away. How does the telegraph carry the words?"

"Well, they stretch wires from the capital to, say, our city. When they want to send a telegram they pinch, or twist the wire in a certain manner at the capital. The wire at our end then turns in the same manner. Each twist or turn means a definite letter. How's it possible to get an immediate response from such a distance, at the other end of the wire? Well, that shouldn't surprise you. You've seen big dogs. It may be several feet from the tip of a dog's tail to his mouth. Still as soon as you twist this tail, his mouth begins to bark."

Yosl-Zisl never lacked an answer. Sometimes the boys asked ethical questions. "*Rebe*, suppose you found a pocketbook with 50,000 rubles. Would you return it?"

"Well," answered Yosl-Zisl, "I'll be honest with you. I'd inquire very carefully as to who lost the money. If a rich man lost it, say a Rothschild, I'd ask for a reward. But if a poor man had lost it, say a man like Ruvn the Watercarrier, who hasn't a shirt on his back, I'd return it immediately, to the last kopek! I wouldn't take a reward even if it were offered. Who wants to take money from a pauper?"

Solomon Simon, pp. 66–67.

10. REB MIKHL DOVID THE MELAMED

He was a small, jolly fellow with a sparse beard and a mercurial personality. While he taught us, he would whittle at the same time, carving snuff boxes for elderly, confirmed snuff addicts and *esreg* cases for *sukes*. He had what were in those days called golden hands. He could repair watches, forge new links for chains, and make figurines from clay for the children in the *kheyder* who liked to play chess.

A boy standing in front of I. Mandelbaum's shoe repair store in Lublin.

Mostly he carved holders for the cigarettes that he smoked until his fingers were stained a deep yellow-brown. He also made colorful paper lanterns for us to take along on the way home from *kheyder* on dark winter nights. He would teach in a cheerful chant, snapping his fingers in joyous accompaniment. The mistresses of the houses in which he ate his meals adored him, since he praised all their dishes. The *khasidim* loved him for his tales of saints and wonder rabbis.

He really found his forte during holiday banquets. He sang in a high tenor, matched round for round with every celebrant, and danced without growing tired. Above all he enjoyed dancing on tables.

He would also regale us, his pupils, with fantastic stories about miracle workers who could leap mighty distances, make themselves invisible, and perform other such stunts. These miracle workers had to wage an eternal conflict against gentile warriors and priests who took the guise of werewolves and sought to do Jews harm. But the Jewish miracle workers drew holy circles around the villains and made them helpless.

We cherished these stories. With the coming of *purim*, Reb Mikhl Dovid deserted the Talmud altogether to make preparations for the holiday. First, he drew with a candle stub on the eastern wall of the *besmedresh* large letters and drawings. At first, what he had drawn there wasn't evident, since the tallow was white and so was the wall. But he dipped a rag in ashes and went over the tallow, and soon the drawings and legends came to life. The first inscription read: "The beginning of the month of Adar is the time for happy hearts." Below, was drawn a bottle of whiskey and two hands making a benediction. And true to his convictions, Reb Mikhl drank several rounds of whiskey with the *khasidim*. In the *kheyder*, he studied the *megile* with us, the story of Queen Esther; and at the same time he carved for us the most beautiful *gragers*, noise-makers, which children twirl during *purim* each time "Haman" is mentioned, to drown out the name of the hated foe of the Jews.

Both on *purim* and on the day that followed, Reb Mikhl Dovid almost literally turned the shtetl upside down. When the *megile* was read in the *shul*, he gathered all the boys around him and led us in twirling our *gragers*, waving with enthusiasm the giant *grager* he had carved for himself. He also stamped his feet, not only for Haman, but also for Haman's wife Zeresh and for their ten sons. He went completely beserk at the mention of Haman's youngest son, Vajezatha. The sight of a grown, bearded man waving a *grager* in the *shul* filled us boys with delight. We almost wrecked the building in our enthusiasm. It was *purim*, a time of Jewish rejoicing!

After the *megile*, Mikhl Dovid made a house-to-house tour, drinking a toast at each one. On the following day, he gathered the *khasidim* to continue the revels. They bought a keg of beer, roast geese, cakes, fish and traipsed from house to house eating, guzzling and dancing. The boys ran behind. The *misnagdim* gazed disapprovingly at the revelers. The *khasidim* couldn't have cared less and sang even louder out of spite.

Mikhl Dovid danced in the streets, seemingly inexhaustible from the drinking, singing, and rejoicing. "A plague take Haman and his ten bastards!" Mikhl Dovid clamored for food, another keg of beer, compote. Two of the men turned their caps inside out, seized sticks, and, squatting on the ground, began to sing beggars' songs, and in Polish at that!

Mikhl Dovid then jumped on top of a table and started to dance. "And to hell with Haman and his ancestors all the way back to Amalek himself!" He leaped down from the table and draped the table cloth around his body. "I am

Hersh Ostrov the melamed with his children in front of the Kolbushov besmedresh, 1929. Courtesy of David Salz.

the Angel Michael!" he cried. "Give me two feather dusters and I'll make wings of them." He ran into the kitchen, plucked two goose feathers, affixed them to the table cloth with a piece of string. Wearing this costume, he ran into my father's study and swung into his version of an angelic dance. He floated and soared like a spirit; the men clapped their hands and encouraged him. Suddenly, he spread his arms like wings and flew right through the window!

He was carried back into the house, one of his merry, twinkling eyes closed and bleeding.

I. J. Singer, pp. 63–68.

UNIT SIX
SHUL AND BESMEDRESH

A view of the fabulous wooden shul in Zabludeve.

1. KHELM BUILDS A SHUL

It was announced in Khelm one *shabes*, in all the houses of prayer, that the rabbi was calling a meeting at his house right after *havdole*. And so, as soon as *shabes* was over, the most respected householders gathered in the rabbi's house to hear what he had to say.

"Householders of Khelm," he began, "God has been good to us and we are happy. We are well-fed. Our children have clothes and shoes. We are well supplied for the winter with potatoes and carrots, cucumbers and beets, peas and beans. There is bread and herring for all. There is even a piece of meat to be had, thank God. We are well off, but it's not good enough."

"What's wrong?" asked those assembled.

"What's wrong is that we have forgotten that we are Jews."

"What do you mean, we've forgotten that we are Jews!" they asked in amazement. "We pray don't we, we say the proper blessings, we study and we observe the commandments."

"All well and fine," says the rabbi, "but what's a town without a *shul*?"

"Without a *shul*? Why we have a tailors' *shul*, a cobbler's *shul*, a cold *shul*, an old *shul* on the main street and a small *shul* on Church Street."

"Yes, that may be so," he replied, "but where, pray tell, is the Khelm *shul*? Khelm ought to have a *shul* of its own."

"That's right," they all agreed, "we ought to have a Khelm *shul* as well."

"Then let's build ourselves a Khelm *shul*," said the rabbi. "We've plenty of trees on the hill, there's money to buy nails. Tomorrow morning let's all gather on the hill and we'll start chopping down trees. We'll prepare the logs for the *shul*."

"We'll be there, rabbi, we'll be there!" shouted all the householders, and they were joined by all the other Jews who were standing outside at the rabbi's window.

* * *

At the break of day all of Khelm gathered on the hill to chop down the choicest trees for the new *shul*. Not knowing that trees are round and that round things roll, they proceeded to carry the huge logs down the mountain, twelve men to each log. But that's another story. Then, once the logs were at the bottom of the hill, they couldn't decide who should go first, the right end or the left. They ran to the rabbi for advice, and he instructed them to cut off the left end, so as to leave only one end of the log. But as much as they cut, there were always two ends to the log. Then the good rabbi advised them to carry the logs breadthwise into town so that both ends would be first. That would indeed have solved the problem were the road into town not so narrow. It was finally decided to tear down the buildings on both sides of the road leading to the *shul* so that the men could carry the logs with ease. But that too is another story.

* * *

Once the logs were brought to the new site, building began in earnest. They laid the foundation, erected the walls, put in windows and doors. They covered the roof with brown shingles and the drain pipes were made of tin painted bright red. The result was a fine piece of work, a real doll house.

All along work progressed smoothly, without arguments. But how long can Khelm go on without an argument? A problem arose once planks had to be prepared for a floor. One half of Khelm argued that the planks had to be sanded completely smooth, otherwise they were inviting disaster.

For as everyone knows, on *yonkiper* and *tishebov* Jews walk around in *shul* in their stocking feet. Unless the floor is smooth, someone would surely get hurt.

The other half said: We admit that people might get splinters in their feet if the planks aren't smooth, but there is a far greater danger in having a smooth floor. On *simkhes-toyre* Jews dance with the Torah scrolls in their hands. Suppose someone slipped and fell on the smooth synagogue floor. Not only would the Jew suffer a broken leg, or worse, but all of Khelm would have to fast because a Torah scroll would have fallen down.

The rabbi heard both sides of the argument and decided that since both sides were right, a compromise had to be reached: The planks should be sanded because Jews could indeed injure their feet on *yonkiper* and *tishebov*, but the planks should be laid smooth-side down, so that Jews won't slip and fall when they dance with the Torah on *simkhes-toyre*.

Both sides agreed to the compromise and the *shul* was duly completed. At the festive opening of the new *shul* the Khelmites were as proud as could be. Everyone was ecstatic, all except the rabbi. "What's wrong?" the Khelmites asked, and the rabbi explained his concern.

"As you all know, the King of Thieves has been here once before. You remember, of course, how he stole the moon out of a tightly sealed barrel. Now as soon as he finds out that we've built a brand new *shul*, he'll be sure to come on a dark night and steal it!"

"What should we do, rabbi?"

"My children, I haven't the slightest idea. That's why I'm so worried."

"Not me!" shouted Fayvl, the smartest man in Khelm. "Come back tomorrow and I'll show you what's to be done."

Next day Fayvl called the house painter and said: "Take a brush and, with extra large letters, paint the following words on one entire wall of the *shul*: ZE HASHUL SHA-

YAKH LE'KHELM—which is Hebrew for 'This here *shul* belongs to Khelm.'"

When the rabbi saw the finished product, he nearly jumped for joy. "What an idea!" he exclaimed. "Now let those thieves take the *shul*. What good will it do them? Wherever they take it, everyone will know that the *shul* is stolen property!"

*   *   *

Khelmites liked praying in the new *shul*. It was always packed with people both from Khelm and from neighboring towns. One morning the *shames* came in and noticed that thieves had stolen the charity box. Even though the box had been nailed to the wall with twelve nails, they had managed to make off with it. What could be done? If another box were nailed in, the thieves would be sure to steal it; not to replace it—what's a *shul* without a charity box?

The *shames* brought the matter to the rabbi who promptly decided:

"*Shames*, hang the box from a chain attached to the high ceiling. That way the thieves will never reach it."

The *shames* did so, but the very next day the well-to-do Jews complained to him:

"Hanging the box up high is a good idea as far as thieves are concerned, but how are *we* supposed to reach it?"

"Don't ask me," said the *shames*. "Ask the rabbi."

The householders explained their case to the rabbi who agreed that they were right. He then instructed the *shames:* "Go out and buy a ladder that will reach from the floor to where the box is hanging. Whoever wishes to throw a coin into the box will just climb up the ladder and do so. . . ."

F. Freed, pp. 50–58.

2. THE WOODEN SYNAGOGUE

The wooden synagogue was the unique creation of Polish Jewry. Many of them were architectural works of art, but

Another view of the Zabludeve shul.

even the simplest among them were far superior to the makeshift version in Khelm.

Talmudic laws governing the construction and upkeep of a synagogue were as strictly observed in seventeenth-century Europe as in ninth-century Babylonia: A *shul* should not be used for shelter against heat or cold, or as a short-cut thoroughfare. No eating or drinking is allowed in a *shul*. It is not proper to demolish a *shul* and build another on the same site. (If the *shul* is burned down or non-Jews destroy it, a new *shul* should replace it on the same site.) If a *shul* is sold it must be on condition that the new owners will not use it as a bathhouse, a laundry, or a tannery. One talmudic ruling, that the *shul* should stand in the highest part of town above all other buildings, could not be enforced in Europe. The Catholic church would not allow synagogues to stand out and passed strict laws limiting their height. One way of increasing the inner height was to lay the *shul* floor deep in the ground, as was the case in the main synagogue of Vilne.

The wooden synagogues of Eastern Europe occupied a very special place in the Jewish imagination. It was said, for instance, that the magnificent wooden *shul* in Zabludeve, in the Grodne province, was built without using a single piece of metal, a single nail. The reason this fact was so important is that the Temple in Jerusalem was also built without the use of metal!

Perhaps another reason wooden synagogues were so special is that they were so vulnerable. Fire prevention was virtually nonexistent until modern times. At the slightest whiff of smoke, the town would immediately fear the worst. Here is one of many tales of just such a fire.

THE SHUL IN RADZIVIL AND THE MARVELOUS ARK

The large *shul* in Radzivil was famous throughout the

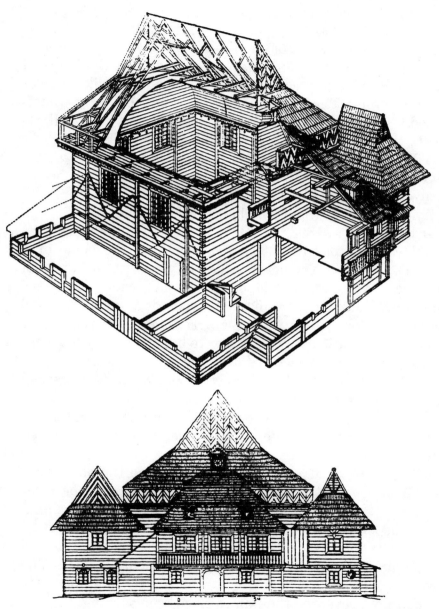

Diagrams of the Zabludeve shul. From **Maria** and **Kazemierz Piechotka**

177

Ukraine for its magnificent architecture. Though made entirely of wood, it was built very high with beautiful hand-carved ceilings and elaborate balconies. A curved staircase led to the womens' balcony and higher still to the windows of the square tower on the very roof. Built on top of the tower was a dome that looked like a large satin *yarmlke*.

The inside of the *shul* was decorated with the signs of the zodiac, with biblical passages, and all in striking color combinations. The letters were large and brightly illuminated. The community *pinkes* (register) of Radzivil records the visit of the famous Reb Velvele Zbarzher who couldn't believe his eyes when he stepped into the *shul*. On leaving the town he blessed the *shul* that it never be destroyed and never fall victim to a fire.

And as it turned out, his blessing held true.

It happened in 1883. Sunday, 10 o'clock in the morning a terrible fire broke out. The fire began at the home of a butcher who was frying fat. The day was sunny and hot and the flames soon enveloped the whole town. Most of the houses in Radzivil were made of wood and some even had roofs of straw—these were the first to go. The remaining houses, made of brick, took longer to burn, but they too went up in smoke. For two days and two nights the fire raged. The entire population of Radzivil, with their few rescued belongings, camped out in the cemetery, a fair distance from town. Everything was destroyed. Everything, that is, except for the old wooden synagogue. The *shul* survived without a scratch.

All the houses of prayer that surrounded the old *shul*— the Husiatin *shtibl*, the Trisker *shtibl*, the rebe's *besmedresh*, the Braner *besmedresh*—all burned to the ground, while the *shul* itself was untouched by the flames.

Eye-witnesses later reported that when the fire reached its height, flocks of white doves flew in from all sides. The doves took up positions over the roof and by flapping their wings they prevented the flames from approaching.

* * *

The ark of a synagogue in Pren, Romania.

Ten years after the Great Fire, another wonderful thing happened in the same *shul*. By then the town had been completely rebuilt thanks to the generosity of Jews from other towns. As trade and business were going well, kahal decided that in memory of the great miracle that happened to their *shul* and in honor of the rescued Torah scrolls from the other houses of prayer that were evacuated to the *shul* during the fire, a large new ark should be built to house them.

The heads of kahal promptly set out for Kremenits and brought down with them a famous engraver who was known throughout the Ukraine for his great artistry.

The artist-engraver spent an entire year working on the ark and the result was a rare masterpiece: carved lions and leopards, deer, eagles and doves, creatures of all shapes and sizes. Specialists would come from far and wide just to see the results of his handiwork. And the carver, once he had completed the job, carved, at the very bottom of the ark, his own name: "Oyzer son of Yekhiel, work to be proud of."

Five months later, on the first day of *shvues*, two o'clock in the afternoon, a thunderstorm broke loose. A flash of lightning burst through the dome on the roof, entered the *shul* and scorched out the words at the bottom of the ark. There was no other damage done. People were amazed. Why should the artist be deprived of the right to sign his name to a work that justly deserved to be called "work to be proud of"?

But the truth was revealed a short while later. The same engraver had made similar carvings in a Catholic church. This was seen as blasphemy. The heavens decided to strike out his name in punishment.

Abraham Rechtman, pp. 39–41.

3. HOW THE SHTETL WAS REALLY RUN

Folklore and literature alone cannot provide an accurate picture of the inner workings of the shtetl. For if they were our only source, it would seem that each town was made up of a mindless mob of Jews who dutifully followed their leader—the rabbi. In difficult matters, perhaps, Fayvl the Genius would come to bail them out. In fact, nothing could be further from the truth. A shtetl was not run by the *rov* nor by the masses but rather by an elite group of well-to-do householders who controlled the town council called kahal.

The power structure of the shtetl can be summed up by the three K's:

1. Kahal, the central authority.
2. *Khevres*, the real action on the grass-roots level. A *khevre* is a voluntary association organized around work, study or charitable functions.
3. *Kley-koydesh*, which means literally, "the holy vessels." These were the only paid officials of the community, and indispensable for the religious work they performed: rabbi, *shames*, *gabe*, *shoykhet*, *khazn*, watchman, scribe.

The only source of information we now have on the civic affairs of a shtetl is the *pinkes*, a register in which the minutes of the kahal and *khevre* meetings were recorded. Through the pages of a *pinkes* we can see how the town was run, how the various groups related to each other, how one community related to the next, and how the Jews related to the surrounding gentile world.

The *pinkes* was always considered and kept as a holy object. There were even some people who believed that a house in which a *pinkes* was kept would always be preserved from fire and that the women of the house would never have trouble giving birth. Until recently, there was a custom in the *shtetlekh* of the Ukraine, to place a *pinkes* under the pillow of a woman who was having great labor pains.

Almost all of the old *pinkeysim* were made of parchment and were bound in fine leather with gold lettering. The size was that of a Talmud. Most were written by a professional scribe, in the same script as a Torah scroll. The title page of a *pinkes* as well as the first letters of each paragraph in the regulations were illuminated with exceptionally fine ornamentation and drawings. Sometimes each page of a *pinkes* was enclosed in a beautiful, colorful frame.

There were three types of *pinkeysim:*

1. The community registers which recorded the decisions and regulations of kahal.
2. The registers of the social and educational *khevres* such as: Visiting the Sick, the Burial Society, Welcoming Visitors, Welcoming the Bride, the Godfather Society, the Great Charity, Free-Loan Association and Redeeming the Captives.
3. The registers of the workers' *khevres:* tailors, cobblers, hatmakers, tanners, and so on.

From the *pinkeysim* of the *khevres* we learn that it was no easy matter getting accepted to any one of them. One had to pass through several stages before qualifying as a full-fledged member. Even after achieving the preliminary qualifications, there was often a waiting period of a few years before being accepted, because new admissions to the *khevre* were very limited. In some cases, the limitations were so great that the *khevre* admitted no more than two new members a year! In other *khevres*, a deadline was set for the 15th of Kislev (late November, early December) for all new admissions.

Pinkes of the Gmiles khasodim (Free Loan) Association in Pilten,
Kurland, founded in 1889. The biblical motto on top "For I
have said, a righteous world shall be built" includes the key
word khesed from the association's name.

Special admission privileges were given only to scholars, especially those who mastered the post-talmudic commentators. These scholars were often admitted over and above the limit. Once admitted, they enjoyed seniority over the other members.

4. THE WORKERS' KHEVRES, A FIRST-HAND REPORT

We could not always find the registers for the workers' *khevres* in the smaller towns of the Ukraine. Nevertheless, our historical-ethnographic expedition did manage to locate a few of these valuable documents.

The title page of these workers' registers usually bore an appropriate biblical or rabbinic quotation which emphasized the importance of work: "For you shall eat the labor of your hands; happy shall you be and it shall be well with you" (Psalms 128:2) or "Blessed are you in this world and it will be well with you in the world to come" (Berakhot 8). On the combined *pinkes* of the shoemakers, tanners, and hatmakers of Mikolayev (which was famous for its leather goods) the title-page had the following motto: "Greater is man's pleasure from his labor than from worshipping the Lord" (Berakhot 8).

These registers contain three types of regulations:

1. Matters pertaining to their profession: price control, labor disputes between workers and employers.
2. Matters of internal organization and leadership.
3. Religious affairs.

Elections for the workers' *khevres* took place once a year during the intermediate days of *peysekh*, just like all other elections in the shtetl. New members were chosen either through an "electoral college" or directly by ballot box.

Besides the regular positions that were held in every *khevre* such as chairmen and trustees, the workers' *khevres*

would also elect a special seven-man board who were given
absolute jurisdiction to represent all the member workers.
These seven drew up and signed the contracts; they controlled prices; they granted permission for a worker to go
into business for himself; they punished law-breakers and
even had the right of excommunication. All their decisions
were duly recorded in the *pinkes*.

Working hours were also regulated in quite a modern
way. In the tailors' *pinkes* of Loytsk (1721) the following
was recorded: No one, not even a self-employed tailor can
work late into the night. On the eve of the Sabbath and
holidays, all work must be laid aside at two p.m. If, however, someone was forced to work overtime—because of a
wedding or because the local *porets* badly needed the garment—that someone must pay two groschen to charity for
each hour of overtime and must also pay his own workers
extra.

To avoid competition, the seven-member council enforced
price control. From time to time they would issue a price
list which would be posted in all the synagogues and houses
of study. These lists were very detailed and stated exactly
how much should be paid for a new piece of work and how
much to repair an old garment.

The council of seven was also responsible for watching
over the apprentices. They decided how many years the
apprenticeship should last, what type of household chores
they had to perform for their boss and what salary they
would receive. The contracts drawn up between the apprentice and his employer were approved by the council
and recorded in the *pinkes*.

Religious matters take up a large part of the workers'
pinkes. Almost every workers' *khevre* had its own house of
prayer or study, its own *gabe*, *shames* and *khazn*. When
hiring a *khazn*, each *khevre* made sure to chose a *khazn*
who was one of them. Cobblers chose a cobbler; tailors, a
tailor. Only the Burial Society could not have a *khazn* from

185

its own ranks, in accordance with the age-old principle: "It is forbidden for someone who takes care of burials or for a doctor to pray in front of the ark, because they cannot in all honesty represent the congregation when reciting the prayer 'Heal us, oh Lord,' for they make a living from the dead and the sick."

Workers handled the distribution of synagogue honors quite differently than other groups. Each worker was of equal standing before God. In their *khevres*, no *alies* were ever sold, so as not to allow the richer members to outclass the poorer ones. Instead, members were called up to recite the blessing on the Torah in alphabetical order. Exceptions were only made in special cases: a man who had *yortsayt*, a mourner, a groom, a father celebrating a *bris*, and so on. The same egalitarian system was used in deciding who should carry the Torah around the ark on *shmini atseres* and *simkhes-toyre*.

The money for the upkeep of their *shul* was collected from all on an equal basis. From the *pinkes* of Loytsk we learn that each member had to contribute one groschen every Sabbath eve and two groschen on the eve of a new moon. Each week a collector made the rounds of all the members' houses to collect the dues. If anyone was unable to pay up, the sum was recorded and had to be collected before the yearly elections. For failure to repay such a debt, the council of seven had the right to confiscate something from the individual and pawn it. That year he would not be eligible to run for office in the *khevre*.

The individual *khevres* did not always have their own *shul*. In this case the practice was that in the main synagogue the *alies* on a given Sabbath were reserved for a particular *khevre*. For instance, on the Sabbath after *simkhes-toyre*, when the Torah reading starts from the beginning, the Talmud study group was called up to recite the blessings. On the Sabbath of "Lekh-Lekho" when the passage "And you shall circumcise the flesh of your foreskin" (Genesis 17:11) is read, the circumcisers were called up. The story of Abraham inviting the three angels belonged to the Welcoming the Visitors Society. The portion of Mishpotim concerning money-lending was reserved for the Free Loan association. The *khevre* that supplied Jewish soldiers with kosher meat was called up on the Sabbath which included the passage: "These are the beasts which you shall eat among all the beasts that are on the earth" (Leviticus 11:2). Likewise, the passage "The Lord removed from you all illness" was reserved for the Association of Visiting the Sick.

5. INSIDE KAHAL

Kahal elections took place on the intermediate days of *pey-sekh*. The chairman-for-the-month called the election and the majority of eligible electors had to participate. The election results and the names of the new appointees were recorded each year in the community *pinkes* and the out-going members had to sign their names. The list always read the same way: "In a joyous hour did election take place on _____, the __th day of the intermediate days of *peysekh* in the year ____, as is customary in all the communities."

First, four "heads" were chosen, then three treasurers and finally seven elders. Then the rotating chairmen were elected, a bookkeeper, heads of the various communal institutions such as the Talmud Torah School, the hospital, the charities, a keeper of the *pinkes*, and a special scribe.

The four kahal heads were the managers of the community. They were responsible for all religious institutions: the synagogues, houses of study, *yeshives*, the ritual bath. They decided on the budgets, hired a doctor, a bath-house attendant, and the like. When necessary, they also negotiated with other communities.

The treasurers took care of finances. They would submit

proposals to raise funds, to economize; they supervised tax collecting. The elders were advisers to kahal. Whenever a new project was undertaken, say the building of a new *besmedresh*, the heads would consult with these elders before reaching a decision.

The community registers are full of entries describing various lawsuits of one individual against another, of the individual against the community, and the community against an individual or a group. A whole range of complaints was recorded: one witness reports that so-and-so tore up books in the *besmedresh*; another testifies that someone was spreading false rumors about a Jewish girl; a third person is called up for breaking the laws of his *khevre*.

The usual punishment was to expel the guilty party from his *khevre* or to deprive him of community privileges—forever, or for a specified amount of time. Kahal was able to enforce the law in almost every case, and this without any Jewish police force or prisons. Some of the penalties that kahal could impose were the following:

1. No honors in the *shul*.
2. No participation in town celebrations.
3. No one is allowed to rent the criminal an apartment or a store.
4. A woman or the wife of a criminal may not use the *mikve*, the ritual bathhouse.
5. No one may give him work.
6. No marriage arrangements with his family are allowed.
7. No one may sell him kosher meat.
8. His children can be expelled from school.
9. He must pay more taxes.

There were even instances in which kahal imposed the death sentence on a Jew and carried it out. This was for the most despicable crime of all—that of informing against Jews to the government.

The stairs leading up to the balemer or platform in a shul in Lite.

6. AUSTERITY REGULATIONS

It seems that the fabulous wealth of the Ukrainian land-owners eventually began to rub off on those Jews who did business with them. These Jews began to imitate the life of the *porets:* fancy furniture, horse-drawn carriages, and especially lavish celebrations. These celebrations would last several days and did more harm than good.

First, this would arouse the envy of the non-Jews. They couldn't help but wonder: Where in the world did those Jews get such fancy clothes? They're just a bunch of crooks!

Secondly, it caused a split among Jews themselves. The poorer people, not wanting to fall behind the richer ones, also arranged for magnificent feasts which they could really not afford and which dragged them into new debts and new sorrows.

Thirdly, these long celebrations often led to drunkenness and to general loud behavior.

The spiritual leaders of the Jewish communities in the Ukraine began an all-out campaign to stop these excesses. There is hardly a community register that we managed to find that did not have some sort of ruling to stem the tide of this easy life. The following regulations were recorded in the *pinkes* of Bar:

A. At a reception for the groom, whether a local fellow or a stranger, and at the celebration on the day after the wedding, preserves should not be given to anyone except the very closest relatives.

B. At a wedding feast: If the person sponsoring the feast is a wealthy man (the status to be determined by how much a man paid in taxes each year), he may invite no more than twenty guests not counting relatives, religious leaders, and poor people.

C. If the sponsor is a middle-class householder, he may not invite any strangers, but only religious leaders, poor people, and the closest relatives.

D. If the sponsor is not well-to-do, he may invite only the religious leaders and his closest relatives.

E. At the feast of a circumcision, a wealthy man may invite twenty guests, relatives included, but excluding the religious leaders and poor people.

F. A middle-class householder may invite only ten guests including his relatives, with the same exceptions.

G. Someone who is not well-to-do is forbidden to have a circumcision feast. He may only serve preserves, honey cake, and whiskey.

Sections 3–6, Abraham Rechtman, pp. 195–221.

7. THE HOLY VESSELS

Of the *kley-koydesh* the rabbi was first on the list. But there was more than one type of rabbi. First, the *rov*. He was closest to 'rabbi' in the English sense. He is an authority on Jewish law. Even if more learned men could be found in town, people still consulted the *rov* for advice. The plural is *rabonim*.

Second, *reb*. This is a title for any male Jew who is older or wiser. When a stranger came to town, he was addressed as 'Reb Yid'—Reb Jew. The name *reb* can also be used in a sarcastic way, to make fun of the person: "Listen, Reb Yid, are you gonna pay up or not?"

Third, *rebe*. Meaning, a teacher of children. Students always referred to their teacher as *rebe*, and the word carries more respect than *melamed*. A *rov* could also be addressed as *rebe*. Sometimes both terms could be used together. In the shtetl of Orinin, province of Podolia, an especially popular and talented teacher was called "Rebe reb Meyer the melamed." The plural form of *rebe*, used mostly by children, is *rebes*.

Rebe also means a khasidic leader. A *rebe* is considered to be a holy man by his followers even if he isn't as learned as the local *rov*. He commands authority not because of his scholarship but because of his qualities as a leader, because

191

he is considered to have an 'in' with the Almighty. The plural form: *rebeim.*

Abridged from Gershon Zev Braude and B. Segal.

Until 1835 *rabonim* could only serve a community if they were appointed by kahal. They received a salary, usually for life—unless they moved on to another shtetl. The *rov* had two functions: 1) to be an expert in ritual law, advise people on kosher meat, *matse* baking, the employment of non-Jews on *shabes,* and so on; 2) to be an arbiter and counselor in civil and family disputes. In other words, his job was highly specialized, and would not include decisions on how to lay a synagogue floor, sick calls, teaching or leading the prayer service.

Next in line of the *kley-koydesh* was the *shames* who in day-to-day life was even more important than the *rov.* A *shames* often had to serve as bailiff, policeman, notary, recorder, clerk, stove lighter in the *shul,* charity collector, the leader of prayer services, and even Torah reader. The smaller the town, the more a *shames* had to serve as Jack-of-all-trades. As usual, there is a Khelm story to describe the role of a *shames:*

The town of Khelm was once confronted with a great problem: their *shames* had grown old and could no longer make his rounds at night to rouse the people for midnight recitation of the Psalms.

So the Khelmites met in solemn council and decided that since their *shames* was not strong enough to perform his duty, all the window shutters were to be stacked near his house, so that he might bang on them all at one time.

Irving Howe and Eliezer Greenberg.

The accompanying chart and artist's rendition give the structure of the Vilne kahal and *kley-koydesh* during the seventeenth and eighteenth centuries. Vilne and other

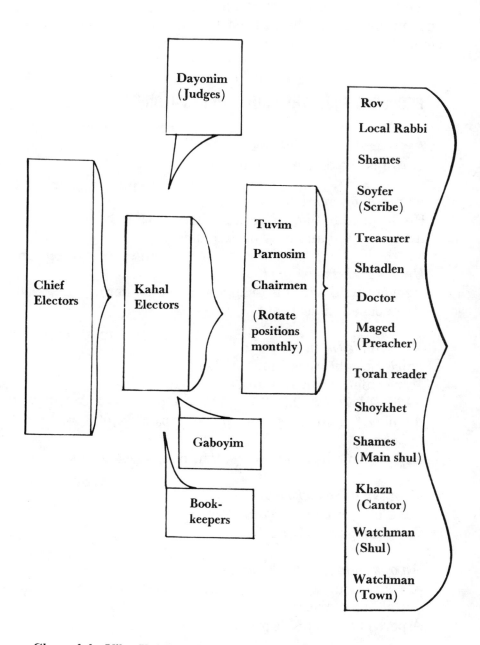

Dayonim (Judges)

Chief Electors

Kahal Electors

Tuvim

Parnosim

Chairmen

(Rotate positions monthly)

Gaboyim

Book-keepers

Rov

Local Rabbi

Shames

Soyfer (Scribe)

Treasurer

Shtadlen

Doctor

Maged (Preacher)

Torah reader

Shoykhet

Shames (Main shul)

Khazn (Cantor)

Watchman (Shul)

Watchman (Town)

Chart of the Vilne Kahal in the Seventeenth and Eighteenth Centuries

large cities were able to support a large kahal. But even
the smallest shtetl had at least eight members in its town
council.

8. PROVERBS FROM THE SHUL AND BESMEDRESH

תּוֹרה איז די בעסטע סחורה.

Toyre iz di beste skhoyre.
Torah is the best merchandise.

אַרײַן װי אַ יװן אין סוכה.

Arayn vi a yovn in suke.
He dropped in like a Greek soldier into a *suke.*
An unwanted and unexpected visitor.

ער האָט זיך צעגראַגערט.

Er hot zikh tsegragert.
He went wild with his gragger (noise-maker).
He knocked himself out.

מער שוחטים װי הינער.

Mer shokhtim vi hiner.
More slaughterers than chickens.
More chiefs than Indians.

אַז מען האָט ניט קיין אתרוג דאַרף מען קיין פּושקע ניט האָבן.

*Az men hot nit keyn esreg, darf men keyn pushke nit
  hobn.*
If you don't have an *esreg,* you don't need an *esreg* box.

נעם צו דעם של־יד.

Nem tsu dem shel-yad.
Take off your hand *tfiln.*
Get your paws off me.

אַן אָפּגעשלאָגענע הושענא.

An opgeshlogene heshayne.
A beaten-out willow twig (at the end of the Hoshanah
  Rabbah service).
A person shorn of his glory.

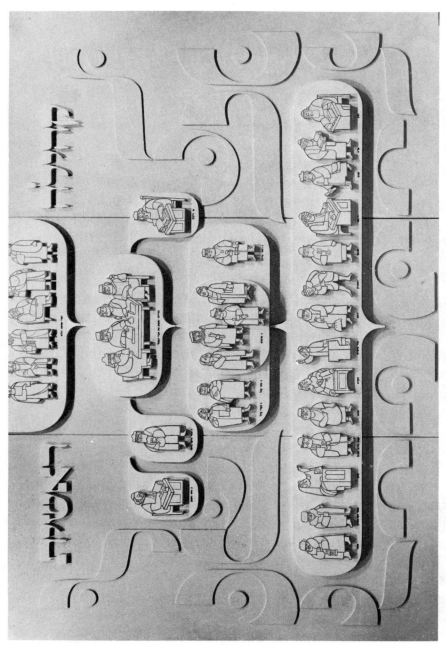

Woodcarving of the Vilne kahal, seventeenth and eighteenth century. The artist is Dan Gelbert. Courtesy of Beit Lochemei HaGetaot, Israel.

ער מאַכט שבת פֿאַר זיך.

Er makht shabes far zikh.
He makes *shabes* by himself.
He's his own boss.

ער זאָגט אָמן אויף אַלץ.

Er zogt omeyn oyf alts.
He says Amen to anything.
He's a yes-man.

אַן אָקס האָט אַ לאַנגע צונג און קען קיין שופֿר נישט בלאָזן.

An oks hot a lange tsung, un ken keyn shoyfer nisht blozn.
An ox has a long tongue and can't blow a *shoyfer*.
You do need a long tongue to blow a *shoyfer*, but obviously, that isn't the only requirement.

9. BESMEDRESH

On the south side of the *besmedresh* separated by an arcade stood the Husiatin *shtibl*, also called the Rizhiner *shtibl* because the Rizhiner were the ones who used it most. This *shtibl* was almost a continuation of the *besmedresh*. Boys who studied Talmud in the *besmedresh* would often move into the *shtibl* where it was much quieter. Even men who came to pray would move from one place to the other in order to get a *minyen* together.

A few steps removed from the *besmedresh*, right opposite the *rov's* house which actually was an annex of the *besmedresh*, was Khaye-Neshe's soup kitchen. The juiciest aromas imaginable came from that kitchen enticing everyone who passed by. The soup kitchen supplied the Rizhiner *shtibl* with whiskey and snacks whenever they had a celebration. The *besmedresh* students would come here for a bite to eat during the long winter evenings of constant study: crackers, marinated herring, sour pickles, *knishes* with onions or *kashe*. *Kheyder* children would also buy their snacks here: candies, mint caramels and poppy cakes. Other regular customers on winter evenings were the Tailor's *khevre* who would come in after evening prayers

196

The inside of a besmedresh showing the library and a grandfather clock.

for roast duck with a bit of whiskey and other appetizers. Winter was the season the tailors raked in a lot of money from patching up peasant jackets and fur coats. This inspired them to get together and have a good time. But they couldn't just throw a party, so they took advantage of every religious occasion: the completion of reading Psalms, celebrating the acquisition of something new for their tailors' *shul* and so on. Members of the burial society would also come in for a good bite to eat following the burial of a rich man. In short, Khaye-Neshe's soup kitchen provided physical sustenance to the holy congregations of the shtetl so that they might devote themselves to spiritual matters.

Southeast of the *besmedresh* stood the main synagogue made out of brick. According to tradition, it was over 600 years old. On the women's balcony, which was added on to the northern wall, there was an inscription stating that this section was renovated in the year 1573. Only the lower-class merchants and poor artisans prayed in the main *shul* and even then, only on *shabes* and holidays. We used to call those Jews who prayed in the *shul* regularly: *shul-yidn* (synagogue Jews). Every *shabes* and holiday, Tall Refoel, the *shul shames* who was a bootmaker by profession, would go out into the middle of the marketplace, place one hand under his right ear and shout: *"In shul arayn!"* (Into the *shul* with you!) and the whole shtetl would know that the time for prayer had come.

It was in this main synagogue that each new Torah scroll which any khasidic *shtibl* had made to order was welcomed with music. From there the scroll would be escorted with great pomp and ceremony, songs and dances, to its holy destination. The *bris* of a rich man's son was often celebrated in the main *shul*. For this purpose a leather upholstered armchair always stood ready which was called Elijah's chair and another armchair called the Godfather's chair.

The *shul* was decorated on the inside just like the Temple

in Jerusalem, or at least that's what the *kheyder* and *besmedresh* boys would say. The ceiling was painted with a circle which represented the heavens where angels played various instruments in a heavenly orchestra. On the inner circumference of the circle, Psalms chapter 150 was written in large script. Outside the circle to one side were two huge lions who faced each other with ferocious lifelike growls. On the other side two large deer with twisted antlers were painted facing each other. And underneath these pictures was the passage: "Be as strong as the leopard, brave as the lion, and light as the deer in performing the will of your father in heaven." The walls were decorated with the legendary wild ox, the Leviathan and the twelve signs of the zodiac. The Leviathan held his tail in his mouth, for as everyone knows, were he to let go of it, the entire world would be destroyed.

The *shul-yidn* insisted that these drawings as well as the figures of doves over the ark and deer over the platform were made by Italian artists who fasted and bathed during the entire period of their work. Another legend had it that the mound right outside the *shul* was really the grave of a bride and groom who were murdered under the wedding canopy.

On the west side of the *shul* was an overgrown garden with tall trees. The trees bent over the iron fence that surrounded the garden. There were benches in this garden. Here the members of the *shul* and *besmedresh* came out for a chat or a cigarette between services. On holidays they would come here during the reading of the Torah. *Kheyder* children would carve whistles and pipes out of the branches of the trees. All shtetl weddings were performed between this garden and the *shul* (except if the bride was a widow or a divorcee). The entire shtetl would accompany each bride to the rhythm of a merry marching tune. This was called "leading the bride to the *shul*."

10. INSIDE THE BESMEDRESH

Surrounded on all sides by these communal institutions, including the mysterious, magnificent *shul*, stood the familiar, weekaday *besmedresh*. Every day of the year, for each and every male Jew, the *besmedresh* was the home away from home. From early morning until twelve noon there was always an available *minyen*. One group would finish praying and the next one would begin. During afternoon and evening prayers, especially in the winter, the *besmedresh* was simply packed from wall to wall.

Between afternoon and evening prayers one often heard a passing preacher deliver a sermon and one of the charity collectors would stand at the door with a plate. If the preacher were any good the crowd would be all ears and he could hypnotize them with his moving chant and wonderful stories. For weeks afterwards the *besmedresh* Jews would hum his tune and retell his tales. This type of preacher would stay for *shabes* and would deliver his sermon on Saturday afternoon, winter—in the *besmedresh*, summer— in the main *shul*. In summer the women would come to hear him and fill up the women's balcony. During the winter some would stand, wrapped in shawls, along the walls of the *besmedresh*. Other women would fill up the entrance to the *besmedresh*, and older women—whose piety was unquestionable—would bravely make their way into the room itself and stand behind the oven to hear the sermon.

If, on the other hand, the preacher turned out to be an "infantry preacher," that is, one who did the rounds of all the *shtetlekh* on foot, then the *besmedresh* would turn into bedlam. Everyone did whatever he pleased and the preacher just about preached to himself. If he happened to have an idiosyncrasy or a funny trait such as a stutter or a nasal voice, and if he had the habit of quoting stories that had nothing to do with anything, then the *besmedresh* boys would listen very attentively. Later they would imitate him without mercy.

Every khasidic *rebe* who would visit our shtetl would preside in the *besmedresh* on Friday night. He would leave the *khasidim* with a new tune which they would bring back to their respective *shtiblekh*.

All shtetl meetings would take place in the *besmedresh* between the afternoon and evening prayers, meetings about giving the *rov* or the *shokhtim* a raise, about paying the tuition for orphans, about collecting money for *matses*, for poor brides, for the sick. The *besmedresh* was also the place where the Russian authorities would come when they wished to inform us of the latest decrees—that made our lives more miserable.

Here in the *besmedresh* the *rov* would deliver his yearly sermon on the *shabes* before *peysekh* concerning the laws of that holiday. The *shames* would also get up on the platform from time to time and announce the latest prohibitions in his hoarse voice: "On order of the rabbi I am empowered to proclaim that no one is to carry during this coming Sabbath because the *eyrev* has been torn"; or "On order of the *rov* and of kahal I hereby announce and proclaim that meat slaughtered by outsiders is absolutely forbidden. Anyone who bought meat from these outside slaughterers should appear before the rabbi to find out if her utensils are still kosher."

The whole week long there was no set order in the *besmedresh*. Anyone sat or stood wherever he pleased or wherever he could. But on *shabes* and holidays the *besmedresh* belonged to a group of "regulars" who consisted of artisans, peddlers, and poor storekeepers. Then each of them had his own set place at one of the tables. The scholars and wealthy Jews usually prayed in their own *shtibl* on *shabes* and holidays. The *besmedresh* and the main *shul* belonged to the simple folk, or, as they were sometimes called, "King David's Brigade"—the ones who recited Psalms. Just as the older scholars and *besmedresh* boys would get up at dawn and come to the *besmedresh* to study, the simple folk would come to the *besmedresh* and study Psalms together.

The actual building was one large rectangular room with windows on three sides. The two doors were on the north side. As soon as you entered the room the first thing you saw was the huge tiled stove which stood between the doors. On three sides of the stove were benches and on the southern side stood a long wooden table. On winter evenings the porters and water-carriers would sit at these benches and warm their frozen bodies after a whole day out in the cold. Here, next to the stove and behind it, wandering Jews found their resting place.

The stove was also the place where all folktales were told: tales about ghosts and spirits, elfs and demons and—not to mention them in the same breath—*lamedvovniks* and other saintly Jews, or even Elijah himself. Chief among the storytellers was Mekhele Shvarts who doubled as assistant *shames* in the *besmedresh* and assistant gravedigger of the shtetl. His prime story-telling time was between the afternoon and evening prayers on weekdays and at dusk on *shabes*. His audience consisted of regulars and occasionals. The regulars were cobblers like himself who belonged to the same guild, while a tailor or passing traveler would listen in occasionally. The *besmedresh* students would also lend an eager ear from time to time.

Many of Mekhele's stories were inspired by his second job as gravedigger. His favorite story, of course, was about the grave of Zhamele the Messiah of Tishevits. His gravestone was encircled with white lime and no one dared approach it. Whenever a khasidic *rebe* visited the town, he would get down on his knees a few feet from the grave and pray. Then he would approach in stocking feet and place a note on the grave, by attaching it to the end of a twig. The only thing that could interrupt Mekhele's stories was the slam of the *shames*'s hand on the table followed by his hoarse cry: *MAYREV!*

202

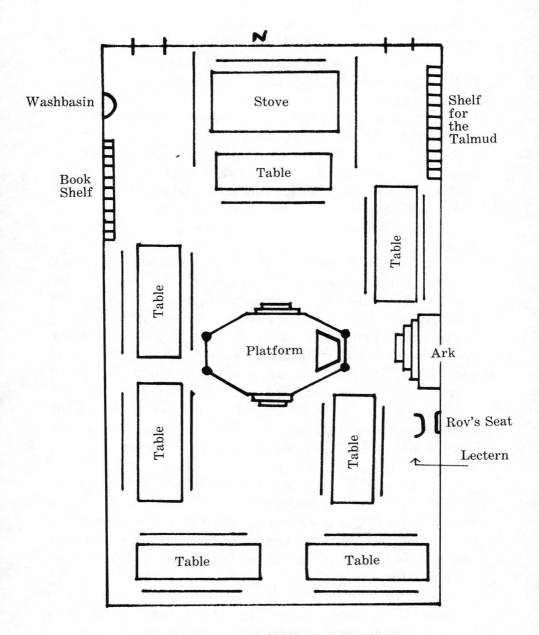

Washbasin

Book
Shelf

Shelf
for
the
Talmud

Stove

Table

Table

Table

Platform

Table

Ark

Rov's Seat

Lectern

Table

Table

Table

FLOORPLAN OF THE TISHEVITS BESMEDRESH

Opposite the stove, beside the western wall, stood a wash-stand where the men would wash their hands before prayer. They would let the water drip off their hands into the barrel behind the stand, then wipe them on the hem of their caftans or on a towel. Besides the study tables and benches along the walls, there was a special place set aside for the *rov* which was marked by an inscription on the wall: The *rov's* place.

On top of the platform opposite the ark stood a large brass menorah where candles were always burning. Preachers would stand on the steps leading up to the ark when giving their sermons. Each sermon ended the same way: "And a redeemer shall come unto Zion" followed by the mourner's *kadesh*.

The hundreds of books in the *besmedresh* always needed to be repaired. The students had a special *khevre* whose job it was to collect money for new books and for rebinding the old. The boys would go out collecting from house to house every Friday. Most of the money collected in the *besmedresh*, however, went to support the impoverished families of Tishevits. A large, black iron alms box hung over the main door for charity given in secret. Only the wardens of the Great Charity *khevre* knew to whom the money would be distributed. These were the anonymous poor, people who had once lived well and were now embarrassed to show that they needed help.

The *besmedresh* was dominated by the platform in the middle. Four wooden columns kept the railing in place and steps led up to the platform on two sides. The Torah was read from the slanted table on this platform. The platform also served as a soapbox for the local bigshots who led the communal meetings.

The ruler and despot of the *besmedresh* was Yoshe *shames*. Yoshe never played favorites and never discriminated between young and old, rich and poor. Yoshe was also the undertaker ever since Shoel Gravedigger got too old for the job.

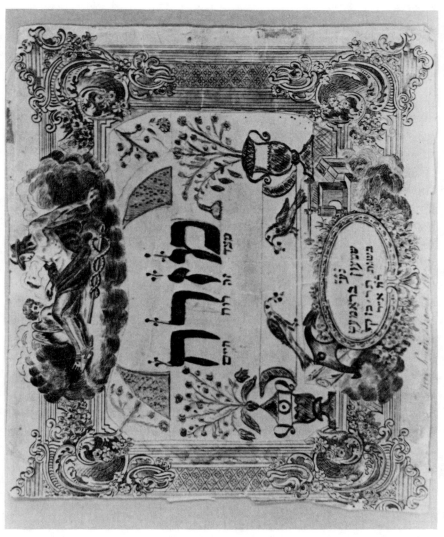

The artist Shimen Bromet took the title page of a non-Jewish book, complete with a Roman god, and made it into a mizrekh! Dated, 1867.

205

Yoshe ruled with an iron hand. He constantly kept watch over the *besmedresh* students lest they get too rowdy or let their candles drip over the pages of the Talmud. Yoshe also gave orders to the *shabes-goy* who would sweep the *besmedresh* every Friday and scrape away the mud. He saw to it that the *shabes-goy* and his wife scrubbed the brass menorah and chandeliers clean and washed the floors before each holiday.

On winter evenings there was always trouble over the potatoes the students would leave baking on the oven coals. The baked potatoes with their burnt crusts were the absolute favorite food of all *besmedresh* boys from time immemorial. For that reason Yoshe never accomplished anything, but he still went right on grumbling. Behind his back the boys would call him Yoshe Krepl because besides being hoarse and speaking with a nasal voice, Yoshe was also hard of hearing and one of his ears was folded over like a *krepl*. The only way the boys had of getting back at him was to call him by this nickname, but never dared do it to his face.

Yoshe's assistant and messenger boy was the quiet, good-natured Mekhele Shvarts. Mekhele was the one who would invite the guests to all the shtetl celebrations or, may this never happen, was the one to follow behind a funeral procession with an alms box and shout: "Charity saves from death!" Only when V.I.P.'s were involved would Yoshe himself deliver the invitations. But the job of calling, waking, and reminding Jews day in and day out to observe their faith and to come serve the Lord—this job was in Mekhele's hands. Each and every Friday afternoon, Mekhele would do the rounds of the entire shtetl and rap three times on every Jewish door and in this way he let the shtetl know that it was time to light the Sabbath candles.

On *shvues* morning Mekhele would wake the shtetl with a trembling voice: "Wake up dear Jews to recite the Psalms.

It's King David's *yortsayt!*" On winter mornings before the sun had risen, Mekhele would take his position in the center of the marketplace with a lantern in one hand and a staff in the other and chant ever so mournfully: "Wake up, dear Jews, wake up! Arise and get yourself up! It's time to serve the Lord!"

It would be a terrible mistake to think that all the *besmedresh* boys did all day and night was—study. At a moment's notice the *besmedresh* could turn into a clubhouse complete with acrobatics, fistfights, and chess games. In addition, every possible occasion was an excuse for a feast. Whenever the Book-Repairing *khevre* collected enough money to buy a new set of the Mishna, Talmud, or Midrash, the books were brought into the *besmedresh* with the accompaniment of musicians, and then everyone sat down for a huge meal.

Nothing could compare with the celebrations on the *yortsayt* of a khasidic *rebe*. These celebrations took place in the *shtibl* named after the deceased *rebe*. Since the Rizhiner *shtibl* was right next door to the *besmedresh*, boys from both buildings would go around collecting candles for the *yortsayt* celebration. Usually the younger kids would do the rounds. All they had to do was walk into a house and say: "The Rizhiner's *yortsayt*" and the owners would donate a candle or two.

These younger boys were also responsible for making a large wooden star of David which they would hang from the ceiling directly over the platform. Then they would arrange candles in all the windows and the *shames* would light the candelabra. When it came time for afternoon prayers, the *shtibl* would be lit up from wall to wall. After evening prayers would come the feast during which the older *khasidim* would tell stories about the Rizhiner *rebe* and would repeat some of his teachings. The stories and teachings were accompanied by khasidic melodies sung with or without words. Much later, after the grace after meals, the *khasidim* would start a circle dance, each man holding on to the other man's *gartl*. At first the men danced to their own singing, but as they got into it, song was no longer needed, and they continued dancing in total silence.

Meanwhile the *kheyder* children would remove some of the candles, attach them to shingles and go marching and singing through town on their way to the river. They would choose a quiet spot on the river and place the shingles in the water. The floating flames looked like illuminated spirits that were setting out for the farthest reaches of the earth. They seemed to carry with them secrets of far-off places, secrets that were both familiar and strange.

This ritual of the floating candles was one of the most meaningful and most mysterious experiences a child would ever have.

Yekhiel Shtern (1950 B), pp. 91–121.

UNIT SEVEN

THE SHTETL AFTER DARK: ENTERTAINMENT

A Jewish orchestra at the turn of the century in Ostrovtse, Kelts province. The angry violinist with the white beard seems to be the leader of the group. Notice that none of these men has his head covered.

The *kheyder* combined individual instruction with a general free-for-all. In the *besmedresh* teenage boys studied, joined in communal prayer, baked potatoes and played chess. Similarly, the khasidic *shtibl* was a place for adult celebration as well as for prayer. The *khevres* combined their specific functions with every possible excuse to have a good time. Play and entertainment were not something to do *after* work or *after* school but were part and parcel of the scheme of Jewish life. Children's games made use of the everyday aspects in a child's life: the Bible, the alphabet, the customs of grownups. Some were games that older children passed on to younger ones; others were taught by the *melamed* or *belfer*. Celebrations in the *shtibl* or *besmedresh* took place at specific times, relating to the Jewish calendar. Even such obviously universal forms of entertainment as card playing and theater were Judaized by attaching them to special dates. The most lavish of all celebrations—the wedding—did not depend on the calendar so much as on the decision of one's parents.

1. CHILDREN'S GAMES IN TISHEVITS: BAKNBROYT

Four children stand in the corners of a square. A fifth child, the one who's "It," stands in the center. He begins the game by going to one corner "begging": Give me *baknbroyt*. The child standing in the corner points to another corner. "It" goes to the second corner. The child in the second corner sends "It" to another corner, and so on. But meanwhile the corner players try to change places behind "Its" back. "It" must try to jump into a corner once it is free. The child left without a corner then becomes "It," and must go around "begging."

2. SHELI-SHELKHO

A group of children make a long line, holding hands. One child, the "prince" faces them. They call out to each other.

Children: What do you wish, Prince?

Prince: The prince wants the princess in the palace.

Children: We are the palace guards. We don't let anyone pass.

Prince: But I, the brave prince, will take out my sword and go through.

Children: We will fight to the last drop of blood.

Prince: Here comes the prince.

The prince runs into the line, once, twice, three times. On the third time, the children let him through. Then everyone chases him and the one to catch him becomes prince for the next round.

3. IKS, MIKS, DRIKS

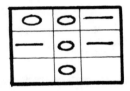

Played with chalk on anything writable. The marks used were a line and a circle. The winner calls out: *Iks, Miks, Driks!*

Yekhiel Shtern (1950 B), pp. 23–24, 27.

4. KHUMESH GAMES: THE WEEKLY PORTION GAME

Any page of a traditional *khumesh* (Bible) has two possible outstanding features: *alie* markers and concluding letters. *Alie* markers are the words "second, third, fourth, fifth, sixth, seventh," and "maftir." Concluding letters appear at the end of some weekly portions, either in sets of three or individually.

מוֹעֵד עַל יֶרֶךְ הַמִּשְׁכָּן צָפֹנָה מִחוּץ לַפָּרֹכֶת: וַיַּעֲרֹךְ עָלָיו 23

עֵרֶךְ לֶחֶם לִפְנֵי יְהֹוָה כַּאֲשֶׁר צִוָּה יְהֹוָה אֶת־מֹשֶׁה: ס וַיָּשֶׂם 24

אֶת־הַמְּנֹרָה בְּאֹהֶל מוֹעֵד נֹכַח הַשֻּׁלְחָן עַל יֶרֶךְ הַמִּשְׁכָּן נֶגְבָּה: 1500

וַיַּעַל הַנֵּרֹת לִפְנֵי יְהֹוָה כַּאֲשֶׁר צִוָּה יְהֹוָה אֶת־מֹשֶׁה: ס וַיָּשֶׂם כה 26

אֶת־מִזְבַּח הַזָּהָב בְּאֹהֶל מוֹעֵד לִפְנֵי הַפָּרֹכֶת: וַיַּקְטֵר עָלָיו 27

קְטֹרֶת סַמִּים כַּאֲשֶׁר צִוָּה יְהֹוָה אֶת־מֹשֶׁה:∗ ס וַיָּשֶׂם אֶת־ 28 שביעי

מָסַךְ הַפֶּתַח לַמִּשְׁכָּן: וְאֵת מִזְבַּח הָעֹלָה שָׂם פֶּתַח מִשְׁכַּן 29 100

אֹהֶל־מוֹעֵד וַיַּעַל עָלָיו אֶת־הָעֹלָה וְאֶת־הַמִּנְחָה כַּאֲשֶׁר

צִוָּה יְהֹוָה אֶת־מֹשֶׁה: ס וַיָּשֶׂם אֶת־הַכִּיֹּר בֵּין־אֹהֶל מוֹעֵד ל

וּבֵין הַמִּזְבֵּחַ וַיִּתֵּן שָׁמָּה מַיִם לְרָחְצָה: וְרָחֲצוּ מִמֶּנּוּ מֹשֶׁה 31

וְאַהֲרֹן וּבָנָיו אֶת־יְדֵיהֶם וְאֶת־רַגְלֵיהֶם: בְּבֹאָם אֶל־אֹהֶל 32

מוֹעֵד וּבְקָרְבָתָם אֶל־הַמִּזְבֵּחַ יִרְחָצוּ כַּאֲשֶׁר צִוָּה יְהֹוָה אֶת־ 100

מֹשֶׁה: ס וַיָּקֶם אֶת־הֶחָצֵר סָבִיב לַמִּשְׁכָּן וְלַמִּזְבֵּחַ וַיִּתֵּן 33 1000

אֶת־מָסַךְ שַׁעַר הֶחָצֵר וַיְכַל מֹשֶׁה אֶת־הַמְּלָאכָה:∗ פ מסטיר

וַיְכַס הֶעָנָן אֶת־אֹהֶל מוֹעֵד וּכְבוֹד יְהֹוָה מָלֵא אֶת־הַמִּשְׁכָּן: 34

וְלֹא־יָכֹל מֹשֶׁה לָבוֹא אֶל־אֹהֶל מוֹעֵד כִּי־שָׁכַן עָלָיו הֶעָנָן לה 500

וּכְבוֹד יְהֹוָה מָלֵא אֶת־הַמִּשְׁכָּן: וּבְהֵעָלוֹת הֶעָנָן מֵעַל הַמִּשְׁכָּן 36

יִסְעוּ בְּנֵי יִשְׂרָאֵל בְּכֹל מַסְעֵיהֶם: וְאִם־לֹא יֵעָלֶה הֶעָנָן וְלֹא 37

יִסְעוּ עַד־יוֹם הֵעָלֹתוֹ: כִּי עֲנַן יְהֹוָה עַל־הַמִּשְׁכָּן יוֹמָם וְאֵשׁ 38

תִּהְיֶה לַיְלָה בּוֹ לְעֵינֵי כָל־בֵּית־יִשְׂרָאֵל בְּכָל־מַסְעֵיהֶם:

חזק

סכם פסוקי דספר ואלה שמות אלף ומאתים ותשעה: אָרְ"ט סימן: וחצרו
אלהים לא תקלל· ופרשיותיו אֶחָד עָשָׂר· אִי זה בית אשר תבנו לי
סימן· וסדריו עֶשְׂרִים וְתִשְׁעָה· וְלַיְלָה לְּלַיְלָה יְחַוֶּה דַּעַת סימן:
ופרקיו אַרְבָּעִים· תורת אלהיו בלבו סימן: מנין הפתחות תֵּשַׁע
וְשִׁשִּׁים· והסתומות חָמֵשׁ וְתִשְׁעִים· הכל מאה וששים וארבע
פָּרָשׁוֹת: ישלח עזרך מקדש ומציון יסעדך סימן: ..

A sample page from a khumesh.

Rules of the game: Each *alie* marker is worth 100 points. Of the concluding letters, three *peys* or three *samekhs* are worth 1,000 points. If only one *pey* or *samekh* appears—500 points.

Number of players: unlimited. Before the game begins the players decide on a time limit and on how many points are needed to win. Whoever manages to get the most points within the time limit or whoever first gets the maximum points—wins.

How the game works: Berl opens the *khumesh* at random. If he finds any of the above markings in the page open before him, he records its numerical value. If he cannot find either an *alie* marker or a concluding letter, he gets a second try by announcing how many pages forward or back he intends to turn. If, on the second try, he finds a marker, he records the points and continues playing. If not, the *khumesh* is passed on to Motl and so on.

When time runs out, the players add up their points and the one with the most points wins.

Chaim Gilead.

5. MOYSHE GAME

Number of players: unlimited. Rules of the game: The word "Moyshe" is worth 1,000 points. A *mem* alone—500 points; a *shin*—100 points; a *hey*—50 points.

How to play: Berl opens the *khumesh* at random. If, on the right-hand page, at the beginning of the top line, he sees the name "Moyshe"—he wins 1,000 points. If he finds any of the three possible letters he wins the respective number of points. If not, he turns three pages either forwards or back and he must now guess which is the third letter in the third line. If he guesses right, he takes another turn. If not, he passes the *khumesh* to Motl and so on. Whoever has the most points at the end—wins.

It often happened that players got so good at this game that they could guess which word or letter appeared on any given page of the Bible. Once all the players had memorized the pages this well, they would find another edition of the *khumesh* where the text was laid out differently, or better yet, they would use a Mishna or a volume of the Talmud.

Chaim Gilead.

6. NOYEKH WITH SEVEN "MISTAKES"

A common riddle is: *Vi shraybt men Noyekh mit zibn grayzn?* How can you write the word "Noah" and make seven mistakes? Some possible solutions are the following:

נווייאק ; נוויאעכ ; וְאֶוּיאַהך

The trick, however, is that the Yiddish word for "mistakes," *grayzn*, also means "circles." The answer to: how to write the word "Noah" with seven *circles*, is very easy:

Dov Sadan.

7. MATHEMATICAL PUZZLES; GEMATRIA

Each letter in the Hebrew alphabet is also a number. The first letter of the alphabet, *alef*, equals one; *beys*, equals two; *giml*, three; and so on. This characteristic of the letters makes many types of puzzles possible.

Since letters have both a language and a mathematical meaning, you can "figure out" the mathematical value of any word or phrase written in Hebrew characters. A favorite pastime of both children and adults was finding phrases or words with equal mathematical values—and wondering what this relationship could mean. Some examples:

"Blessed is Mordekhay" equals "Cursed be Haman"

$$502 = \text{ארור המן} \quad = \quad \text{ברוך מרדכי}$$

Kortn (Yiddish for playing cards) equals "Satan"

$$359 = \text{שטן} \quad = \quad \text{קרטן}$$

Some people say, this proves that Jews are forbidden to play cards.

8. MAGIC SQUARES

Take this passage: חכם אחד וגם גדול הדור
זה דבר טוב בעולם

To be a wise man and the greatest of a generation, this is a good thing in the world.

If you take the first letter of each word and place it in a square arrangement you have the following:

ו	א	ח
ז	ה	ג
ב	ט	ד

Two New Year's cards from the turn of the century. The one of the two kheyder-yinglekh smoking on the sly was so popular that it was included in the second one by the Warsaw artist Khayim Goldberg (look right next to the window). The ditty on this card reads: We found a shoyfer somewhere/and we're having a good time/We wrap ourselves in daddy's tales / and do the blowing just like grownups.

217

And their numerical values equal:

8	1	6
3	5	7
4	9	2

Any direction you add up the letters in this "magic square" you will get 15. In addition: 15 = יה ; which stands for the name of God.

Yekhiel Shtern (1950 B), p. 45.

9. MAKE-BELIEVE WEDDINGS; THE CIRCLE DANCE

A good many Jewish dancing games are based on actual wedding dances. Circle and dance games are the first kind of games that children play in groups.

Sherele: All the children join hands in a line. They pass under the arms of the first two girls in the line—forming a chain. Then they twist back under and return to their original positions. This is what they sing:

Ver hot dikh geheysn khasene hobn?	Who asked you to get married?
Ver hot dikh geheysn di kop bagrobn?	Who asked you to be buried alive?
Keyner hot dir nit geneyt,	You know that no one forced you.
Host zikh aleyn di kop fardreyt.	You took this madness on yourself.

The name "sherele" is the diminutive form of the old "sher" or "shir" which used to be danced at weddings by two rows facing each other. While singing the rows would come together and then move apart. This dance is similar to one of the old Polish national dances, the Polonaise. As far as the lyrics go, they are part of a longer song actually sung by grown-ups at weddings.

Shmuel Zanvl Pipe.

10. KHOSN-KALE

This song is sung while the children pantomine a wedding:

Yakh bin der khosn	I am the groom
Du bist di kale.	And you the bride.
Tantsn veln	All the little girls
Meydelekh ale.	Will join in a dance.
Yakh bin der meylekh	I am the king
Du bist di malke.	And you my queen.
Veln mir zikh shpiln	And so we will play
In bobe-lialke.	Gramma-dolly.
Yakh vel zayn bobe	I'll be granny
Un du vest zayn lialke	And you'll be dolly.
Yakh vel zayn keyser	I'll be the king
Un du vest zayn malke.	And you'll be the queen.
Zingts, zingts	Sing out and sing
Yingelekh ale.	All you boys!
Yankele iz der khosn	Yankele is the groom
Feygele iz di kale.	And Feygele—the bride.

From the shtetl Sokhatshev, Warsaw province.
M. Vanvild, p. 121.

11. WEDDING BIRDS

Often, in the summertime, flocks of sparrows fly together singing. The children thought that the birds were celebrating a wedding. When the birds flew past, the children would jump and sing after them:

Bom tshi-tshe	Bom tshi-tshe
Khasene feygele.	Wedding birdie.
Gib mir a shitkele lekakh.	Give me a piece of honey cake.

From the shtetl Shebreshin, near Khelm.
M. Vanvild, p. 130.

12. ARTS AND CRAFTS FOR THE HOLIDAYS

Days, sometimes weeks, before each holiday the *belfer* in *kheyder* would help the children make toys. For *tishebov* these would be wooden guns and swords. For *lagboymer*, bows and arrows. For *khanike, dreydlekh*. For *purim, gragers* (noisemakers to drown out the sound of Haman's name during the reading of the *megile.*) For *peysekh* children would decorate *matse* hole-punchers. For *shvues* the children would gather branches of greenery to decorate their homes and make paper cutouts. On *simkhes-toyre* there were flags to make. The children also made lanterns to carry to weddings which were held at night.

Directions for *peysekh* toys: Pierce an egg. Empty the contents carefully. Draw a string through. Glue feathers on and hang or swirl like a bird.

It was customary to give children walnuts and colored eggs on *peysekh*. These were given by parents and close relatives. The eggs were not to be colored with paint, because paint is *treyf*—and, besides, it might contain leaven. Instead, they could be boiled with hay or onion skins and would come out green or yellowish brown.

From the shtetl Sislevitsh.
Beatrice Weinreich (1960).

13. KHANIKE

Dreydl games were popular in *kheyder* all winter long. The *belfer* helped the children carve these four-sided tops. On each side a Hebrew letter was painted or carved: *nun, giml, hey, shin.*

How to play; Game number one: Each player must bring to the game a pile of coins, buttons, or nuts. Everyone puts one coin in the center. Berl spins the *dreydl*. If the *dreydl* drops with the *nun* on top, it means *nisht*—Yiddish for "nothing." So he doesn't do anything at all. Then it is Motl's turn to spin, and so on. If the *dreydl* stops with *giml* on top, it stands for *gants*—which means "all"—and the player takes all of the coins. *Hey* stands for *halb*—

220

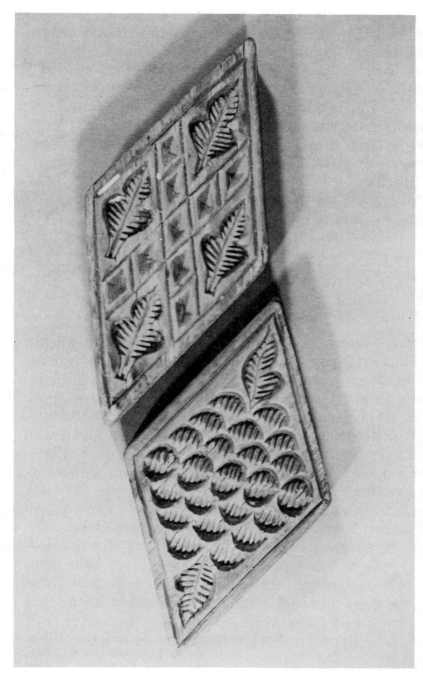

Purim cooky cutters from Yorshev, Podolia province, 1895. Notice that some eighty-year-old dough is still stuck to one mold.

"half"—and the player only takes half of the coins. *Shin* stands for *shtel*—"put" and the player must put another coin into the center pile.

There were many other interpretations of the *dreydl* letters in the different areas of Eastern Europe. For instance, a *giml* sometimes meant *gib*—"give" another coin; and a *nun* might stand for *nem*—"take" all the coins.

How to play; Game number two: On a large sheet of paper the *belfer* would draw a *pey* as shown here: He draws a string of rings over the *pey*. The players spin the *dreydl* one after another. A *giml*—3 points; a *hey*—5 points; a *nun*—15 points; a *shin*—30 points. The game goes on until one player accumulates as many points as there are rings around the *pey*.

Yekhiel Shtern (1950 B), p. 50.

14. SHVUES

The Jewish paper cutouts were usually made only by schoolboys and men. Paper cutouts were used for both religious and decorative purposes. The designs included flowers, animals, passages from the Bible, menorahs, crowns, six-pointed stars, soldiers, the ten commandments. Cutouts for *shvues* are called *shvueslekh*. Those that are round and look like flowers are called *reyzelekh*, roses. This folk art was only known in Galicia and the neighboring regions of Poland and Russia.

My family in Strusov always had a small guest house for traveling Jews. They never charged any rent from these guests. However, one way a guest could "pay" for this hospitality was to teach the children something, help them make toys or entertain them. I learned how to make these *reyzelekh* from one such stranger. We used to hang them in the window at *shvues* time.

From the shtetl Stursov near Tarnopol in eastern Galicia.
Uriel Weinreich (1954).

Instructions: Fold a round piece of paper into 8
sections. Draw the design on one side of the folded
paper. Tack onto a board. Cut out the design with
a sharp knife.

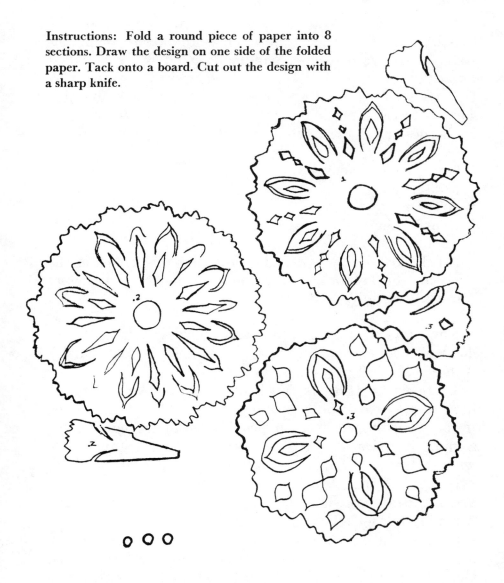

Reyzelekh

15. CARD PLAYING

Jews did not use popular playing cards because of the crosses and other Christian symbols found on them. Instead, there were special, handmade Yiddish cards called *Lamed-alefniks* or *kvitlekh*. The cards were decorated with Hebrew letters (standing for numbers), common objects—such as teapots, feathers, and sometimes portraits of biblical heroes. Each card had a special name. For example:

6, was called a Vover.
7, Zayner
9, Teser
Hearts, Lev
Trump, Yontef
A full card deck was called a *shas* (meaning: a set of the Mishna or Talmud) or a *tiliml* (also meaning a booklet containing only the Psalms).

Nowadays a game of cards is an everyday affair. Where don't we play cards nowadays? When don't we play cards? And who doesn't play cards nowadays?

There was a time, if you know what I mean, when we used to play cards only once a year—at *khanike*. That is, if you want the whole truth, people used to get together for a game in those days too—a real game, a hot game! But where? In a secret chamber, behind locked doors.

In winter, in *kheyder*, between the late-afternoon and evening prayers, when the teacher was at the synagogue warming himself by the stove and we were left alone; or in summer, in a dark corner of the stable, near a thin crack in the wall; or at other times of the year when we bribed Getsl, the *shames*, and locked ourselves up in the synagogue high up in the women's balcony, turned a lectern facedown for a table, and dealt out a hand of Starshy Kozir or Thirty-one, or Turtle-murtle.

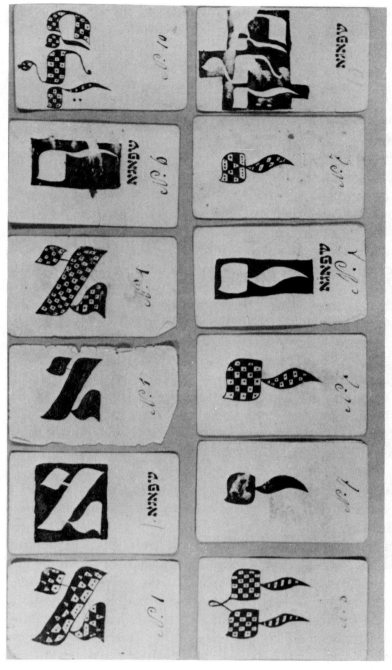

Khanike kvitlekh (playing cards) from the nineteenth century. Made by Efrayim Shoykhet from Dubosar, Moldavia. The khes (no. 8) is made up of two zayins joined together, just as is done in a Torah scroll.

One day Riva-Leye, the *gabe's* wife, of blessed memory, found a strange object in her lectern and almost fainted dead away. Who could have planted a thing like that—in her lectern? Aghast, she ran out of the synagogue into the street, shouting at the top of her voice: "Help, fellow Jews! Help! A misfortune has come to pass! A calamity! A plot! Come with me and I'll show you!"

What was the calamity and what kind of a plot? You couldn't get any answer from Riva-Leye. Only this: "Come, come with me and I'll show you." And before long she had drawn around her a fine assemblage, consisting of the rabbi, the *shoykhet*, a few of the elders, and the cantor, together with a liberal sprinkling of the town notables.

Naturally, when the rest of the people saw Riva-Leye proceeding up the street followed by the rabbi, the *shoykhet*, a few of the elders, and the *khazn* and so many of our leading citizens, they joined the procession too. And then the women and boys, and the little children, torn by curiosity, fell in behind, and together they marched into the synagogue. At the head, came Riva-Leye, and behind her, the townspeople.

You can imagine what a terror gripped the town. People thought—it must be something serious. Either someone had left a baby, or some poor woman had been found hanging from the rafters, or God forbid, someone had been murdered.

Worried and frightened, they clattered up to the women's balcony—Riva-Leye first, followed by the rabbi, the *shoykhet*, the *khazn*, with the rest of the town after them.

"Where—where is it?" the crowd asked Riva-Leye, and listened for the cry of the baby and looked for the hanging body or the trail of blood leading to the corpse that some unknown enemy had left there to bring trouble on our town.

And then imagine how astounded they all were when, instead of a baby or a bleeding corpse, they found this strange and ominous object in Riva-Leye's lectern; a picture of a bearded man—obviously a Russian Orthodox priest, but two priests and two crosses, one priest upright, and the other one standing on his head. . . .

They all bent down and peered into Riva-Leye's lectern, first the rabbi, then the *shames*, then the *shoykhet* and the elders and the *khazn;* then the leading citizens; then the common people. They looked and drew away. For to touch the thing with their hands—for that no one was bold enough. That is, no one except one man, Velvl Ramshevitsh, the *khazn's* son-in-law.

When Velvl Ramshevitsh looked and saw what it was, his face lit up, and then with a laugh, he cried, "It's nothing! What's there to get excited about? It's just the king of clubs!"

"And what is the king of clubs?"

"A card. A card—that you play with."

"How did it get here?" they wanted to know. "In the lectern of Riva-Leye, the *gabe's* wife, in the women's balcony of the synagogue? That's one thing. And the other is, how does it happen that you, the cantor's son-in-law, know what a card is and that it's called the king of clubs? And that it's a game that people play?"

At this our Velvl realized that he had fallen into a trap. And he turned every color imaginable and began to babble and to make sounds like a sheep or goat, sounds that no one could understand, no human being, at any rate. . . . There was only one lucky week in the year when we could play cards freely and openly. That was the week of *kanike.*

Sholom Aleichem (1946).

16. PURIM-SHPILN

Jews in Europe had a one-day-a-year theater season: Purim. Since Purim celebrates the events described in the Scroll of Esther, one would expect these events to supply the plot of the *purim-shpiln*. Except that Jews never had a theatrical tradition of their own. They may have worn masks on Purim and celebrated the holiday with special dances and song, but a full-fledged play with actors and costumes could only have been borrowed from the surrounding culture.

Sure enough, in the first documented *purim-shpiln* there is a comic figure called Prince Mondrish who comes straight out of seventeenth-century German theater. Mondrish, in turn, is the German version of the Italian Harlequin and the English Pickelherring (the "English comedians" introduced professional theater into Germany in the 1590s). Mondrish was a downright vulgar character who preferred ad-libbing his lines and talking about current events rather than sticking to the script.

Granted that Purim is a day on which Jews are commanded to get drunk and live it up, but surely there's got to be Jewish content in all this merriment! This is where Midrash helped fill in the gaps to create a theatrical form that was uniquely Jewish.

Why was Haman so mad at the Jews? The Babylonian Talmud provided the answer: They tried to short-change him in the marketplace! What is the real reason Vashti (Ahasuerus' first wife) was punished? The Midrash explains: because she forced her Jewish maids to work on *shabes*.

It seems that the first *purim-shpiln* based on biblical themes were performed in Western Europe, in Prague and Frankfurt, by *yeshive* students in the *besmedresh*. It wasn't until later that the *purim-shpil* was "democratized" so that tailors and cobblers might go around performing them from house to house. With time, the repertoire of plays also expanded. If Purim tells the story of a Jewish girl who made it big in a Persian palace, why not dramatize the story of little Joseph making good in Pharoah's palace? And so it was that "The Selling of Joseph" eventually became the most popular *purim-shpil* of all time.

Orphans performing the play, "Pleasure from One's Children" in Oshmene, Belorussia, August 18, 1923.

THE TAILOR'S SOCIETY OF YANOVE PRESENTS:

Di Mekhires-Yoysef-Shpil (The Selling of Joseph)

Starring:

> Berl Tailor as Young Joseph
> Motl the Apprentice as Big Joseph
> Yankl Journeyman Tailor as Jacob and The Turk
> Fayvl Cobbler as Mother Rachel and the Wolf
> Shloyme Cobbler as The Clown and Benjamin

The tailors and cobblers of Yanove, Lublin Province, performed "The Selling of Joseph" in the year 1913. Men and boys played the male and female parts. Here are some of the costumes:

Jacob: A long beard, a satin *kapote*, a *shtrayml*, a red kerchief around his neck and sandals over white stockings. In other words, he was meant to be a take-off on a *khasidic rebe.*

Clown: Dressed entirely in red with a yellow stripe running down his trousers. With a dunce cap on his head.

Brothers: Each wears a cardboard hat with his name on it: "Reuven ben Jacob, Asher ben Jacob" and so on. Each carries a wooden sword.

Turks: (who buy Joseph from his brothers) Dressed like Russian Cossacks, with red shirts and red turbans.

Wolf: (who is accused by the brothers of having torn Young Joseph to bits—also based on midrashic sources). Covered with furs.

Big Joseph: Appears before Pharoah in torn "prison" clothes.

The first performance, directed by Zalmen the Tailor, was so successful, that two years later, in 1915, the *yeshive* students performed the same play in the women's section of the *besmedresh*. And this is how the play begins. The lines are sung or chanted.

Enter Clown.
Clown: Hello the Clown I am the Clown
       A bread of rye, a bread of wheat
       And grab a bite
       Tra-la-la-la-la.
       Hello the Clown!
       Listen to a tale full of wonders
       The adventure of Joseph and his brothers.
       Listen to a tale full of splendor
       A marvelous tale you will always remember.

Enter Jacob, *led by his servant.* Jacob *sits down center stage and yells:*
Jacob: Oy-oy-oy-oy-oy! Servant!
Servant: What is it, boss?
Jacob: Get the chickens out of here!
Servant: (at the imaginary chickens) Shoo, shoo, shoo . . .
Jacob: Go out and buy me a pack of Petersburg tobacco.
Servant: What kind of tobacco?
Jacob: You heard me! Petersburg tobacco!
Servant: Oh yah, Betersturg. . . .

                  Shimon Khalamish (1964, 1965).

17. JEWISH WEDDING DANCES

Broygez Tants: Quarrel dance. Two or more participants pantomime a feud. They eventually make up, but only after several false starts.

Kosher Tants: Most dances are for either men only or women only. The kosher dance, however, is done between a man and woman: the bride and groom, parents of the bride or groom, the rabbi and bride. Since holding hands in public between men and women is forbidden, the partners hold the corners of a handkerchief between them. No other dancing takes place at this time and everyone watches.

Koyletsh Tants: Bread Dance. A woman dances before the bride, holding a long, white braided bread in her hands.

Bezem Tants: Broom dance. A man dances with a broom, pretending it is a gun or a horse.

Flash Tants: Bottle dance. A man dances and does gymnastics with a bottle balanced on his head.

Bobe Tants: Grandmother dance. The grandmothers of the bride and groom dance together.

Mekhutonim Tants: Relatives' dance. The parents of the bride and groom dance.

Dance of death: A man dances as the angel of death. He chooses someone to dance with him and act out his leaving this world.

Heydn-Deydn: Two men dance. Each man places his right hand on the other's right shoulder. They kick their legs as high as possible. Everyone sings, "heydn-deydn." Then they change to their left hands and left shoulders.

18. THE BATKHN: PINKE OF KAPULE

. . . Speaking of the bathhouse it would be a crime indeed not to say a few words about Pinke the bathhouse keeper, particularly since he was a peculiar and versatile person. In addition to his two positions as bathhouse keeper and manager of a candle factory, he combined in his person two

A Jewish wedding by Issachar Ryback. The bride and groom are seen holding candles.

more offices, which were exactly opposite in character; undertaker and *batkhn*. I don't know what kind of an undertaker he was. I suppose, however, a pretty good one, for it was not known that any of the people he had buried ever came back. A *batkhn*, however, he was of the first order. Before he led the bride and the groom under the wedding canopy he preached to them, pointing out the great significance of this step in their lives and warning them not to rejoice too much, for everything in life passes like a dream. If the bride and groom were orphans he would remind them of death to prove to them that man is like a flower of the field; today it flourishes and grows up and tomorrow there is no trace of it. All this he would recite with great pathos in serious tone, so that not only the bride and the groom, but all the guests would start crying.

After the wedding ceremony, when the bride and groom and the important guests were seated around tables covered with all kinds of food and drink, Pinke would suddenly become a juggler, a wit, who so amused the guests that they would split their sides laughing. Emptying glass after glass to the accompaniment of the musicians, tell merry tales and stories, jokes and puns—and all in rhyme! He would also perform all kinds of tricks, swallow ribbons, and the like. He could impersonate a person with two faces, dividing his face in two, with one half he laughed and with the other he cried.

From the city of Minsk, 1840s.
A. J. Papierna.

19. A MIXED MARRIAGE

How Aunt Itke, the family rebel and one of the guiding lights of the haskole in Kutne was married off to Berish, an heir of the Zdunska-Volye khasidic dynasty.

While everyone in Kutne, except for grandfather Reb Moyshl, tried to forget that Aunt Itke had become a bride to Zdunska-Volye, time took its natural course. Grandma Leye didn't even show Aunt Itke the wedding gifts that had been brought from Zdunska-Volye by a special khasidic messenger. Once more an active correspondence was struck up between Kutne and Zdunska-Volye and the *mekhutonim* began to discuss the wedding date.

Meanwhile, little red hairs began to sprout on Berish's, the groom's chin; and all day long he would pull at his chin to speed up the growth of the little, red khasidic beard that appeared just in the nick of time. Soon the little beard began to show a bit on his throat and a bit on his chubby cheeks. Wedding preparations began in earnest and the groom was outfitted with several dressing gowns and a broad silk *kapote* with velvet khasidic-style laces. From Kutne, grandfather Reb Moyshl sent the groom a *shtrayml* and Berish began to wear it on *shabes*. And though he still did not pray in a *tales* he already hung around the married young men. Even Reb Mendele himself had a new dressing gown made in honor of his son's wedding, and his wife had a new headdress sewn for herself.

Preparations were in full swing in Zdunska-Volye, but in Kutne no one said a word. Aunt Itke was avoided altogether and everything was done in secret. Grandma Leye hoped for a miracle—that the wedding be canceled. At night she wept into her pillow and consoled herself with the knowledge that even the *khupe* wasn't the last word and that God had created divorce to rescue the daughters of Israel.

But time moves onwards and the date of Aunt Itke's wedding arrived. We came from Lodz for the wedding. It was just before *peysekh*. There was still snow on the fields. Grandfather Borekh and Grandma Khaye brought along several cages of top-quality chickens. Simkhe Gayge arrived and brought a small barrel of butter as a wedding present. Simkhe Gayge ignored everyone, and joked with the women as if *he* were the one marrying off his daughter. Aunt Itke did not appear at all. She saw what was going on and the wheels in her head stopped spinning. For hours on end she sat in her chair and allowed everything to be done with her. Every now and then Grandma Leye entered her room fearfully and looked into her eyes. Aunt Itke answered with a stubborn silence. She didn't ask for food and it seemed as if Aunt Itke were fasting the whole time.

Then the day actually arrived. First thing in the morning guests appeared from Lodz who introduced a bit of clatter in the otherwise gloomy atmosphere. Aunt Shifre-Mirl arrived with her two daughters Yokheved and Sortshe. They chatted loudly between themselves passing judgment on Aunt Itke's trousseau and on the small Kutne houses.

Soon thereafter, Synagogue Street was disturbed by a clamor marking the return of the Zdunska-Volye wagons full of guests. Half of Zdunska-Volye, women in headdresses and all sorts of *khasidim*, poured out of the covered wagons with shouts and curses. They all shouted in a special brand of Yiddish and amidst the bedlam there emerged a number of familiar faces: Reb Mendele wrapped in large shawls and with a crumpled *rebe's* hat. The groom's red beard made a frightened appearance on his chubby face and his belly bulged rather visibly underneath his new khasidic overcoat. Though he was fasting the traditional wedding-fast, you couldn't tell.

Once again Kutne houses were filled with noise and with strange, pushy Jews. Reb Shimen and his son-in-law took refuge in the corners. The musicians could barely make their way through the *khasidim* and when they struck up the customary tune of greeting, the guests weren't interested and interrupted the music by shouting and jostling the players. No sooner had a few chords been heard then Reb Mendele yelled out in his strange Yiddish dialect to cut the senseless racket because he and Reb Moyshl still had the dowry and the boarding terms to discuss.

Thus the wedding day passed in a clatter and a din. Aunt Itke was entirely forgotten. Not until early evening was some order made and the tables set. The *khasidim* were everywhere. Candles were lit and only with great difficulty were the men quieted down and seated at their tables.

The scene was the same among the women. The place was swarming with khasidic headdresses. The female relatives from Kutne were barely visible in the midst of the seething mass. Grandmother Prive, the distinguished widow, got a headache. Even the aggressive *rebetsn* of Kolish was cowed into silence by the noise of the khasidic women. No one listened to her. Even once the candles were lit, the bride's chair moved into the center, and encircled with branches, even then the khasidic women continued arguing and shouting. The musicians began playing but the women went right on with this racket.

In the midst of this bedlam Grandma Leye led in Aunt Itke dressed in a white wedding dress and a white veil. The bride passed by the female relatives like a pale sleep-walker with wide-opened eyes that stared and saw nothing. She let everything be done to her and was silent. The women congratulated her but she didn't hear them. When Reb Mendele's wife approached her and wished her a *mazltov*, Aunt Itke replied by staring at the deep folds of her future mother-in-law's headdress. Aunt Itke was seated in the bride's chair and as she sat there, pale and dazed, her forehead looked ghostly underneath the white veils. Grandma Leye was afraid to look at her only daughter. Then the wailing tune was played, a *batkhn* began addressing his rhymed sermon to the bride and Grandma Leye started to wail.

And so, Aunt Itke's unusual wedding finally came to a close. Late at night, after the *mitsve* dance, two old *khasidim* took the groom by the hand and led him off somewhere. The frightened groom scratched his beard while the old men mumbled Hebrew phrases about how a Jew should behave on his wedding night. They pushed the groom into a dimly lit side room. He stood still in confusion in the sudden stillness. Through the walls the shouting and dancing of the guests could still be heard. Suddenly the groom noticed two white featherbeds on the far side of the room. Recalling what the two *khasidim* had said, he began to undress.

When all he had on was his undershirt, his long *tales-kotn* and the velvet *yarmlke* on his head, he went up to the bed nervously. The first bed was empty. Then he approached the second bed and found it empty as well. He bent over the white linen as if in search of a lost object.

The frightened groom shook his head and grabbed hold of his long *tales-kotn*. A kerosene lamp cast a dim light over the room. He bent over the bed for a second look. All of a sudden, he raised his head and caught sight of Aunt Itke, sitting doubled up on a high dresser, still wearing her wedding dress and her veil. Her glazed eyes stared like those of a hunted animal.

The groom grabbed hold of his *yarmlke* as if it were trying to fall off his head. He looked up at Aunt Itke on the dresser and he seemed to hear the two *khasidim* mumbling to him in Hebrew and threatening him with damnation. He felt a sweat break out beneath his boyish beard. He raised his head even higher and with a khasidic melody addressed Aunt Itke:
"Well? . . ."
The white bride on the dresser was as silent as a corpse.

Abridged from I. J. Trunk.

Children playing in front of the rabbi's house in Kolbushov, 1929. Note the well in the foreground.

UNIT EIGHT

THE LIVING AND THE DEAD

Tombstones in Berzhan, near Tarnopol.

For Jews in Eastern Europe death was part of the natural cycle, a continuation of life. Nothing dies completely, for something always remains. How do you know when one instant is over and the next begins? Isn't the second instant merely a continuation of the first?

There are many ways in which Jews emphasize the continuing importance that death and the dead occupy in their lives: by holding memorial services; by building specifically Jewish cemeteries and visiting them regularly; by carving Jewish tombstones; by telling tales about the angel of death —by tricking him. As we saw in earlier units death was a subject for the *kheyder*, for kahal, for the burial society, the *khevres*, and even weddings. With the very act of remembering the dead we bridge the difference between them and us.

1. THE ANGEL OF DEATH: WHAT DOES HE LOOK LIKE?

A rabbi does not lie down and die so easily. He, who had always been frail and sickly—partly because of too much fasting and partly from undernourishment—finally took to bed in his old age. For over a year he lay paralyzed without eating or drinking a thing—only studying, praying, and struggling with the angel of death. Shmulik swore to his friend with all kinds of oaths that every evening at twilight, between the two evening prayers, "That One" flew in through a crack in the window, stationed himself at the rabbi's head, and waited to make a grab for his soul should he ever stop praying. But the rabbi was too clever for him. Not for a single moment did he stop praying—he simply went on praying and studying, studying and praying.

"What does he look like?"

"Who?"

" 'That One'."

"How should *I* know?"

"You said he comes every night, so you must have seen him."

"Stupid! Anyone who lays his eyes on 'That One' won't live to tell about it! How could I have seen him?"

"Then how do you know he comes?"

"What do you think he does? Sit in the sky waiting for an invitation?"

The day of the rabbi's death was a holiday. The rabbi had a beautiful funeral such as only a small-town rabbi can permit himself. The shops were closed, the schools deserted, and the whole city accompanied him to the cemetery.

Sholom Aleichem (1955), pp. 22–23.

When can he be seen?

If you would watch a funeral procession through the eye of a needle you would see the angel of death with his sword. But you had better not do it if you want to live for another year.

Descriptions

Our sages tell us that the angel of death reaches from heaven to earth and that he is full of eyes from head to foot. Some other reports are that he looks like an

old man with a poisoned sword,
a beggar,
a peddler,
an Arab,
he's married to Lilith,
a wanderer,
a cat,
an old grandfather,

a spy,
a soldier,
he has a metal-colored beard,
he has no body at all,
he carries a wooden sword,
he strangles with his thumb,
he disguises himself as an animal.

2. HOW HE TRICKS MAN AND MAN TRICKS HIM

Once upon a time there lived a man called Dima son of Abaye, who was on friendly terms with the angel of death. One day the angel of death said to his messenger: "Go and bring me a woman called Miriam, who is a women's hairdresser." The messenger misunderstood him and brought another Miriam who was a children's hairdresser. Then the angel of death said to him: "I sent you to bring me the Miriam who dresses the hair of women and you brought me the Miriam who dresses the hair of children." The messenger replied: "Return her to me and I will bring her back to life." Said the angel of death to his servant: "How were you able to kill her, since the time for her death had not arrived?" And the messenger replied: "I will tell you. When I came to her, I found her sitting in front of the fire with a poker in her hand ready to rake the fire. She put the poker into the fire, and it was burnt, and with that her luck was also burnt, and I took her life." Then Dima asked: "But have you the power to do so?" And the angel of death replied: "Yes, is it not written in the book of Ecclesiastes: 'Some die without judgment'? That is, men die before their time. But I do not put them among the dead until the time arrives which has been fixed for their death. I keep them with me until I can put them among the dead."

Therefore women must be careful not to burn their pokers, for they burn their luck with it.

Moses Gaster.

245

It chanced once that a great calamity almost befell the angel of death. He came pretty near losing the knife with which he severs the life of man. When Rabbi Joshua ben Levi was at the point of death the angel of death came to see him.

"Show me first my place in paradise," pleaded Rabbi Joshua. "That will make it easier for me to depart from this life."

"Come, I will show you," answered the angel of death.

And so they ascended to the celestial regions. On the way, Rabbi Joshua said to the angel of death, "Do give me your knife. I am afraid that you will frighten me with it while we are on the way." The angel of death felt pity for him and gave him his knife. When they at last arrived in paradise the angel of death showed Rabbi Joshua the place reserved for him. A great yearning then seized Rabbi Joshua and he sprang forward within the gates. But the angel of death seized hold of his coat and tried to pull him back. Having the knife in his possession Rabbi Joshua refused to budge from his place. "I swear I will not leave paradise!" he cried.

Then a great tumult was heard among the angels. It seemed very much as if death were about to be abolished from the world and people would be able to live forever, like the angels. The angel of death didn't know what to do. The holy man had sworn that he would not leave paradise, and who could violate the oath of such a man? So the angel of death went to complain to God himself. And God said, "I decree that Rabbi Joshua must return to earth. His time has not come yet."

The angel of death came again to Rabbi Joshua and demanded in a terrible voice, "Give me back my knife!"

"I will not give it back to you!" cried Rabbi Joshua. "I want to abolish death forever!" Suddenly the voice of God was heard sternly commanding, "Return the knife, Joshua! Man must continue to die."

Babylonian Talmud, Ketuboth 77b.

The old cemetery was in a state of almost total ruin. The tombstones were washed out by the rain and many were broken into countless pieces. There remained only one legible inscription. Though half of the tombstone had sunk into the ground, the following words could be made out: "Here lies . . . the holy Rabbi Eliezer Liber . . . who died in the plague of 1771."

This is how it happened. In 1771 a terrible plague broke out in Barditshev that took hundreds of victims each day. The Barditshev rabbis and community leaders took all the traditional measures: special prayers were composed; the fence around the cemetery was repaired; they even arranged a "black wedding" in the cemetery. The plague raged on.

When the saintly Rabbi Liber realized that the whole city stood at the brink of destruction, he called together the *dayonim*, the heads of the *yeshive*, the community leaders, and in their presence he took it upon himself to be the sacrifice for the entire population.

That very night Rabbi Liber died and the plague subsided the next morning.

Abraham Rechtman, p. 132.

3. OMENS AND AMULETS

The *khazn* of Khelm read in an old book of *kabole* that on the night of *hoshane rabe*, after midnight, when the moon moves to the center of the sky, a man may learn his fate. One need only look at one's own shadow: if the shadow is whole it means he will have a good year. If, God forbid, the shadow is headless, the man will surely die within the year. If the shadow is missing a hand it means that he will be sick. Everything depends on the shadow cast by the moon.

On the night of *hoshane rabe*, the *khazn* went off to the large *shul* to recite Psalms with great devotion. When the recitation was over it was already one in the morning, just when the moon moved into center sky. The *khazn* made

Tombstones in **Kelme** besoylem.

sure to be the last one out so as to be absolutely alone when examining the state of his shadow.

As he walked outside and caught sight of the bright *hoshane rabe* moon, his heart was seized with fear: Should he look and risk seeing a headless shadow or should he not look and miss his chance altogether? Finally, he couldn't resist and, with eyes half-closed, he looked down and saw the shadow of an animal (who happened to be chewing contentedly nearby).

The *khazn* barely made it home and collapsed onto his bed, crying bitterly.

"What happened?" asked his wife in amazement.

"Help!" he cried, "I'm a beast. I saw my shadow cast by the moon on this night of *hoshane rabe*."

His wife examined him carefully. The *khazn* called for the mirror and when he saw himself unchanged he still couldn't calm down. "Sooner or later I'm sure to become a beast," he said.

They cried the whole night through. The next morning he decided not to appear in *shul*. "If I am fated to turn into a beast, it might as well happen at home," he argued, and to himself he thought: "God forbid, if I became a beast while praying before the ark it'll be all over. The community leaders will have a fit and the butchers will take me away to be slaughtered."

Meanwhile the congregation had assembled to say the *hoshane* prayers and their *khazn* was nowhere to be seen. The *shames* came to fetch him but he refused to budge. The *shames* came a second time and said that if he didn't appear he would lose his job. This was too much—no matter what happened, he still had to earn a living. Luckily, he came up with a clever plan which he shared with his wife:

"Listen, I'm going off to *shul*, but you come with me. Take along a rope and go up to the women's balcony. Keep an eye on me at all times and as soon as you see me turning into a beast, come right down, tie me up, and take me home."

The *khazn* was met in *shul* by the jeers of the angry community leaders. He took his place before the ark in a state of confusion and fear. He imagined everyone was staring at him in a funny way. He began to feel dizzy and his voice stuck in his throat. Instead of shouting *"hameylekh*—the king," all he produced was "hame-e-eh" with such a shriek that the entire congregation burst out laughing.

Their laughter added to his confusion and to make matters worse, the children crowded round him and begun taunting him with "meh—heh—heh!" The *khazn* was at his wits' end. He threw back his head and cried out with all his might:

"Help, Yente! Bring the rope quick! Take me away from here!"

Yente his wife appeared at once, threw the rope around him and began dragging him out, crying:

"Woe is me, woe to our fate, the *khazn* has turned into a beast!"

The *khazn* let himself be dragged out and he went on praying: "Hameh ... hameh." All of Khelm ran out after him.

F. Freed, pp. 130–132.

4. NAMES

If a person is seriously ill, one way to protect him from the angel of death is to change the patient's name. Certain names are especially effective: Alter (old one), Zeyde (grampa), Bobe (gramma), Khayem for a male or Khaye for a female (both mean "life").

Your name is the essence of your life. One day, when that day comes, you will have to report it to the angel of the grave. Woe to him who forgets his name! His soul is doomed to endless exile.

In order to insure against such calamity, a child is given a biblical verse the first and last letters of which correspond to the first and last letters of his name. For example, the name Yisroel:　יִשְׂרָאֵל

יָמִין ה' רוֹמֵמָה, יָמִין ה' עֹשָׂה חָיִל.

Psalms 118:16. The right hand of the Lord is exalted: The right hand of the Lord doeth valiantly.

A child said this passage three times a day after praying.

5. WHY DOES ONE DIE?

It's determined on the day you are born.

When you've used up the number of words you were allowed in your lifetime, you die. (From the shtetl Rishkan.)

Ninety-nine percent of all people die from the evil eye.

It is as hard to separate the soul from its body as it is to thread a thin needle with a fat string.

When I was still a *kheyder-yingl*, the teacher's child took sick. One night we heard sounds from the attic, sounds of someone climbing to the roof. And all at once there was a tremendous crash, as if someone had fallen. Just at that moment, the child died.

From the watchman of the Vilner besoylem.

Why does a human being have his hands closed at birth and open at death? Because when a man is born, he cannot satisfy his wants and tries to take in the whole world. At death—he's had enough.

If several persons are present when a person dies, they must form two rows, as if greeting a bride, to allow the angel of death to leave. No children should be allowed to see this.

From the shtetl Kartuz-Bereze.

6. THE PEASANT WHO COULDN'T DIE

In 1913, I happened to be in the town of Lentshits at the home of Reb Yosef Landau when a young peasant from the neighboring village burst in. Mukha was his name. He dropped a hammer into Reb Yosef's hand. The latter had no idea what this was all about and stared at the peasant in amazement. After a long, embarrassing pause, Mukha finally got up enough courage to explain:

"Twenty years ago my father stole this hammer from you. For the past three days he's been lying on his deathbed, and death won't take him. A few hours ago he confessed and the priest suggested that I search you out and return the hammer. Only now will he be able to die."

Both sides took this matter very seriously.

Y. Zelkovitsh (1938), p. 153.

7. THE BEREAVED

Doctor Kazchkovsky came to visit Mother when she was already hopelessly ill, a fact confirmed by his flushed face, which had turned even redder than usual. "What can I do?" he asked. Was he not doing everything possible? "Here's whom you should ask for help," and he pointed toward the ceiling. But Grandma Minde didn't need that advice. She had already been to the synagogue. She had hired people to read the Psalms day and night. And she had visited the cemetery, trusting in the powers of her ancestors to intervene for her. . . . "A saint like Khaye Esther must not die! No, dear Lord, you are merciful, you will not allow it!"

Yet, though God was merciful and kind, little Khaye Esther never rose from her sickbed. She died on a *shabes* morning while Jews were still praying in the synagogue.

She died. . . . This was a second blow for the children, the first had been the death of their teacher, Moyshe the Slaughterer. Their suffering was great. True, their mother had

Woman mourning at her relative's grave in Lite.

not been as gentle as most mothers. She had slapped them plenty. But now all that was forgotten. All they remembered was how Mother would dig into her pocket to find a penny for each of them; how her little hand would feel their foreheads when they were ill; how every Friday she would wash their hair; how on *peysekh* she would laugh when the children became tipsy with wine. . . . This they remembered, and each child buried his face in his pillow, crying bitterly. When they heard Father weep, the sobs became louder and stronger. How was it possible for *Father* to weep! Grandma Minde, was also weeping, and conversing with the Lord to the melody of a prayer.

Suddenly, the door opened and Uncle Pinney burst into the house, *"Gut shabes!"* When Uncle Pinney saw everyone weeping and wailing, he began to scold Father and Grandma Minde, "What's this! Weeping on *shabes?* Have you gone mad? Have you forgotten that it's forbidden to weep on *shabes?"*

As he said this, he turned away, pretending to be wiping his nose, and stealthily cast a glance into the room where Mother was lying on the ground, covered with black with candles surrounding her. He dried his eyes quickly, so that no one should see he was crying, but now he spoke more gently, and tears trembled in his voice.

"Stop it, Nokhem. Come, come, stop it. . . ."

But, unable to control himself, he sat down at the table, laid his head on his left arm, and burst into tears, wailing in a shrill voice, like a little child:

"Khaye Esther, Khaye Esther. . . ."

Sholom Aleichem (1955), pp. 169–171.

8. FUNERAL AND BURIAL

A shroud should never have any knots, so that the dead person will be able to easily free himself when the Messiah comes.

A funeral procession nearing the cemetery in Aleksander-Kuyavsky.

255

The funeral procession takes the longest, most complicated route to the *besoylem*. This is to confuse the dead person so that he won't be able to find his way back to haunt his family.

When a learned man dies his corpse is carried to the *besmedresh* where he prayed. He is carried between all the benches. Then a eulogy is said.

At the grave the mourners rip a piece of their clothing. They wear this shredded clothing for 30 days; or for a dead parent, for a whole year.

As the mourner leaves the cemetery he fills his shoes with sand and pulls some grass out of the ground at the entrance of the cemetery and throws it back towards the graves. He says: "And they of the city shall flourish like grass of the earth" (Psalm 72:16).

Y. Zelkovitsh (1938), p. 172.

9. THE BURIAL SOCIETY

The tailor's burial was associated with yet another incident. He had two sons, one in Lutomiersk and one in Lodz. As soon as the tailor was dead, the son who lived in Lutomiersk concealed all the pledges and promissory notes that had been in his father's possession. The other son came to the burial society, complaining that his brother had robbed him of his inheritance. The association decided to intervene on his behalf. The deceased tailor had prepared his own shrouds in his lifetime. After his death, he was dressed in these shrouds. The members of the association stripped the dead man of his shrouds. Fearing that the police might force them to surrender the shrouds, they ripped them and concealed the pieces in the cellar among the discarded books. Not before the greedy son had produced the pledges and the promissory notes were preparations begun for the burial of the deceased. The burial society not only performed funeral functions but saw to it as well that no one was wronged.

Y. Zelkovitsh (1951), pp. 262–263.

10. THE DEDICATION OF A CEMETERY

Zundl, the chief trustee of the burial society, who had complete charge of the cemetery, came to the mayor in alarm. He reported that the cemetery, which was God knows how old, was practically filled. New burial grounds had to be dedicated in a hurry.

A town meeting was immediately called. The elders sat about a round table while the rest of the townspeople stood in the hall. And the debate began. All agreed that new burial grounds must be dedicated. The question was, where? The young generation held that the new cemetery should be located on top of the hill, beside the watermill. It's a nice spot and the dead would have a beautiful view. From the front of the cemetery the whole town of Khelm could be seen by the dead, so they could keep an eye on it and protect it.

But the older people argued, "True, the top of the hill is a beautiful spot. But every family has at least one member resting in the old cemetery. When the month of Elul arrives and we must visit the graves to pay respect to the dead, it will be a great hardship. First we must lie on the graves of our beloved in the old cemetery, and then, after a good cry, which wrecks every bone and muscle, we'll have to climb the hill to the new cemetery. No, it's impractical! The new cemetery must be near the old one."

The older generation won, but no one had the slightest idea what the length and breadth of the new cemetery should be. True, they could take the old one as a guide, but it had been dedicated when Khelm was a village, whereas it is now a city, and still keeps growing.

Gimpl the mayor came up with an idea; "All of us, but all of us—men and women, old and young, children, even babes—must go to the field and lie down, near one another, flat on the ground. Of course, the men and women will lie separately, and the children in the special children's section. The learned and the important citizens shall stretch them-

Visiting the grave of Rabbi Avrom Arn Teitelboym. A fence was put up because this was considered a holy grave. Kolbushov, 1929. Courtesy of David Salz.

selves on the ground at the front rows of the graves and the plain people in the back rows. We should allot a large plot for transients. Then Shloyme the mathematician can measure the whole area. And that is that."

It was so logical that the whole assembly rose to cheer. Everybody, that is, but Shloyme the mathematician. "Wait a while! Don't cheer yet! It's a well-known fact that when people get older they gain weight. Some get very bulky. If we measure the cemetery to the size we are now, it will be filled before you wink."

So, on a nice, hot summer day, all Khelm—men, women, children, and infants—bundled up in heavy woolen underwear, in suits and dressed with thickly padded linings and on top of all that, heavy winter overcoats. They trudged to the new cemetery, sweating and panting. All stretched themselves out on the ground as prearranged—men and women separately, children in the youth section, infants in a corner, and the learned and the important citizens in front. Shloyme measured the area, including a plot for himself, and drove stakes into the ground as markers for its boundaries.

To reward Gimpl for his brilliant idea it was resolved, at a special town meeting, that he should have the honor of being the first person buried in the new cemetery.

Solomon Simon, pp. 50–53.

11. MAGICAL TOMBSTONES

IN TISHEVITS

Near the *kheyder* there was an unfinished house in which were stored stone and wooden tombstones. The teacher's son was a tombstone engraver and he would do his work here. The place was always full of youngsters who would follow the work of the engraver with curiosity and then try to imitate him by drawing with chalk on the walls either hands in the position of the priestly benediction or other figures found on tombstones. When the engraver was not present the boys would practice climbing on the stone.

The closeness of the tombstones to the *kheyder* gave rise to fantastic tales about ghosts and migrating souls. No one dared venture into the ruins at night. During the winter we had classes at night and we were afraid to go through the hall because of the tombstones. The reflection through the door of a white and snow-covered stone seemed certain to be a ghost in shrouds. The teacher, therefore, would lead the children out through the hall.

Yekhiel Shtern (1950 A), p. 154.

IN MEZHBIZH

Not far from the Bal Shem Tov's (Besht) monument in Mezhbizh we found a tombstone from 1865 with the inscription:

HERE LIES RABBI ISRAEL MES WHO DIED WHILE STILL ALIVE

The following tale is told about this inscription: Odl, the Besht's daughter, had three children: Moyshe-Khayem Efroyem Sudilkover, Reb Borekh of Mezhbizh, and a daughter, Feyge, the mother of Nakhmen Bratzlaver.

After Rabbi Israel Bal Shem Tov passed into the other world, it became customary for the Jews of Mezhbizh not to name a newborn son Israel, because of the sanctity of the Besht's name. A child who was given the name Israel did not live out his years.

And it came to pass that Feyge, the Besht's granddaughter gave birth to a male child. Soon thereafter the Besht appeared before his daughter Odl in a dream and asked that the newborn child be called—Israel.

But Feyge, the child's mother, refused. She did not want to risk his life. Odl, however, was determined to fulfill her father's request and on the day of the *bris*, when the *khazn*

Tombstones from Kelme besoylem. The animals represent the names of the deceased. A deer and wolf for Tsvi Zeyv (right) and lion and deer for Arye Leybl (left).

called out: "And his name shall be called in Israel," Odl promptly stood up and called out: "ISRAEL." The *khazn* repeated the name after her and so it remained, against the mother's wishes.

Three days later the child died. Poor Feyge took her dead child and brought it to her mother. She placed the child in front of Odl and said tearfully: "Mother! You are to blame for my child's death! Here's the child and do with him as you please!"

Odl picked up the child and took it to the cemetery and put it down on the Besht's grave saying: "Father! You ordered me to name the child after you and now it is dead. Take him back—he's yours!" She stood there crying for a while and then returned home.

It snowed all night through. In the morning, when the undertaker went outside, he heard a baby's cry coming from the cemetery. He followed the voice until he reached the Besht's grave. There he found the crying infant.

The town was in an uproar. Feyge, the child's mother came running as fast as could be and took back her child who was healthy and unharmed.

For this reason the child Israel was called "Israel Mes"— Israel the dead one—for the rest of his life. He lived to the age of 100 and was buried not far from his great-grandfather, with the inscription: HERE LIES ISRAEL MES, WHO DIED WHILE STILL ALIVE.

Abraham Rechtman, pp. 123–24.

12. KADESH AND YORTSAYT

Never before in my life have I been the privileged character I am now. What is the reason for this? As you know, my father, Peisy the cantor, died the first day of *shvues*, and I was left an orphan.

The first day after *shvues* my brother and I began to say *kadesh*, the prayer for the dead. It was my brother Elye who taught me how to say it. My brother Elye is a devoted brother, but a poor teacher. He is quick tempered and he beats me. Taking the prayer book in his hand, that first day after *shvues*, he sat down with me and began to teach me the words: "Yisgadal v'yiskadash shmey rabo." He expected me to know it by heart right away. He repeated it with me one time after another from beginning to end and then told me to say it by myself. I tried, but it didn't work.

The first few lines weren't bad, but after that I always got stuck. Every time this happened he prodded me with his elbow, and said my mind must be elsewhere (how did he guess?). I started out like a flash, but again, after a few lines, I got stuck. The words wouldn't come. So he grabbed me by the ear and shouted, "If Father could only get up from his grave now and see what a stupid child he had! . . ."

"Then I wouldn't have to be saying *kadesh* for him!" I said, promptly. For this I caught a juicy slap on the cheek. Hearing the noise my mother cried out, "God be with you! What are you doing? Whom are you slapping? Have you forgotten that the child is an orphan?"

Congratulate me. I know the whole *kadesh* by heart now —every bit of it. In the synagogue I stand on a bench and rattle it off without a pause. I have a good singing voice— inherited from my father—a real soprano. All the boys stand around me and envy me. The women weep. Some of the men give me a kopek. Yossi the *noaed's* son, Henekh with the squinting eye (who is by nature very jealous), stands in front of me and sticks out his tongue. He is eager —he is anxious—he is dying—to make me laugh. But just to spite him I won't laugh. One time Arn the *shames* caught him at it, and grabbing him by the ear, led him to the door. Served him right!

Sholom Aleichem (1946).

13. THE SPIRITS CONGREGATE

The spirit is like a flame, that is why flickering lights can be seen in a cemetery at night. Spirits converse together, study, and do pretty much what they did in this life. Occasionally a spirit council is called to judge disputes between the latest arrivals and other members of the company. On the new moon and the seventh day of *sukes* and probably on other nights as well, they congregate in prayer meetings, when they talk about the living. Some nights they gather in the *shul*, where, clothed in ghostly prayer shawls, they conduct their own weird service. Once a man who fell asleep in a *shul* and was locked in by the *shames* awoke to find himself in the midst of such a spirit congregation. To his amazement he discerned the forms of two men who were still among the living. Sure enough, within a few days these two passed away. The custom of knocking on the *shul* door before entering in the morning probably intended to warn the spirit worshipers that it was time to leave.

Joshua Trachtenberg.

14. THE SPIRITS CELEBRATE

Karpl the Fiddler was a very pious Jew. He would play only at poor weddings and took no pay. He made a modest living as a dyer. Purim was the happiest day for him. He would take his fiddle in hand and go from house to house regaling his friends. Everywhere he went people treated him to a glass of wine and a piece of cake.

One Purim evening, Karpl drank one *lekhayem* too many and got lost on his way home, until he found himself in front of the big *shul*. From there he knew the way blindfolded, for what Jew doesn't? Just as he was about to return home, he noticed that the windows of the *shul* were all lit up and that sounds of prayer were coming from inside. He was reminded of the saying: "Do not avoid the Lord when you pass His holy abode." Thereupon, he promptly stepped into the *shul* forgetting that on the night of Purim Jews never pray Ma'ariv together and certainly not at such a late hour.

In he went to find the *shul* packed with people and the place as brightly lit as paradise. Everyone was in a festive mood and when they caught sight of his fiddle they led him up onto the *bime* with great rejoicing. But Karpl was seized with fear. He couldn't lift a muscle—whom should he see around him but dozens of friends who had long since passed away! Only now did he realize that he was surrounded by dead souls. He remained paralyzed until several of his former friends approached him and, with friendly smiles, asked him to play the same Purim melody that he used to play at their homes when they were still alive. "Fear not," they said. "You should only be as secure among the living as you are now among the dead. Play, and we will reward you far more than the living ever did."

These words comforted him and he played his Purim melody very well, so well in fact, that he was asked to replay it three times. Then they recited hymns and asked him to play other tunes. Karpl was such a success that he was brought before the rabbi who thanked him heartily, saying:

"God shall bring you as much joy as you have brought us on this Purim. Tell me, how shall we repay you? You know who we are. We have no money and we know that you never accept payment."

"There is something I want," said Karpl. "Firstly, I want to know who it is I'm speaking with. Secondly, I want to receive a definite sign so that I can prove to the townsfolk that I actually met you, and, thirdly, I want you to teach me some of the melodies that are sung in heaven. I promise that I shall perform these melodies only for the sake of heaven at poor weddings and at special celebrations."

"All three wishes shall be fulfilled," replied the old man. "You wish to know my name. I am Reb Sholem Altarus and, some seventy years ago, I was rabbi in this city. As for a definite sign that you met me personally, I shall tell you a sermon that I delivered on the last Purim before my death. Reb Hirsh Feld who is now an old man of ninety was present." And Reb Sholem did indeed relate his sermon to Karpl the Fiddler. Then Reb Hershl the *khazn* was brought forward and though he was as hoarse as a rusty saw (having died of a lung disease), his melodies penetrated into Karpl's very soul. He taught Karpl a half-dozen melodies, among them the Messiah's triumphal march; the suite which is played when a *tsadek* is escorted into heaven; the song that pilgrims used to sing on the way to the temple in Jerusalem. The remaining three were holiday tunes.

By this time it was almost three in the morning. The bright lights began to dim and the figures became indistinct. Karpl felt a weariness overtake him and he fell asleep on the spot. When he awoke it was well into the morning and the congregation had begun reciting the morning prayers. Karpl found himself behind the door of the *shul* and would have dismissed the whole thing as a dream if not for the sermon and the melodies that he remembered. He repeated the sermon to ninety-year-old Reb Hirsh and played him the wonderful music. Reb Hirsh was in seventh heaven. Soon the whole town knew about it and Karpl was acclaimed a saint. He vowed never to drink on Purim any more.—This is how we know that the dead souls celebrate in *shul* just as we mortals do.

Ayzik-Meyer Dik, pp. 27–32.

15. THE HISTORY OF A SOUL

A soul migrates until it returns to heaven as pure as when it left.
The soul of a *tsadek* becomes the soul of a fish.
The soul of a butcher who eats *treyf* meat becomes the soul of a black crow.
The soul of a dishonest *khazn* becomes the soul of a dog.

Because his prayer was as pleasing to the Lord as a dog's bark.

The soul of an informer becomes that of a parrot. Because he acted like a parrot: spoke the wrong things at the wrong time to the wrong people.

Y. Zelkovitsh, pp. 157–8.
(1938)

UNIT NINE
BREAKUP

Immigrants on their way to America getting a free meal in Warsaw.

1. THE STATISTICAL MISSION (1890)

My first stop was Tishevits. The marketplace is a large square. It is surrounded by blackened, crooked houses, some roofed with straw but the majority with shingle. All are single-story buildings, with wide arcades supported by rotten, yellowed beams. In front of the arcades, not far from each other, stand the market-women over their stalls of bagels, bread, peas, beans, and various fruits.

We walk from house to house, starting from number One. I can see for myself which houses are inhabited by Jews and which by non-Jews. A glance at the window is sufficient. Yellowed windows are a sure sign of the Chosen People, especially broken panes replaced by pillows and sacks. On the other hand, flowerpots and curtains are clear signs that the owner does not have the same claim to poverty. . . . There are exceptions.

A large, strange wooden house makes the worst impression of all. It is larger but also blacker and filthier than all the other houses. The frontage leans over heavily and looks down upon its likeness—also an old, blackened ruin—upon an elderly, emaciated, rickety woman who is busy haggling with her customer—a servant girl with disheveled blond hair—over an addition to a pound of salt.
The *shames* points the old woman out to me: "She is the owner of that house." I was amazed. She's much too poor to own such a house.

"Actually," explains the *shames*, "the house is not exactly hers. She pays only one sixth of the rent. She's a widow, you see, but the heirs, her children, don't live here. So she is called the owner."

"How much rent does the house take in?"

"Nothing."

"How much is it worth?"

"About 1500 rubles."

"And takes in nothing?"

"It's empty."

"Why's that?"

"In our town almost everyone owns his own property. If there is someone who needs to rent, he doesn't want to heat a room of his own. He usually pays a few rubles a year for the corner of a room in someone's home. Who needs such big rooms for himself?"

"So why did they build such a big house in the first place?"

"Who knows—in the old days! Today there's no need for such a—."

"Poor woman."

"Why's that? She has her own salt stand and earns a few rubles a week, of which 28 rubles a year go for property tax and the rest is enough to live on. What else does an old woman need? She's sewn her shrouds already. . . ."

2. THE MASKIL

Don't ever think Tishevits is the end of the world! No sir, they've even got a local *maskil*. An honest-to-goodness *maskil*, one of the old kind. He's never studied, never read, no books, not even a newspaper, but he's a *maskil* out of the blue. He isn't clean-shaven. In Tishevits it's enough that he actually trims his beard. But rumor has it that he cuts and combs his hair even during the days before *yonkiper!* His dress isn't particularly modern. After all, even the barber in Tishevits wears a beard and *kapote* like everyone else. For our *maskil*, polishing his boots and wearing a black ribbon around his throat are quite enough. He keeps a bare remnant of his *peyes* but makes up for it by wearing a

Poor Jewish children around the kitchen table in Lite.

square cap. People refer to him, saying: "He's in the money, a first-rate business. Imagine, all he has are three kids. What more does he need? He's a *maskil!*"

Exactly what qualified him as a *maskil* was hard to discover. Everyone knew he was a *maskil*. That was enough. The whole town calls him a *maskil* and he himself admits it. Most important is his tongue which he lashes out "against God and his Messiah."

As I later discovered, the *maskil* considered me as an ally and was certain that I would stay at his house or, at the very least, that he would be the first to be "written up."

But when the mountain did not come to Mohammed, simply because he didn't know about him, Mohammed came to the mountain.

He caught me as I was interviewing a widow and he barged into the house.

"My dear sir, what are you doing here?"

"Where do you mean?" I asked.

"Do you think I'm one of the peasants? Just because I live in Tishevits doesn't mean that I'm an idiot, that I don't know what's happening in the world. I may live in the dumps, but I know what's going on."

"If you know so much, then why ask?"

The *shames* listened attentively, as did the idlers who had been following my every step. Their faces lit up with ecstasy and I could imagine they were thinking: "Let's just see how two *maskilim* have it out with each other."

"What do I care if you laugh?" he answered angrily. "I can answer back. And whom should I be afraid of?— Tishevits jackasses? Just look at these dumb-heads, will you!"

I was on the spot. I couldn't very well come out and defend Tishevits. The townspeople standing at the window and the door were enjoying the fact that I was having a hard time.

"Tell me, why don't you, just what's all this writing about?"

"Statistics."

"Statistic—shmistic! We've heard that before. But what exactly are you after?"

I explained, not so much for him, but to give the whole community a clearer idea about statistics.

The *maskil* burst into a vulgar laugh. "Go tell that to Tishevits jackasses, not to me! Why do you record how a person lives, if he has a floor or not? What do you care if a person lives without a floor?"

"The point is to show how poor Jews are, because there is a widespread belief—"

"No such thing," he says, cutting me short. "And even if there were, why do you have to know exactly the number of sons and daughters, each one's age, and why record all those illnesses?"

"People doubt whether enough Jews actually serve in the army; you know of course that the official records are false, so we have to prove—"

"Fine, I agree with you. But what about business licenses? Why do you write down whose got one and for how much?"

"To show that—"

But the *maskil* didn't let me finish and shouted angrily:

"Like hell! Meanwhile they'll find out that so-and-so has a license for less than he's selling and they'll fix him good!"

No sooner had he said this than the crowd at the window vanished. The *shames* too beat it and the *maskil*, who probably meant no harm, was left dumbfounded.

The crowd was simply afraid. A few hours later all of Tishevits was buzzing. I was already suspected of being an agent for the tax bureau. They figured that the tax collectors decided that a Jew would uncover crooked dealings better than one of them.

Now I wandered all alone around the market. The shtetl was keeping its distance. Only the *maskil* followed me, step for step. He wanted to talk to me but I couldn't stand the sight of him. As the faces in the street became darker and more somber I began to think of escaping. They were looking at me sideways and plotting something in secret.

Then I decided to make one last try. I remembered that the present *rov* of Tishevits was once a *dayen* in our city and would certainly recognize me or would, at least, swear that I wasn't what they thought I was.

"Where does the rabbi live?" I asked the *maskil*.

He answered joyfully: "Come, I'll take you."

3. THE RABBI OF TISHEVITS

Whoever has not seen the Tishevits rabbi's housecoat will never understand why his third wife, the *rebetsn*, a middle-aged woman, wears thick glasses on her nose. The housecoat looks as if it were patched together from a few threads.

"Two gulden more a week," he sighs, "if the town would only give me that much of a raise, I'd make ends meet. Otherwise it's very bad. I'll win my case yet. They can do without my *dintoyre*. The khasidic *rebeim* take care of that. Also the civil courts. As for questions about kosher food, any *melamed* can handle that. Then there are women's matters, that would be silly to hold out on. But I'll get my way, if I can just wait until elections. They can't possibly hold elections without a *rov*, and what's a town like this, a worthy congregation of Israel, going to do without elections! And if even that won't help, I'll refuse to examine the slaughterers' knives! No meat for anyone! Yes indeed, I've got them now."

It was difficult to distract the *rov* from his own problems. But when the *maskil* promised to make every effort to intercede with kahal on his behalf, he offered us a seat and heard our request.

"Nonsense," he says, "I know you. Tell them, the fools, that I know you."

"They run at the sight of me!"

"What do you mean they run? Who runs? All right; if

you say so, I'll go down with you myself."

"What will you wear?" calls out a woman's voice from behind the stove.

"Well, hand me over the *kapote*," he replies.

"Hand it to you? I just undid the seams!"

"Oh well," says the rabbi, "it's not so terrible. We'll go tomorrow."

I try to explain that it's now only noontime and that I'd hate to waste the rest of the day.

"So what would you like me to do?" asks the rabbi, folding his arms. "Right now the *rebetsn* is fixing my *kapote*."

"Call them up to you!" I plead.

"Call them? Why not? But will they come? They'll heed me like they would any rabbi! Maybe I'd be better off going down in my housecoat?"

"That would not be proper," says the *maskil*. "The Russian watchman is patrolling the streets."

"If it were up to me, I'd do it," says the rabbi. "But if you say no, I won't."

We finally decided that all three of us would call in the crowd from the window. It was no easy thing, however, opening the window. It hadn't been opened in fifteen years. But we finally managed, and the *rov* placed himself in the middle with the *maskil* and myself on each side of him, and the three of us started calling.

The market was full of people and in a few minutes they filled up the room.

"Friends," said the *rov*, "I know this man."

"There'll be no more writing!" several voices called out at once.

The rabbi lost his courage immediately. "If you don't want to, you don't have to," he said quietly.

But the *maskil* jumped up on the table and shouted:

"Jackasses! You have to cooperate! It's for the good of all of us!" And he began telling a pack of lies: that he had discussed the whole matter with me, that he had been joking before, and that I had shown him recommendations from rabbis.

"From which rabbis?"

"From the Parisian rabbi," he went on spouting. "From the Parisian rabbi (he couldn't come up with anyone better), from the London—."

"Jews, let's go home!" yelled someone, cutting him short. "He's not one of us."

"The crowd left us quickly as they had entered. The three of us stayed plus the *shames*, who approached me and said:

"Give me something—for the day."

I gave him a few ten kopek coins. He didn't count them, threw them into his pocket and without saying good-bye—left.

4. THE EMIGRANT

I open the door.

A one-room house without beds, without utensils, the floor covered with hay and straw. In the middle of the room—an overturned barrel surrounded by four grimy children with unkempt hair. On the barrel, a large yellow clay bowl of sour cream. The children scoop from it with moldy green tin spoons in their right hands. In their left hands each child has a piece of bran bread.

In one corner sits a pale woman, tears trickling down on a potato she is peeling. In the opposite corner, the "man of the house" is stretched out on the ground.

"You've troubled yourself for nothing, mister," he mutters to me without getting up. "You've come for nothing. I don't belong here any more."

But seeing my reluctance to leave, he picks himself up ever so slowly.

"Well, where do you want to sit?" he asks regretfully.

I assure him that I can write just as well standing up.

"You won't get anything from me because I'm just waiting for a ship ticket. As you can see, I've already sold everything, even our silverware."

Jewish immigrants on a stop-off in Warsaw.

"Are you a worker?" I ask him.

"A tailor," he replies.

"And why are you leaving?"

"Hunger."

And in fact, hunger was etched out on his face, on her face, and, especially, in the burning eyes of the children over the bowl of sour cream.

"Can't you find work?" I ask.

He shrugs his shoulders as if to say: We don't even talk about that any more.

"Where are you headed for?"

"London. . . ."

Y. L. Perets.

5. THE FIRST JEWISH IMMIGRANTS TO AMERICA FROM EASTERN EUROPE

In 1869–70 the population of northern Poland suffered a severe famine. This food shortage was the cause of the first organized emigration of Jews out of Eastern Europe. Three hundred and seventy-one Jews passed through Prussia: two hundred and ninety-three on their way to New York, two to Paris, one to Constantinople, and the rest to England.

According to the records of a relief station in Prussia these were the occupations of the immigrants.

1 *khazn*	6 clerks	2 butchers
5 *melamdim*	21 merchants	7 shoemakers
2 *shokhtim*	3 carpenters	1 string maker
4 *yeshive-bokherim*	1 candle maker	2 locksmiths
	1 apprentice	7 blacksmiths
9 workers	2 painters	6 tailors
4 tinsmiths	2 farm hands	1 writer
3 bakers	4 dyers	2 musicians
1 wine distiller	1 fisher	5 bricklayers
1 tanner	1 barber	1 miller
2 glass makers	1 cigar maker	1 metal worker
2 maids	4 hatmakers	

Z. Szajkowski.

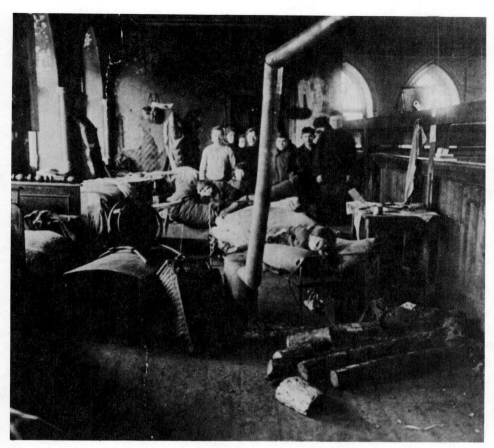

A refugee family camping out in the women's section of the shul. Brisk-de-Lite, 1922.

6. SHLOF, MAYN KIND

Sleep my child, my comfort and beauty,
Hush and go to sleep.
Sleep my life, my only *kadesh*.
Sleep, my little son.

At your cradle sits your mama,
Sings a song and weeps.
Someday, you may know the reason
And what was on her mind.

Your daddy's in America
Little son of mine,
But you are just a child now
So hush and go to sleep.

America is for everyone,
They say, the greatest piece of luck,
For Jews, it's a garden of Eden,
A rare and precious place.

People there eat *khale* in the middle of the week,
Little son of mine,
I'll cook chicken broth for you—
So hush and go to sleep.

Dad will send us twenty dollars
And his picture, too,
And he'll send for us, God bless him,
And bring us there to him.

But till it comes, the magic letter,
Hush, and go to sleep,
Sleep is a precious cure,
So hush and go to sleep.

Sholom Aleichem (1972).

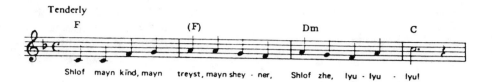

Shlof mayn kind, mayn treyst, mayn shey · ner, Shlof zhe, lyu - lyu - lyu!

Shlof mayn le bn, mayn ka dish ey - ner,

Shlof zhe, zu ne nyu;

Shlof mayn le bn, mayn ka dish ey ner,

Shlof zhe, zu ne nyu.

Shlof mayn kind, mayn treyst, mayn sheyner,
Shlof zhe, lyu-lyu-lyu!
Shlof mayn lebn, mayn kadish eyner,
Shlof zhe, zunenyu.

Bay dayn vigl zitst dayn mame,
Zingt a lid un veynt.
Vest a mol farshteyn mistame
Vos zi hot gemeynt.

In amerike iz der tate
Dayner zunenyu,
Du bist nokh a kind lesate
Shlof zhe, shlof, lyu-lyu;

שלאָף מײַן קינד, מײַן טרייסט, מײַן שיינער,
שלאָף זשע, ליו-ליו-ליו !
שלאָף מײַן לעבן, מײַן קדיש איינער,
שלאָף זשע, זונעניו.

בײַ דײַן וויגל זיצם דײַן מאַמע,
זינגם אַ ליד און וויינם,
וועסם אַ מאָל פֿאַרשטיין מסתמא
וואָס זי האָם געמיינם.

אין אַמעריקע איז דער מאַמע
דײַנער, זונעניו,
דו ביסם נאָך אַ קינד לעת-עתה,
שלאָף זשע, שלאָף, ליו-ליו !

283

Dos amerike iz far yedn,
Zogt men, gor a glik,
Un far yidn a gan-eydn,
Epes an antik.

Dortn est men in der vokhn
Khale, zunenyu,
Yaykhelekh vel ikh dir kokhn,
Shlof zhe, shlof, lyu-lyu.

Er vet shikn tsvantsik doler,
Zayn portret dertsu,
Un vet nemen, lebn zol er,
Undz ahintsutsu.

Biz es kumt dos gute kvitl,
Shlof zhe, zunenyu.
Shlofn iz a tayer mitl,
Shlof zhe, shlof, lyu-lyu.

דאָס אַמעריקע איז פֿאַר יעדן,
זאָגט מען, גאָר אַ גליק,
און פֿאַר ייִדן אַ גן־עדן,
עפּעס אָן אַנטיק.

דאָרטן עסט מען אין דער װאָכן
חלה, זונעניו,
ייַכעלעך װעל איך דיר קאָכן,
שלאָף זשע, שלאָף, ליו־ליו.

ער װעט שיקן צװאָנציק דאָלער,
זײַן פּאָרטרעט דערצו,
און װעט נעמען, לעבן זאָל ער,
אונדז אַהינצוצו.

ביז עס קומט דאָס גוטע קװיטל,
שלאָף זשע, זונעניו,
שלאָפֿן איז אַ טײַער מיטל,
שלאָף זשע, שלאָף, ליו־ליו.

7. THE SHTETL UNDERGROUND

To maintain order, Sislevitsh had a chief of police and a constable. In 1905 eight policemen joined that force. The chief of police was the ruler of the town; his word was law. Frequently, this official would tyrannize the shtetl, but we almost always found a way to calm him down. As a rule, he was not opposed to little gifts. In 1903, a new chief of police came to our town. He started a vigorous campaign right away against "subversive" elements, particularly among the young people. His zeal knew no bounds. Once he found two young men on the outskirts of the town, reading a book. He had them arrested and questioned for two weeks. Subsequently, they were released. Another time, he raided a meeting in the forest of the illegal Jewish labor organization, the Bund, and arrested ten young men and three women. The young people maintained that their gathering was a harmless outing and, since no forbidden literature was found on them, they were released. The young roughnecks of the town decided to teach the chief of police a lesson. On a dark night they set fire to the woodshed of a school on the outskirts of the town. By law, the chief of police had to be present at a fire. A group of young people ambushed him and beat him up. This experience considerably diminished his zeal for discovering conspiracies. The constable, too, who had started to peer into closed shutters, was given a beating while somewhat drunk.

Controversies in Town

The town, consisting exclusively of *misnagdim* (opponents of Khasidism), had a synagogue and three houses of study in which services were conducted three times a day. There were excellent libraries in each of the holy houses and, at dusk, between the afternoon and evening services, numerous groups were busy studying the Bible, the Talmud, or some ethical text. Those who needed it had a teacher who taught them the weekly portion of the Bible on Friday evenings and Saturdays. The older men were strictly orthodox, but they tolerated the younger generation who were liberal in their religious views. The young people, too, avoided publicly offending the orthodox.

On one occasion, however, a sharp conflict broke out between the young and the old generations. A wandering preacher came to town. He could speak well and strongly opposed "progressives," whom he attacked in his sermons. These sermons led to arguments between some of the parents and their children. Once, several young people entered the *besmedresh* and interrupted one of the preacher's customary speeches against them with "boos." Some of the older people defended the preacher and a fight began. During the fight a butcher called out that the young people were right and the preacher was causing trouble in the community. The older people revenged themselves on the butcher by prohibiting him from selling kosher meat. The prohibition would have ruined the butcher if the Jewish Labor Bund had not sent an ultimatum to the trustees of the *besmedresh* to repeal the prohibition, or else. . . . The trustees were frightened and lifted the ban.

Political Parties

The first political party in our town was the Zionist organization. On a winter night, some time in 1898 or 1899, the Jews were called to the *besmedresh* where an out-of-town preacher and some local men spoke to them and sang Hebrew songs. As far as I can remember, the speakers asked the audience to become members of the Zionist organization, and the response was good. The work of the organization consisted mainly in collecting money for the Jewish National Fund. Before every Zionist Congress there was some activity in town concerning the election of delegates. The Zionist organization also opened and maintained the Hebrew school in town.

The Jewish Labor Bund got started in our town about 1900. By 1905 it had grown into a powerful organization whose members came from all classes of the Jewish population. The organization called and conducted the strikes in the leather factories and in the shops.

The heroic date in the history of the Jewish Labor Bund in Sislevitsh was the year 1905. In the fall of that year a peculiar tension was felt in town. People waited eagerly for mail to arrive to find out the latest news. Rumors of pogroms spread and there was talk of organizing a Jewish self-defense force. Money was needed to buy arms, and the following way of obtaining the funds was decided upon, although the organization was, in principle, opposed to stealing.

The town had two government stores for the sale of liquor and the Bund decided to stage a hold-up in one of these stores. Once a month there was a fair in town, where

286

A May Day rally of the Labor Zionist movement in Khelm, 1932. The well- dressed demonstrators are carrying red flags and Yiddish placards: Long live the first of May! Long live Labor Zionism!

peasants and merchants would come from the neighboring villages and towns. During the fair the government stores made a lot of money. The day of the fair was, therefore, chosen for the hold-up. Sometime in October 1905, in the evening following the day of the fair, as soon as the front door was closed, several of the members of the Bund entered the store, held up the salesgirls, and left with the money. Although the street was full of people and police, no one noticed what had happened. When the salesgirls shouted that they had been held up, no one believed them. There were rumors that the girls took the money themselves and concocted the story of the burglary. It was only after the Bund published a proclamation taking responsibility for the crime that the girls were released.

The attack was well organized, except for one serious slip. The men did not wear disguises, and everyone in the shtetl knew everyone else. So the salesgirls identified them. One fled abroad; the other was arrested and faced a long term at hard labor. After several months' imprisonment, he was freed on bail of five hundred rubles and then left the country. With the help of the chief of police a false death certificate for the arrested was written. The certificate was given to the district attorney, and he returned the bail money. In the end the whole affair cost considerably more than it had brought in.

8. STRIKES AND LOCKOUTS

In 1900–1901 the Bund called the first strike in the leather factories in town. Members of the organization assembled a large number of workers and together they made a list of their demands. These included higher wages, and a twelve-hour workday, from seven in the morning to seven in the evening, with a break of one and half hours for breakfast and one hour for lunch. A general assembly of the workers was called where these demands were discussed. Each worker then swore on a pair of *tfiln* that no one would go back to work until all their demands were met.

When the strike committee presented the demands to the factory owners, there was no reaction. The latter regarded the entire affair as a boyish prank. On the following day, however, when not a single worker reported for work, the factory owners began to take a serious view of the strike. They tried to break the solidarity of the workers by promising higher wages to the older workers. The workers remained unmoved by the tempting offers. The oath on *tfiln* acted as a powerful deterrent.

The strike lasted only a short time and ended with complete victory for the workers. The factory owners gave in to their demands.

A second general strike in the leather factories took place in the summer of 1904. This was during the Russo-Japanese war, when the profits of the factory owners were high and the cost of living had gone up. The Bund was by that time firmly established in town and conducted organizational and educational activities for the workers. It was therefore not difficult to call a strike. The Bund called a general assembly of leather workers in a forest one and a half miles from town. A speaker from the neighboring town of Wolklowysk was invited. The speaker presented the demands to the workers for their approval. These demands were: 1) a raise of about 34% in wages; 2) a nine-hour workday, from eight to five; 3) job security—that is, no worker could be fired without good reason; 4) medical insurance—the employer had to pay the medical bills of a worker who was sick.

That evening the demands were presented to the factory owners. They were ready to talk about a reduction in working hours and a raise in pay, but not about the other two demands. They were particularly angry with the demand for job security which to them seemed unfair. The strike committee refused to discuss some demands without the others, and they called a strike. It lasted three weeks and again ended in a victory for the workers. The new working conditions were in effect until the end of 1907. The period of 1904–1907 was known as the good years for the workers in the leather industry.

In November 1907 the tide turned against the workers. The factory owners called a meeting of the workers where they announced that of the four conditions they had won in the previous strike, all but one would be abolished. If the workers refused to agree, all the factories would close down. The workers refused to give in to this blackmail and called another strike. This was going to be a strike to end all strikes, because the factory owners were using it as a test case for the entire region. Likewise the workers asked the tanners' union for help and were sent a professional organizer to advise and guide the strikers. He was an energetic young man and a good speaker who inspired confidence. He also traveled throughout the district to collect funds for the strikers.

Most of the strikers did not need help. Before the strike, they had earned decent wages and managed to accumulate some savings. A few of the unskilled workers, whose earnings were considerably lower, needed help. They were given one and a half rubles a week, if single, and three rubles, if married. To keep up the spirit of the strikers, daily meetings were held. Since it was winter, and assemblies in the open were impossible, the strikers met daily, except *shabes*, in the *besmedresh*. The trustees of the *besmedresh* didn't object. The majority of the Jewish population sympathized with the strikers.

There were at first no problems with the police. At the time of the strike the chief of police was a quiet and liberal man. He promised not to interfere as long as the strike was conducted peacefully. It was difficult, however, to conduct the strike peacefully, and a clash took place between the strikers and the police. The strikers had pinned their hope

The German army entering the Jewish quarter of Mlave (near Warsaw) during World War I.

on the factory owners' need for money to cover their outstanding loans. Instead, the factory owners decided to raise cash by selling half-finished leather. This led to the clash. In the seventh or eighth week of the strike, the strikers were told that a factory was shipping half-finished leather to other towns. A group of strikers left for the factory to prevent the loading of the leather. At the entrance to the factory yard several policemen refused to let the strikers enter. When they tried to force their way into the yard, the police fired a shot in the air. The strikers withdrew and marched to the homes of the factory owners, demanding that the police be removed from the factories. One factory owner was beaten up. The chief of police called for soldiers to patrol the streets. Tension continued to mount.

Fortunately, the strikers' committee kept calm. An ultimatum was presented to the factory owners to withdraw the police and the soldiers from the factories and the streets, or they would bear the responsibility for the consequences. Soon the police and soldiers withdrew, and the strike continued peacefully.

When the strike entered its fifteenth week, the spirits of the workers were low. Aid from the neighboring towns was irregular. *Peysekh* was approaching and the strikers needed money. The demands for a settlement became more urgent. The factory owners, too, wanted a solution. A week later the strike was settled with a compromise on wages. The workers won the other demands.

What really happened was that both sides lost. The workers, sixteen weeks' wages. The factory owners, the loss of production and, above all, the loss of markets. During the strike some of the merchants who had formerly bought their leather in Sislevitsh found other sources of supply and kept these connections even after the strike was over.

Abraham Ain (1949), pp. 89–112.

9. THE REVOLT OF THE TALES WEAVERS IN KOLOMAY

The revolt of the *tales* weavers in Kolomay was the signal for class struggle in the Jewish community of Galicia. The strike caused terrific excitement in the non-Jewish world. Four hundred Jewish workers, prayer-shawl makers, mostly elderly people, Jews with beards and *peyes*, went out on strike. A description of the strike is found in the telegrams sent by newspaper correspondents.

No. 15. August 1, 1892. Correspondence from Kolomay

A strike of 400 Jewish weavers, *tales* workers, has broken out here. There is general solidarity and the need is terrible.

No. 16. August 15, 1892

The strike of the Jewish weavers. The inevitable class struggle has broken out among the Jews. Who could have imagined that wretched men, weak from disease and tuberculosis, would rise up to strike? These religious workers were forced to strike against their exploiters who are just as orthodox as they are. The wretched conditions of the Silesian weavers is child's play compared with the poverty of the Jews here. They earn 1–3 gulden per week for 15 hours work a day. On July 24, two hundred workers met in the rabbi's house. Comrade Zetterbaum gave a speech which lasted an hour. He described the woeful plight of those assembled. Trembling and emaciated old men supported him and called out that they will beat up those who do not want to strike, even if they have to pay for it with months in jail.

In order to make sure that no one would go back to work before all the demands were met, the committee demanded that all workers take an oath on the holy Torah.

No. 17. September 1, 1892

The successful development of the weavers' strike in Kolomay is thanks to the rabbis of the town. They put all the workers under oath that, on the pain of a curse, they dare not go to work as long as their demands have not been met.

No. 23. December 1, 1892

Kolomay. The strike is broken. Ten *khasidim*, mostly fathers of families with five or six children, broke their oath upon the holy Torah with the excuse that they would starve to death and that during the holidays they were forced into debt. The factory owner persuaded them to return to work. The pleas of the workers, their struggles and threats were all in vain. Police guarded the factory during the day and slept there at night. The appeal of the rabbi made no impression upon these "ultra-pious" *khasidim*. Three months of struggle and hunger exhausted the workers. The Jewish owner has shown in this whole business that he will trample upon the laws of the Jewish religion whenever it is in the interest of his business.

Jacob Bross.

10. KHAYEM-LEYBELE THE TOWN ZIONIST

Khayem-Leybele was the chief trumpeter of the Tishevits fire brigade. Actually, he was commander-in-chief as well and ran the group with an iron hand.

"No questions, boys! When there's a fire, follow orders! There can be only one chief and he sees the danger. Consider yourself soldiers and do what you're told!" Then he would end with his favorite phrase: "You don't have to wait until the Messiah comes to learn how to handle your hardware!"

It was just this phrase, which he used whenever possible and in different versions, that earned him the nickname Leybele the Heretic.

He lived in a two-room house with a den on Tanners' Street. In his den he ran a private school. By day he taught girls to read and write Russian and, in the evening, well-to-do boys would come to learn arithmetic.

"These days such things are necessary," said the fathers whose sons were already helping them out in the store. "After all, you can't always rely on Arn-Moyshe's honesty."

Visitors to his house reported that he had a portrait of the tsar hanging in his den, signed in person by the Governor himself. In the main room, near the *mizrekh*, a photograph of a man stared down from the wall. He was wearing a black frock-coat with silver lapels. No hat on his head, and a square trimmed beard just like a nobleman of old. His glowing eyes penetrated anyone who entered the room and they almost forced the visitor to read the inscription over the photo:

"If you want it, it is no fairy-tale."

Khayem-Leybele could stand for hours in front of this portrait. "The greatest Jew of our times," he said, tears forming in his eyes. "He found the true path to redemption."

"Who knows what that crackpot's talking about and what he sees in that face? And what's that bridge in the picture? I could almost swear it's our very own Long Bridge! What's he looking for anyway?"

"The Messiah, no doubt," says someone with a smile.

"But they say that he thought he himself was the Messiah."

"All he needs is a white donkey," says the town jokester.

Once, when the Rizhiner *khasidim* were seated at the late *shabes* afternoon meal, Reb Moyshe Yitskhok put in a good word for Khayem-Leybele.

There's an old story that when the Bal Shem Tov saw that Satan's close watch would prevent him from reaching the land of Israel, he realized that his disciples would be

295

A woman dentist working in the OSE clinic in Mariampol, 1923.

the ones to find the proper path. Later, the Kotsker *rebe* put so much energy into preparing a few select young men to bring the Messiah that he eventually gave up and locked himself into a room. The Rizhiner, of blessed memory, tried to fool Satan by adopting worldly manners in his outward life, but then the other sages were against it. Sooner or later the proper path must be found. Each generation tries its own way. Nowadays young people are trying it, but as long as they do so with faith and true devotion, we mustn't belittle them. It is said that kings and ministers receive them and listen to their pleas. Who knows who will be privileged to be the messenger of God?

And so it was that people had a mixed attitude to Khayem-Leybele and his house. On the one hand they avoided him, on the other—they respected him. Rumor had it that whenever the inspector came to his school, Khayem-Leybele would cover the portrait with some old tapestry. But whenever he finished writing a petition or a document for someone, he would unlock his drawer and carefully take out a small thin box painted blue and white and would present it as if it were a treasure.

"With a few pennies you too can contribute to the effort of redeeming the land of Israel from gentile hands."

If the client threw something into the box, Khayem-Leybele's face would light up. He would gleefully replace the box in the drawer. Then he would take out a stamp with Dr. Herzl's picture and give it to him, saying: "Stick it on to one of your books for good luck."

If the client refused or even attacked Khayem-Leybele for dragging him into matters that were of no concern to him, then the "Heretic" would turn red with rage:

"It isn't only the land that has been forsaken. The day will come, just you wait, when a child of yours will bless the sweat of those who will till the redeemed soil." Saying this, he would reach into his pocket, take out some of the money the client had just paid him, and drop it into the box.

Jacob Zipper, pp. 297–301.

11. FRADL, THE BLACK SHEEP OF THE FAMILY

Fradl, the only brunette among all her redhaired half-brothers and sisters, was a student in Zvihil. She liked to dress up and speak Russian. From time to time she came to Bilgoray to see her father, but the moment she arrived the arguments began.

This Fradl was considered the black sheep of the family. The *khasidim*, who were my grandfather's enemies, claimed that because of his contempt for their *rebeim* he had been cursed with a heretic granddaughter, a convert who spoke gentile languages and wore patent-leather shoes. To me, the young woman from the strange city was like a visitor from a far-off planet. I gaped when she took a cigarette from Uncle Joseph's box and let the smoke drift from her mouth and nose at the same time, all the while bickering furiously with her father about some mysterious inheritance from her mother that he had allegedly squandered, or about the fact that he didn't care about her.

Uncle Joseph didn't punish his daughter for her un-Jewish ways. But he did say that she was wasting her time by going to school instead of staying in Bilgoray and accepting a match with some eligible young man.

Fradl shrieked in a way no decent Jewish woman would dare in Bilgoray. "Marry some Itshe Meyer and rot in this dump? Not me. I'd rather jump in the river. . . ."

"Then what are you looking for?" her father asked, blowing smoke in her face.

"To study and become a dentist," she shot back, blowing smoke in his face.

The word "dentist" filled me with such pride and awe that I hardly dared breathe. I could only keep staring at this fantastic creature with the cigarette bobbing between her lips and wonder how she could be my blood relative.

I. J. Singer, pp. 124–25.

12. TISHEVITS UNDER AUSTRIAN RULE

From the very first days following his arrival in Tishevits, the town knew that Kommandant Herr von Felsenberg was not one of those officers who achieved fame in the war and whose sole desire was to show off his power in public and rake in the profit in private.

"A tough cookie!" was the immediate reaction when the shtetl saw him take his first stroll through the marketplace and carefully observe the half-empty stores and broken arcades through his monocle. There was something about the way he walked and carried his pointed cane that commanded respect. He walked without guards and unarmed, silent and straight as a rod. He was tall and thin, with carefully trimmed, graying sideburns. It seemed as if he saw through everything, not only by means of the monocle on his crooked nose, but also on account of his entire being which was always on the alert.

"The arcades must be repaired at once," he said turning to Hershke the wartime mayor who followed his every step. "There's no shortage of wood and certainly not of idlers." Then with a smile he added, not in his usual German but in Galician Yiddish: "We can't waste any time, you know, Mr. Mayor. We pay good wages for all work done!"

Having made the rounds he strode back to the Brick House where command headquarters were now situated. In the evening he reappeared on Greblye Street and gave warm greetings to the young people who were making their way across the Old Bridge to the hills and the nobleman's orchard. When he noticed the closed-down water mill he wrote something down and that same evening he called for

An Austrian officer who might be our von Felsenberg, poses in front of a phony backdrop with two Jewish merchants. Deblin, Lublin province during World War I.

Moyshe the Miller. Moyshe's steam mill located in the Yard was operating on a triple shift just for the army.

"The water mill must be reopened for the civilian population," said the Kommandant. "This way you won't have to rob the Kaiser's supplies in order to feed the town and the surrounding villages. There is one condition," he added forcefully, "There must be no smuggling. If not, you will pay with your heads!"

He would allow as much grain as necessary to be brought in, and each flour merchant would receive his due according to the ration cards. But if anyone should try to cheat, let him be warned that von Felsenberg himself was in charge and he would, personally, have anyone breaking the regulations shipped off to Hungary for forced labor.

By ordering the arcades repaired and the water mill reopened, von Felsenberg won the everlasting praise of the shtetl. The smugglers and profiteers, on the other hand, cursed his every move, because whenever something was being smuggled in, he would appear out of the blue. Day and night he kept watch over the town as if he had a thousand eyes. He knew all the tricks of the trade and always showed up just as a wagonload of goods was trying to steal its way in or out of town. He knew about the false bottoms in the wagons, about the hollowed harnesses where soap or tobacco or other lucrative items could be hidden. He wasn't even embarrassed to feel the heavy belts that the smugglers wore then around their broad slacks. And, good-naturedly, he would suggest to the young women who accompanied them to "shake themselves out a bit" so that the trip would be more comfortable. "A woman is not a smuggler, but merely a companion. Isn't that so?" he would say with a smile as he requested her to change into different clothes and try to look somewhat slimmer. Pleas were of no avail. "War is war" was his ready answer as he politely confiscated the contraband and issued a receipt in return. "Everything will be reimbursed." The only exception was for sugar and salt. These items he would not confiscate but would order them to be brought to the stores and would personally oversee that the amount each merchant received was taken off his ration card.

The town had to admit: "He has a conscience after all." He sees to it that the shtetl should not lose those products that were very hard to come by. Naturally, people tried to butter him up by sending him a gift of thanks for his "fatherly concern" for the town. Sure enough, the very next morning he appeared with the gift at the rabbi's house and ordered him to distribute it among the poor. Furthermore he instructed the *rov* to announce on *shabes* in all the houses of study that if anyone repeated the gesture, he would be punished with the full force of the law.

"A tough cookie." There were no two ways about it. The only hope was that he wouldn't last long. Felsenberg did last, however, at least long enough to leave the town with something that, although the elders were dead set against it, the younger generation received with joy, and they learned to regard him as one of their allies.

13. THE SMUGGLERS EXPOSED

One evening, as von Felsenberg, dressed to the hilt, was taking his usual stroll, he stopped in front of Arn-Moyshe's station house and watched one of the wagon drivers pull in with a wagon packed with goods. Arn-Moyshe obviously had a permit to transport these wares and the guards had already examined them at the Long Bridge. Otherwise the wagon wouldn't be moving along in full view. But with the Kommandant standing there, Khayem the Tough was not about to take any chances, and he jumped down from the wagon to show his papers. Herr von Felsenberg answered with a smile and without saying a word pointed his cane to a box protruding from among the sacks and packs. This meant that he wanted the box to be opened in his presence.

And so the wagon pulled into the station house and a short while later out came the Kommandant in a great hurry followed—not by Khayem the Tough and Arn-Moyshe, but by Buniml, Oyzer's son and Yantshe the son of the flour merchant. Both boys were serious Talmud students and had never been mixed up with smuggling. The Jews of the market were astounded and could not for the life of them figure out what the two boys were doing in the dingy station house and why they were following the Kommandant to the Brick House. Until word got out that the box in question contained a few dozen Yiddish and Hebrew books that the older students secretly borrowed from the regional library and planned to distribute secretly and read in *shtiblekh* and attics, far from the prying eyes of their fathers.

This practice had already begun before the war, when the two older brothers of these boys left for Galicia to start a new life. Before leaving they divulged the well-kept secret that in the attic of the Rizhiner *shtibl*, hidden away among the torn volumes and pages of sacred books, was a small shelf with skinny booklets that were worth looking into. How the booklets got there no one knew, but since one secret leads to another, the boys soon discovered that Berish Glazier's attic also contained a similar treasure that his only son guarded with his life. Something new is always added to that collection because when he goes off to the district capital for goods he always returns with library books hidden away among the packages. Of course, not everyone was let in on the secret, but those who had the right to know waited eagerly for Saturday night when their fathers usually gathered in Berish the Glazier's living room for the traditional khasidic feast. The boys came along supposedly to join in the singing, and to learn about Khasidism. But late at night when it was time to go, each of them had a little book skillfully tucked away in his pants.

The first difficult years of the war put an end to this, but as soon as some order was restored, there were new candidates to accompany their fathers to the district capital and to bring back the secular literature. Now Buniml and Yantshe were in charge of operations. No one in their *shtibl* would have guessed it. They were among the most diligent students and hardly ever went out for a walk with the other young people. "The war hasn't affected them," their fathers would say with pride when they heard of other sons who were caught reading secular books. True, there were a growing number of young men and women who had been learning to read and write Russian in Moyshe Elye's house, but these were all tailor and cobbler apprentices and the like. Whatever Russian the Talmud students managed to study was done in secret and late at night in the *besmedresh* or *shtibl*. Since the war, even the children of the well-to-do were showing up for lessons at Moyshe Elye's house, who was now teaching German rather than Russian. As for the young people of the working class, they studied together and no longer feared to go walking arm-in-arm (boys and girls, that is) singing songs in broad daylight.

The children of the khasidic merchants were nowhere near as daring. Boys and girls took separate walks on *shabes* afternoon. On "lover's lane" under the Long Bridge, a boy and girl might "accidentally" bump into each other, but in order to avoid trouble, boys of the same *shtibl* made a point of keeping out of each other's way. Now all the precautions had more or less exploded, once Buniml and Yantshe were caught red-handed. If *they* were suspect, who wasn't?

Had the story of the smuggled books been discovered in a different way, without the kommandant being mixed in, Oyzer the notion seller and the flour merchant would not have made an appearance in the market, but would have locked themselves up with their sons and made it quite clear who was in charge and what the consequences were. But since it hadn't happened in this way, the two fathers, for

The Shtern family. Taken in Tishevits in the early 1930s by the town photographer. From left to right. Bottom row: A niece, Yekhiel Shtern, Avrom Shtern (Reb Avrom the shoykhet in unit IX and Dovid dayen in unit IV), Gitl Shtern (the shoykhet's wife). Sore Shtern (Yekhiel's wife). Top row: Shifre Shtern-Krishtalka, Yisroel Shtern, Hene Shtern-Marder. Missing: Jacob Zipper-Shtern and Sholem Shtern who were already in Canada. Courtesy of Jacob Zipper.

fear of other consequences, rushed off to the Brick House to plead for their sons.

To their amazement, von Felsenberg received them with open arms and their sons were comfortably seated in his office, pleased as can be about something they had just heard.

"Please, have a seat," said the Kommandant. "These are fine sons you have here. Very well-read, indeed." And before the fathers could say another word, von Felsenberg sat down in his armchair and began criticizing them:

"It's disgraceful that, in the twentieth century, books of knowledge should have to be smuggled in. Knowledge is light, and I have long since wondered where the local young people got the little knowledge they have. Now I understand, but the smuggling cannot go on. The young people who thirst for knowledge must have free access to it. I shall take the matter into my own hands. On the middle floor of this building there is a large empty room. From now on this room will be a gathering place and reading room for the youth of Tishevits. They will no longer have to waste their days in foolishness. The Austrian Empire is anxious to spread learning among its people. Young people must be taught!"

The two older men were at their wits' end, having realized that matters were actually much worse than they had imagined.

"But Herr Kommandant!" they blurted out.

"No 'buts' about it. It's all decided. These young men are in charge of setting up a library and hiring the proper people to teach courses, in language, art, and science. . . ."

And this is how the first legal gathering place was established for the young people of Tishevits. We called it the Third Floor *Shtibl.*

Abridged from Jacob Zipper, pp. 104–116.

14. GITL THE SHOYKHET'S WIFE

The townsfolk of Tishevits called her Gitl the *shoykhet's* wife, but for us small-fry she was known as Aunt Gitele. We had mixed feelings about her. On the one hand we loved her, but on the other, we were also scared stiff. That's because whenever we hurt ourselves playing, mother would rush us off to see Aunt Gitele.

Obviously it wasn't Gitl's fault if we had sprained an arm or leg, and we knew that she'd straighten things out, but before the visit was over, we were sure to end up screaming. First she'd rub the injured limb with rubbing alcohol or vinegar. But no matter how gently she rubbed and how carefully she tried to reset the bone, it would hurt like crazy.

It was even worse when Reb Avrom the *shoykhet* was at home, because he would take over from her and she would try to tell him what to do and what not to do:

"Not so tight! Don't you see it's only a child! Good grief, he's ready to pass out." Then she would bandage up the limb and it was all over. Before we left she gave us a biscuit or piece of cake dunked in berry juice to ensure a speedy recovery.

Aunt Gitele would also make sick-calls at our home. That was more fun, because she always prescribed the same remedy: a teaspoon of berry juice and lots of tea. It was only when these two cure-alls didn't work that Aunt Gitele would call a doctor.

The grownups had their own reasons for visiting Gitl the *shoykhet's* wife. They came, not so much for medical treatment, as for advice and consolation. They knew Gitl would not breathe a word to anyone about their visit because "when you speak to Gitl the *shoykhet's* wife, your words disappear like a stone in the sea." She herself hardly spoke at all.

Everything about her was modest. She usually walked through side streets so that no one would see her. She was thin and small. Her dress was simple but clean. She was seldom seen to smile, for as everyone knew "Gitl the *shoykhet's* wife had lost her pride and glory."

The eldest son Yisokher was killed in the First World War. He was at home when the Russian bomb meant for the German arsenal struck him instead. She wasn't even there at the time. She had gone off to another shtetl with the rest of the family. On returning home, she found her husband Avrom standing in front of the ruined house—he had turned gray overnight—and found Yisokher buried in the cemetery.

From then on she took off her marriage wig and wore a simple kerchief instead. She hung up all her festive clothes never to wear them again. She kept her sorrowful eyes from looking at Yisokher's former friends, lest she give them an evil eye. It was only after Reb Avrom the *shoykhet* pleaded with her: "Gitl, you're sinning. God has given and God has taken away. He was our gift only for a while. Have pity on me and on the children"—that Gitl finally suppressed her sorrow. She did the household chores once more, took care of her family, and helped the poor.

There were four *shokhtim* in Tishevits. Three of them were considered paupers. Only of Reb Avrom was it said: "He conducts his household in a grand style." This was because Reb Avrom's home was always open to any visitor in need of a meal or a place to sleep and because Gitl alone among all the slaughterers' wives, gave away the meagre chicken remnants that her husband brought home from the slaughter house twice a week. What no one ever knew was that after giving most of the giblets away to the poor, there was barely enough left to feed her own family.

Gitl brought up her children to follow in her footsteps. Before *peysekh* she would send her daughters to relieve the workers at the *matse* bakery. These bakers had to work non-stop around the clock under the strict supervision of the rabbi. They had to work very fast so that the *matse* dough would not have a chance to rise. The dough had to be kneaded quickly, rolled quickly, cut and punctured quickly and then baked immediately. The hired bakers waited all year for the money they earned in these frantic weeks. But if it weren't for the help of Gitl's daughters, they would hardly be able to stop even to rest.

On Friday evenings, as soon as the candles were lit, Gitl would send her daughters to collect extra *khale* for the poor. Then on *shabes* morning, she would help the daughters divide the pieces into portions which they would hand out.

Gitl observed the Sabbath with her heart and soul. On *shabes* morning she would go with her husband to the Husiatin *shtibl*. She was as loyal a follower of the old Husiatin *rebe* as Reb Avrom was, and she accompanied her husband on his yearly visit to the *rebe*. During services, Gitl was always surrounded by other women who needed help finding the place in the prayer book. And the women knew that if they stayed near Gitl, they had to pray and not gossip. After lunch and the *shabes* nap, Gitl read from the *Tsene-rene*. On the long, hot summer Saturdays, Gitl would often read aloud to her eldest daughter as they both sat outside on the boardwalk. This always attracted women from the neighboring houses who sat around to listen.

Shabes was also the day for paying visits to her close friends. After chanting the traditional Yiddish hymn, "God of Abraham," Gitl would light a candle and welcome the new week of work and sorrow. Besides the standard phrases of this hymn, Gitl would add a personal plea for her son Yankev: "Dear God, blessed be your name, guard and protect all your children, including my forlorn son Yankele who is somewhere in foreign places."

Gitl the *shoykhet's* wife aged before her time. These were terrible years for everyone, especially Jews. Young people couldn't sit still. The shtetl became too small for them, and they set out into the wide world, to the large cities. They wanted to find work, to rebuild society, to steal their way to Palestine, to enter the universities and teachers' colleges. Every so often, Gitl saw off another one of her children as each of them set out into the world—one to another continent, as far away as Canada, the other, meanwhile, only to Vilne. And each time she returned home to stare in silence at Reb Avrom as they both tried to adapt to the ever-growing emptiness. Soon all she had left were the letters and the photographs. Through the mail she became a grandmother; through the mail—a mother-in-law.

Sometimes the house got a new lease on life during *peysekh* or summer vacation when the children came home for a visit. Reb Avrom went over his head in debt to pay their travel expenses—anything to keep Gitl from total despair. He, too, had a hard time making do without the children. He missed them during study, during prayer, during meals. No one left to chat with about politics, about the miserable situation of Jews. Reb Avrom was proud of his children. They could run the world, those sons and daughters of his. Their letters were his consolation.

Meanwhile two of her sons had settled in Canada, and here at home Jews felt the ground burning under their feet. Whoever could had to get out as soon as possible. Gitl and Avrom realized that time was short and they wrote to their sons begging them to bring over the rest of the children. God willing, and if the *rebe* gave his blessing, they too would even join the rest eventually. Her sons' efforts soon saw results. One after another the children left Gitl, "and who knows when we'll see each other again." First the eldest daughter and son-in-law, three days after their marriage. Then the youngest daughter, followed by the third son, his wife and child and, finally—the youngest son.

Gitl and Avrom were left alone. To overcome her longing for the children, Gitl devoted more and more time to helping those in need. She even found the strength to console those other mothers who, like herself, were left without a family.

And when God finally took pity on her and the time came for her to be reunited with her children, Gitl divided up all her belongings among the poor. Some things she distributed to her relatives and close friends. For herself, she took along only the bare necessities.

When the time came for her departure Gitl felt that she was leaving the shtetl to the mercy of the powers of evil. She promised herself and everyone else that she would not rest until she rescued each and every one of them from the impending disaster.

The whole shtetl accompanied her to the Short Bridge where she had previously seen off her own children. There was no one missing in the crowd of well-wishers; even her gentile neighbors were there. Reb Avrom barely managed to drag her away from all her relatives and friends.

He forcibly seated her on the buggy that would drive them to the nearest train station. Shouts and cries accompanied her as the buggy rattled over the bridge and disappeared from sight: "Gitl," they shouted, "How can you leave us here?!"

M. Fisher.

GLOSSARY

álefbeys   The Jewish alphabet.

alíe   The honor of being called up to the Torah reading in the synagogue.

batkhn   Entertainer at a wedding, specializing in humorous and sentimental semi- improvised rhymes.

bélfer   Assistant teacher in the elementary school.

bentshers   Blessers.

besmédresh   Prayer and study house. Small Orthodox synagogue.

besóylem   Cemetery.

bíme   Platform from which the Torah is read.

bókher   (pl. *bókherim*)   Chap, lad, young man.

bris   Circumcision ceremony.

Bund   Jewish Labor Bund, socialist labor party influential in Poland and other East European countries until World War Two.

dáyen   (pl. *dayónim*)   Judge, assistant to rabbi, decides ritual questions and settles disputes.

dintóyre   Law suit before a rabbinical court.

dréydl   (pl. *dréydlekh*)   A top.

éyrev   A wire strung on the circumference of a town to classify it as enclosed private property in which objects may be carried on the Sabbath, according to Jewish law.

farfl   A type of noodle.

gabe   (pl. *gaboim*)   Trustee or warden of a public institution, especially a synagogue.

gartl   Belt worn during prayer.

gemóre   Talmud.

goy   (pl. *góyim*)   A non-Jew, gentile.

gvír Rich man.

haskóle (Haskalah) The Jewish enlightenment movement which flourished in the nineteenth century.

hómentash Triangular Purim cooky filled with poppy seeds and honey or plum preserves.

hosháne rábe The seventh day of Sukkoth, when, according to Jewish lore, every man's fate for the coming year is irrevocably sealed in Heaven.

hoyf (dim. *heyfl*) Yard; court (small yard).

kabóle (Kabbalah) Jewish mystical philosophy.

kádesh (Kaddish) A prayer recited by a mourner, especially by a son for a dead parent.

káhal (also pronounced *kool*) The Jewish community council.

kále Bride.

kaméye Amulet, charm.

kapóte (pl. *kapótes*) Long coat traditionally worn by observant Jews.

khále Challah, a twisted white bread eaten on the Sabbath.

khánike (Hanukkah) The eight-day holiday commemorating the purification of the Temple in Jerusalem by the Maccabees.

khaper Snatcher. A Jew who kidnapped Jewish boys for the Russian draft.

Khásidism (Hasidism) A Jewish religious movement founded in the eighteenth century in Eastern Europe.

khazn (pl. *khazónim*) Cantor.

khévre (pl. *khévres*) Society.

khévre kedíshe Voluntary burial society.

khéyder (pl. *khadórim*) Traditional Jewish elementary school.

khósed (pl. *khasídim*) A follower of Khasidism.

khosn Bridegroom.

khúmesh The first five books of the Bible.

khúpe Wedding canopy; marriage ceremony.

kídesh (Kiddush) Prayer over wine. Sabbath celebration in honor of an occasion.

313

kidesh hashém   Martyrdom; death for being a Jew.

lagbóymer   (Lag B'Omer)   A Jewish spring holiday celebrated by outings.

lamedvóvnik   One of the thirty-six Good Men.

Lilith   Queen of demons in Jewish lore, preying especially on new-born infants.

máged   (pl. *magídim*)   Preacher.

máskil   Follower of the Haskalah.

mátse   (matzah)   Unleavened bread eaten during Passover.

mázltov   Congratulations!

megíle   The Book of Esther, read on Purim.

mekhutónim   Relatives by marriage.

melámed   (pl. *melámdim*)   A teacher of children.

meydl   (pl. *méydlekh*)   Girl.

mezúze   (mezuzah)   A small tube containing an inscribed piece of parchment, attached to the doorpost of Jewish homes.

míkve   Pool for ritual immersion; ritual bath house.

mínyen   Prayer quorum of ten adults, the minimum required for certain religious services.

misnáged   (pl. *misnágdim*)   Observant Jew, opponent of Khasidism.

mitsve   Religious commandment; good deed.

mizrekh   A fixture on the east wall of a Jewish home,   often a picture of Palestine, to mark the direction in which Jerusalem lies.

mogn-dóved   (pl. *mogn-dóvidn*)   Six-pointed star often used as a symbol of Judaism.

párnes   (pl. *parnósim*)   One of the elected heads of the community.

péye   (pl. *péyes*)   Side curl.

péysekh   (Passover)   Jewish holiday commemorating the release of the ancient Hebrew people from slavery in Egypt.

pínkes   (pl. *pinkéysim*)   Book of records, register.

pórets   Lord, landowner.

púrim (Purim) The holiday celebrating the rescue of the Jews from the persecution of the Persian Haman.

púrim-shpil A play performed on Purim.

rébe (pl. *rabéim*) Khasidic master, teacher, rabbi.

rébetsn Rabbi's wife.

rendar Lessee, here, a Jew who leases from a Polish nobleman.

rosheshone (Rosh Hashanah) The beginning of the Jewish New Year.

rov (pl. *rabónim*) Rabbi.

shábes (pl. *shabósim*) Saturday, Sabbath.

shábes-goy Gentile hired to do household chores forbidden to Jews on the Sabbath, e.g. lighting a fire.

shámes Attendant in a synagogue; rabbi's personal assistant.

shmini atséres Eighth day of Sukkoth holiday.

shóykhet (pl. *shókhtim*) Jewish ritual slaughterer.

shtetl (pl. *shtétlekh*) A Jewish market town in Eastern Europe.

shtibl (pl. *shtíblekh*) Small khasidic house of prayer.

shtrayml Fur-edged hat worn by rabbis and khasidic Jews on the Sabbath and holidays.

shul (pl. *shuln*) Synagogue.

shvues (Shavuoth) An early summer holiday celebrating the gathering of the first fruits and the giving of the Torah to the Jews.

síder (Siddur) Daily prayer book.

símkhes-tóyre (Simhath Torah). A Jewish holiday celebrating the completion of the year's reading cycle of the Torah.

súke Booth built during Sukkoth holiday, where meals are eaten.

súkes (Sukkoth) Harvest holiday.

táles (pl. *taléysim*) (Tallith) A striped, tasseled shawl worn by Jews during certain prayers.

táles-kótn Four-cornered tasseled undergarment worn by religious Jews.

tants Dance.

tíshebov (Tisha B'Av) A Jewish day of fasting and mourning to commemorate the destruction of the first and second Temples in Jerusalem.

treyf Forbidden, non-kosher according to Jewish dietary laws.

tsádek (pl. *tsadíkim*) Pious, saintly man; khasidic rabbi.

Tsene-réne A Yiddish translation of the first five books of the Bible, enriched by illustrative stories, traditionally read chiefly by women.

tsholnt A baked dish of meat, potatoes, and vegetables eaten on the Sabbath, kept warm from the day before.

tsítses Tassels of a prayer shawl.

yármlke Prayer cap.

yeshíve School for Talmud study.

yid (pl. *yidn*) Jew.

yíkhes Pedigree, descent, lineage, parentage, aristocracy.

yingl (pl. *yinglekh*) Boy.

yonkíper (Yom Kippur) The day of atonement, most solemn Jewish holiday and fast-day, when every man's fate for the coming year is said to be decided.

yóntef Holiday, festival.

yórtsayt Anniversary of death.

316

SOURCES AND ACKNOWLEDGMENTS

Hirsz Abramowicz, "A Lithuanian Shtetl," Farshvundene geshtaltn. Tsentral-farband fun poylishe yidn in Argentine, Buenos Aires: 1958, 393–396. With the permission of Dina Abramowicz.

Abraham Ain, "Swislocz; Portrait of a Jewish Community in Eastern Europe," trans. by Shlomo Noble. Yivo Annual of Jewish Social Science, IV (1949), 86–114. With the permission of the Yivo Institute for Jewish Research.

Sh. Anski (pseud. Sh. Z. Rappoport), "Mutual Cultural Influences," Folklor un etnografye. Gezamlte shriftn. XV. Vilne–Warsaw–New York: 1925, 257–267.

Ignaz Bernstein, Yidishe shprikhverter un rednsartn [Yiddish proverbs and sayings]. Photo-offset of 2nd ed. Brider Kaminsky, New York: no date, 115.

L. Beylis, "A Local Tale about the Origin of a Proverb," Yidishe shprakh, V (1945), 155–56. With the permission of the Yivo Institute for Jewish Research.

Chayim Nachman Bialik, Aftergrowth and Other Stories, trans. by I. M. Lask. Jewish Publication Society, Philadelphia: 1939, 60–62. With the permission of the publisher.

Gershon Zev Braude and B. Segal, "Rov, rebe, and rabonim," Yidishe shprakh, XXII (1962), 51–52. With the permission of the Yivo Institute for Jewish Research.

Jacob Bross, "The Beginning of the Jewish Labor Movement in Galicia," Yivo Annual of Jewish Social Science, V (1950), 64–65. With the permission of the Yivo Institute for Jewish Research.

Ayzik-Meyer Dik, Alte yidishe zagen oder sipurim [Old Jewish tales] Rom, Vilne: 1876.

M. Fisher [Shifre Krishtalka], "Gitl, the shoykhetke," in Pinkes Tishevits, ed. Jacob Zipper. Irgun yots'e Tishevits b'Yisrael, Tel-Aviv: 1970, 161–169. With the permission of the author.

Joshua Fishman, "Review of Language and Poverty by Frederick Williams." Social Forces, 49, 4 (June 1971), 641–642. With the permission of Social Forces.

F. Freed, ed., Di khakhomim fun Khelm [The wise men of Khelm] Farlag yidish-bukh, Warsaw: 1966.

Devora Fus, Seven Bags of Gold, no. 25 of Israel Folktale Archives Series, ed. by Otto Schnitzler. Haifa, 1969, 15–18. With the permission of Dov Noy.

Moses Gaster, ed., "The Burned Poker and the Angel of Death," Ma'aseh Book. Jewish Publication Society, Philadelphia: 1934, 235–236. With the permission of the publisher.

Mordkhe Gebirtig, "Yankele," translation in A Treasury of Jewish Folksongs by Ruth Rubin. © Schocken Books Inc.: New York, 1950, 30–32. With the permission of the publisher.
Music in The New Book of Yiddish Songs, by Eleanor Gordon Mlotek. © Workmen's Circle Educational Department: New York, 1972, 8–9. With the permission of the publisher.

317

Chaim Gilead, "Bible Games," Yeda-'Am, (May 1959), 13–14.

Eleanor Gordon Mlotek, "In the Days of the Cantonists," Yidisher folklor, I (January 1954), 5. With the permission of the Yivo Institute for Jewish Research.

———. The New Book of Yiddish Songs. Workmen's Circle Educational Department: New York, 1972, iv. With the permission of the publisher.

Naftoli Gross. Mayselekh un mesholim [Stories and parables] with illustrations by Chaim Gross. Aber Press, New York: 1955. With the permission of Chaim Gross.

Marvin Herzog, The Yiddish Language in Northern Poland: Its Geography and History. Mouton, The Hague: 1965. [Chapter two]. With the permission of the publisher.

Abraham Joshua Heschel, "The Eastern European Era in Jewish History," Yivo Annual of Jewish Social Science, I (1946), 100–101. With the permission of the Yivo Institute for Jewish Research.

Irving Howe and Eliezer Greenberg, eds., "How the Sexton went about Awakening the Townsmen for Prayers," in A Treasury of Yiddish Stories. Viking Press, New York, © 1954, 625. With the permission of the publisher. All rights reserved.

Sh. Khalamish (Shlaferman), "Towns in the Lublin District," Yeda-'Am, (May 1951), 22–23.

———, "The Selling of Joseph Play as a Source of Income," Yeda-'Am, (1964), 87–88.

———, "The Selling of Joseph," Yeda-'Am, (Autumn 1965), 132.

Barbara Kirshenblatt-Gimblett, "Moyshe Goy Kodesh" in Traditional Storytelling in the Toronto Jewish Community: A Study in Performance and Creativity in an Immigrant Culture. Ph.D. Dissertation, Folklore, Indiana University, 1972, 127–130. Edited from a taped interview made in 1968. With the permission of the author.

O. Margolis, Di geshikhte fun di yidn in rusland [The history of the Jews in Russia] Moscow: 1930.

Mendele Moykher Sforim, Shloyme reb Khayims in I. Yakhinson, Social-Economic Patterns among Russian Jews in the Nineteenth Century. Kharkov: 1929, 46.

———. The Parasite, trans. by Gerald Stillman. Thomas Yoseloff, New York: 1956, 45–46. With the permission of the publisher.

A. J. Papierna, Zikhroynes [Memoirs]. Warsaw: 1923, 29–31; trans. by Shlomo Noble in E. Lifschutz, "Merrymakers and Jesters among Jews," Yivo Annual of Jewish Social Science, VII (1952), 70–71. With the permission of the Yivo Institute for Jewish Research.

Y. L. Perets, "Sketches from a Tour of the Provinces," in Di yidishe bibliotek, ed. Y. L. Perets. II, Warsaw: 1891, 76–78, 82–93.

Maria and Kazemierz Piechotka, Wooden Synagogues. Arkady, Warsaw: 1959, figures 275–281.

Sh. Z. Pipe, "Progress Report on Jewish Children's Games in the Yivo Graduate Program," Folklore Research Center Studies. vol. 2 eds. Meir Noy and Dov Noy; Jerusalem, 1971, 521. With the permission of Dov Noy.

Berl Rabakh, "Women's Professions in Sonik," Yidishe shprakh, **XXIV** (June 1964), 26–27. With the permission of the Yivo Institute for Jewish Research.

A. Raboy, Eygene erd [Native soil] in I. Yakhinson, Social-Economic Patterns among Russian Jews in the Nineteenth Century. **Kharkov: 1929, 288–290.**

Abraham Rechtman, Yidishe etnografye un folklor [Jewish ethnography and folklore] Yivo, Buenos-Aires: 1958. **With the permission of Fay Storch.**

Ruth Rubin, "Boys' Taunts from Galicia" in "Jewish Life 'The old country'," Folkways Record FG 3801. Permission of Ruth Rubin.

Dov Sadan, "An Old Kheyder Riddle," in Khesed L'Avrom, ed. Moyshe Shtarkman. Yivo, Los Angeles: 1969–70, 685-694.

Elaine Samuel, "Purim shpiln, Purim plays and related customs: An audio-visual lecture." Yivo slide and filmstrip programs, 1972. With the permission of the author.

Beatrice Silverman Weinreich, "Three Songs of the Pogrom Times in Russia," Yivo bleter, **XXXIII** (1949), 241–243. With the permission of the Yivo Institute for Jewish Research.

————, "The Americanization of Passover," Studies in Biblical and Jewish Folklore, eds. Raphael Patai, F. L. Utley, Dov Noy. Indiana University Press, Bloomington: 1960, 341. With the permission of the publisher.

————, "Formal Problems in the Study of Yiddish Proverbs," in For Max Weinreich. Mouton, The Hague: 1964, 389.

Sholom Aleichem, Motl Peysi dem khazns [Motl, the cantor's son] Ale verk fun Sholem-Aleykhem. Folksfond, New York: 1920, 183–184.

————, The Old Country, trans. by Julius and Frances Butwin. Crown Publishers, New York: 1946. With the permission of the publisher.

————, The Great Fair, trans. by Tamara Kahana. Noonday Press, New York: 1955. With the permission of Farrar, Straus and Giroux, Inc.

————, "Sleep My Child," in The New Book of Yiddish Songs, ed. by Eleanor Gordon Mlotek. Workmen's Circle Educational Department. New York: 1972, 152–153. With the permission of the publisher.

Yekhiel Shtern, "A Kheyder in Tyszowce (Tishevits)," trans. by Shlomo Noble. Yivo Annual of Jewish Social Science, V (1950 A), 152–171. With the permission of the Yivo Institute for Jewish Research.

————, Kheyder un besmedresh [Kheyder and besmedresh] Yivo, New York, (1950 B). With the permission of the Yivo Institute for Jewish Research.

Solomon Simon, More Wise Men of Helm, Behrman House, New York: 1965. With the permission of the publisher.

I. J. Singer, Of a World That Is No More, trans. by Joseph Singer. Vanguard Press, New York: 1971. With the permission of the publisher. © Joseph Singer, 1970.

Z. Szajkowski, "The First Organized Immigration from Eastern Europe to the United States: 1869–70," Yivo bleter, XL (1956), 224–225. With the permission of the Yivo Institute for Jewish Research.

Joshua Trachtenberg, Jewish Magic and Superstition. Jewish Publication Society, Philadelphia: 1939, 62. © Edna Trachtenberg.

319

I. J. Trunk, Poyln [Poland] vol. II. Farlag Unser Tsait, New York: 1946, 195–201. With the permission of the publisher.

M Vanvild (pseud. Moyshe Dikshteyn), ed., Bay undz yidn [Among Jews] Pinkhes Graubard, Warsaw: 1923.

Max Weinreich, "The Reality of Jewishness versus the Ghetto Myth: The Sociolinguistic Roots of Yiddish," in To Honor Roman Jakobson. Mouton, The Hague: 1967, 2199–2211.

————, "Yiddishkayt and Yiddish: On the Impact of Religion on Language in Ashkenazic Jewry," in Mordechai Kaplan Jubilee Volume, ed. Moshe Davis. New York: Jewish Theological Seminary, 1953, 481–514.

Uriel Weinreich, "Paper Cutouts from Eastern Galicia," Yidisher folklor, I (January 1954), 12. With the permission of the Yivo Institute for Jewish Research.

————, "Yiddish and Colonial German: The Differential Impact of Slavic," American Contributions to the Fourth International Congress of Slavists. Moscow, 1958, 369–417.

————, College Yiddish. 5th ed. Yivo, New York: 1971. With the permission of the Yivo Institute for Jewish Research.

Yeda-'Am (October 1954), 242.

Leyb Zamet, "Names and Nicknames of Cities and Towns in Lite," Yidishe shprakh, IV (1944), 101–03. With the permission of the Yivo Institute for Jewish Research.

Y. Zelkovitsh, "Death and its Accompaniment in Jewish Ethnography and Folklore," Lodzher visnshaftlekhe shriftn, I (1938), 149–190.

————, "A Picture of the Communal Life of a Jewish Town in Poland in the Second Half of the Nineteenth Century," Yivo Annual for Jewish Social Science, VI (1951), 262–263. With the permission of the Yivo Institute for Jewish Research.

Jacob Zipper, Tsvishn taykhn un vasern [Between Lakes and Waters] Montreal: 1961. With the permission of the author.

KEY TO THE MAP OF EASTERN EUROPE

Yiddish Place Name	Polish Spelling	Map Location
Aleksander	Aleksandrow	3 A
Apt	Opatow	3 B
Bar		4 C
Barditshev	Berdyczow	4 D
Belz		4 B
Bialestok	Bialystok	2 B
Bobruysk	Bobrujsk	2 D
Bratslav	Braclaw	4 D
Brisk (-de-Lite)	Brzesc nad Bugiem	3 B
Brod	Brody	4 C
Chernigov		3 D
Chernobl	Czarnobyl	3 D
Chernovits	Czernowitz	1 C
Chichelnik		1 D
Chortkov	Czortkow	1 C
Danzig		5 A
Dubne	Dubno	4 C
Ger	Gora Kalwarja	3 B
Goray	Goraj	3 B
Grodne	Grodno	2 B
Homel	Gomel	3 D
Horodenka		4 C
Husiatin	Husiatyn	4 C
Kamenets-Podolsk	Kamieniec Podolski	4 C
Kapule		2 C
Karlin	Karolin	3 C
Kartuz-Bereze		3 C
Kelem	Kelme	1 B
Kelts	Kielce	3 A
Khelm	Chelm	3 B
Khmyelnik	Chmielnik	4 C
Kiev		4 D
Kishinev		5 D
Kletsk	Kleck	2 C
Kobrin	Kobryn	3 B

321

Kolesh	Kalisz	3	A
Konigsberg		2	A
Kolomay	Kolomyja	4	C
Korets	Korzec	4	C
Kotsk	Kock	3	B
Kovle	Kowel	3	B
Kovne	Kowno	2	B
Kremenets	Krzemieniec	4	C
Kroke	Cracow	4	A
Kutne	Kutno	3	A
Lemberg	Lwow	4	B
Letitshev	Latyczow	4	C
Lezhensk	Lezajsk	4	B
Lodz		3	A
Lomze	Lomza	2	B
Lublin		3	B
Lubomle	Lumoml	3	C
Lutsk	Luck	2	C
Lyadi	Liady	2	D
Mezhbizh	Miedzyboz	4	C
Mezritsh	Miedzyrzec	3	C
Minsk		2	C
Mir		2	C
Mohilev	Mohylow	2	D
Munkatsh	Mukachevo	4	B
Nay Sandz	Nowy Sacz	4	A
Nemirov	Niemirow	4	D
Nikolayev		5	E
Odessa		5	D
Ostre	Ostrog	4	C
Pereyaslev		4	D
Pinsk		3	C
Piotrkov	Piotrkow	3	A
Plotsk	Plock	3	A
Poltave		4	E
Ponevizh	Panevezys	1	B
Pruzhene	Pruzany	3	B
Pshemishl	Przemysl	4	B
Pshiskhe	Pszysucha	3	A
Riga		1	D
Rimanov		4	B
Rizhin	Rozan	4	D

Rovne	Rowno	4	C
Rubishoyv	Hrubieszow	3	B
Rudem	Radom	3	B
Sadeger	Sadhora	5	C
Satanov	Satanow	4	C
Satmer	Satu Mare	5	B
Shebreshin	Szczebrzeszyn	3	B
Shedlets	Siedlce	3	B
Shedlovtse	Szydlowiec	3	A
Shklov	Szklow	2	D
Shpole		4	D
Sighet (Hungary)		5	B
Sislevitsh	Swislocz	3	B
Slonim		2	C
Slutsk	Sluck	3	C
Smorgon		2	C
Sokal		4	B
Strusov	Strusow	4	C
Suvalk	Suwalki	2	B
Talne		1	E
Tarnopol		4	C
Tishevits	Tyszowce	4	B
Tomashov	Tomaszow Lubelski	4	B
Trisk	Turzysk	3	B
Tultshin		4	D
Uman	Human	4	D
Valozhin	Wolozyn	2	C
Varshe	Warsaw	3	B
Vengreve	Wegrow	3	B
Vilne	Wilno	2	C
Vitebsk		2	D
Vurke	Warka	3	B
Yablenke	Jablonka	2	B
Yas (Rumania)	Iasi	5	C
Yuzefov	Jozefow	3	B
Zabludeve	Zabludow	3	B
Zambrev	Zambrow	2	B
Zamoshtsh	Zamosc	3	B
Zdunska-Volye		3	A
Zhitomir		4	D
Zholkve	Zolkiew	4	B
Zvihil	Nowogrod Wolynski	4	C

INDEX

A. Sources

Zamet, Leyb, 45–48
Zelkovitsch, Y., 252, 254–56, 266–67
Zipper, Jacob, 4–30 , 81–82, 83–85, 107– 13, 114–22, 130–33, 136–39, 294–98, 298–306

B. Subjects

Alefbeys, 149, 151–54, 211
Angel of death, 243–44, 245–46
Ashkenazic (German) Jewry, 33, 34–35, 36, 49

Belfer, 149, 220
Besmedresh, 20, 196, 200, 204, 206, 211, 256
Besoylem, 6, 256, 257
Birth, 143, 149, 181
Blood libel, 85–89
Bris, 143, 186, 198
Burial society. *See Khevra kedishe*

Cantonists, 99–103
Cemetary. See *Besoylem*
Charity, 206
Christians, Jewish relations with, 7–8, 34, 77–79, 83–84, 85–86, 176. *See also* pogroms
Council of the Four Lands, 69

Dances, 218, 231–32, 237
Death, 243. *See also* Funerals and mourning customs

Education. *See kheyder*
Emigration, 42, 44, 278, 280
Eyrev, 4, 18, 21, 201

Foods, 36–39, 40, 121
Funerals and mourning customs, 6, 139, 243, 244, 254–56, 259, 262–63

Generational conflicts, 285
Gabe, 181, 185
Games, 150, 158, 211–18, 220–21, 224

Haskole. See *Maskilim*
Hoshane rabe, 247, 249

Jewish Labor Bund, 284, 286, 288–89

Kadesh, 262–63
Kahal, 9, 69, 99, 187–88, 192, 243
Khanike, 120, 220
Khasidim, Khasidism, 12, 28, 39–40, 49, 76, 77, 110, 120, 131, 191, 201, 207–8, 276, 285, 298
Khelm, 45, 48, 162–63, 171–74, 192, 247–50, 257–59
Khevre, 181, 182, 184–86, 211, 243. *See also pinkes*
Khevre kedishe, 139, 182, 185, 257, 256, 243
Khaper, 102
Khazn, 120, 150, 181, 185, 247
Kheyder, 55, 120, 149–51, 158, 161, 196, 211, 220, 243
Khmelnitski massacre, 49, 68–69, 70–72, 73, 75
Khosn toyre, 154–57
Kidesh, 94
Kley koydesh, 191, 192

Lagboymer, 220
Lamedvovnik, 133–36, 202
Lilith, 143, 146, 149

Magic. *See* Superstitions
Maskilim, 47, 48, 272–75, 277
Marketplace, 25–26, 271
Messiah, 6–7, 254, 266
Melamed, 120, 149, 162, 191, 276
Military service, 99–102, 104
Misnagdim, 40, 285
Mourning customs. *See* Funerals and mourning customs

325

Nicholas I (tsar), 99

Pototski (Polish count), 73

Sholom Aleichem, 54
Singer, Isaac Bashevis, 48
Sobieski, Jan (Polish king), 50

Weinreich, Max, 34

Wisniowiecki (Polish prince), 69

Yoel Bal Shem, 145

Zigismund August (Polish king), 59

JEWISH EASTERN EUROPE
1830–1914

- ✪ Provincial Capital
- ★ Major City
- • Settlement
- ·-·-· Border
- ········· Provincial Border
- ▨ Pale of Settlement
- ▨ Congress Poland

km

0   100   200

© carta, JERUSALEM

POLTAVE

Poltave

Dnieper

Pereyaslev

KIEV

Kiev

Rizhin

Shpole

Talne

Umani

KHERSON

Nikolayev

Zvihil

Zhitomir

Barditshev

Chichelnik

Bratslav

Nemirov

Khmyelnik

Letitshev

PODOLIA

Mezhbizh

Bar

Satanov

Kamenets-
Podolsk

Tultshin

Dniester

BESSARABIA

Kishinev

Yas

Odessa

Black

Sea

Prut

ROMANIA

Danube

Rovne

Ostre

Kremenets

Dubne

Husiatin

Tarnopol

Strusov

Chortkov

Horodenka

Kolomay

Sadeger

Chernovits

Sokal

Belz

Brod

Lemberg

Zholkve

Pshemishl

GALICIA

Tomashov

Lezhensk

Rimanov

Nay Sandz

Kroke
(Cracow)

Carpathian Mts

Sighet

Munkatsh

Satmer

HUNGARY

D

E

C

4

5

6

4

5